About

Where Healing Waters Meet

Ford guides us gently on a mysterious journey through the confluences of mind and body.

Yoga Journal

An accessible, in-depth personal look at how touch and "soma" wisdom may help lead us to natural healing and wholeness.

East West Journal

A rich source of techniques and ideas.

New Age Journal

The leading edge of a trend of convergence between body and mind therapies.

The New Times

Clyde Ford's erudition and gentleness shine through this clearly written intelligent essay on healing.

Massage Therapy Journal

Healing professionals who work with touch-based methods of therapy will find the book a rich source of ideas and techniques; general readers will find it simply inspirational.

Digest of Chiropractic Economics

One of the most worthwhile books in the healing arts in recent years.

Venture Inward

Where Healing Waters Meet will appeal to a wide range of readers--not only psychotherapists and bodyworkers but all those intriqued by the curious way in which life events appear to be impressed in specific body sites.

Brain Mind Bulletin

Where Healing Waters Meet

Touching Mind and Emotion
Through the Body

Clyde W. Ford

Foreword by Marilyn Ferguson

Station Hill Press

Copyright © 1989 Clyde W. Ford.
Foreword copyright © 1989 Marilyn Ferguson.
All rights reserved.
First Paperback Edition 1992

Published by Station Hill Press, Inc., Barrytown, New York 12507.

Grateful acknowledgement is due to the National Endowment for the Arts, a Federal Agency in Washington, DC, and the New York State Council on the Arts for partial financial support of this project.

Produced by the Institute for Publishing Arts, Inc., a not-for-profit, tax-exempt organization in Barrytown, New York.

Cover design and photography by Susan Quasha.
Text design by Susan Quasha and George Quasha.
Illustrations by Patrick O'Brien and Kristen Perry.
Acknowledgements to quoted materials appear at the end of the book under "References."

Distributed by the Talman Company, 150 Fifth Avenue, New York, New York 10011.

Library of Congress Cataloging-in-Publication Data
Ford, Clyde W.
    Where healing waters meet : touching mind and emotion through the body / Clyde W. Ford : foreword by Marilyn Ferguson.
    p.   cm.
    Bibliography: p.
    Includes Index.
    ISBN 0-88268-080-3 (cloth)   ISBN 0-88268-137-0 (pbk.)
    1. Mind and body therapies   I. Title.
    RC489.M53F67   1989   88-36895
    616.89'14—dc19   CIP

Manufactured in the United States of America.

To Emmanuel,
a special joy in my life.

Psyche and body react sympathetically to each other, it seems to me. A change in the state of the psyche produces a change in the structure of the body and conversely a change in the structure of the body produces a change in the state of the psyche.

Aristotle
Physiognomonica

Contents

Foreword by Marilyn Ferguson   *ix*

1   Where Healing Waters Meet   *1*

2   Primordial Connections   *27*

3   Bonds and Bounds of Touch   *59*

4   The Language of Touch   *81*

5   Touching Mind and Emotion Through the Body   *121*

6   The Journey Beyond Body and Mind   *153*

7   Healing Journeys with Exceptional Travelers   *177*

Epilogue   *201*

Appendix   *203*

References   *205*

Bibliography   *215*

Index   *221*

Foreword

In the fourteen years since I began publishing a science bulletin a great many books about body-healing techniques, and an even greater number on mind therapies, have crossed my desk for review.

It's no small surprise to read a book in which these two streams converge so effectively. *Where Healing Waters Meet* is appropriately titled. To his great credit Clyde Ford demystifies these twin aspects of therapy by showing their perfectly logical meeting point. The physical body holds emotional memories. Touch evokes those memories; once aware, the mind can release the tension that produces pain and discomfort. How could it be otherwise? Again, this should be no surprise—we have to learn (or remember) that truth tells us something about the inadequacy of our cultural paradigm of health and dis-ease.

Ford comes to his work with an unusual portfolio. He is a chiropractor well-versed in computer science, neuroscience, and yoga. To make it even more interesting, his undergraduate major was history. And you will find some revealing history in this account of what he calls *somatosynthesis*.

For example, his history of the healing "royal touch" explains a great deal. Knowing that healing by touch was strictly the domain of kings until the Nineteenth Century and that healers risked imprisonment, we can better understand the cultural anxiety we have around the subject to this day. In a way this book urges a democratization of the healing touch; the reader is encouraged to explore somatosynthesis.

Not surprising, given that the author is something of an explorer himself. While enrolled at Wesleyan University he traveled to study the archives to learn about the little-known blacks who came to the Colonies between 1619-1700 as indentured servants, not slaves. Later he was drawn to IBM because he wanted to understand how technological systems could be made to work for people. He pursued an interest in yoga as taught by Satchidananda. When he was weighing the decision to attend chiropractic school he had to reconsider his own image; until then he had been viewed as the scientist and his sister, a midwife, the healer. Nonetheless he felt called to work with the energies of the body.

When I met Clyde Ford he was a computer consultant in Portland, Oregon and attending chiropractic school. Busy as he was, before our meeting he had taken the time to index my newsletter, *Brain / Mind Bulletin*. It is part of his exquisite courtesy that he offers a favor in exchange for a hearing. My co-workers and I were most impressed. Later, when he was awaiting the results of his chiropractic boards, he was persuaded to work for us for a time editing a newsletter, *Leading Edge*, a bulletin of personal and social transformation.

His current work is clearly on that leading edge, for convergence is the direction in which body and mind therapies are heading. Ford asks us to find excitement and meaning in the ambiguity of this convergence by accepting healing as exclusive of neither the body nor the mind. And herein lies the book's deeper message: that enlightened awareness emerges from our ability to work with the tension of opposing beliefs. It is a message of healing we especially need to hear in these times.

Where Healing Waters Meet offers a rich conceptual, as well as experiential, context for its claims and premises. The author, with his scientific curiosity, has asked how certain things can be—and he offers intriguing possibilities. Those with a sophisticated knowledge of the human brain and body will be gratified by the synthesis of research. I daresay this book will inspire other practitioners and researchers to break new ground.

Yet there is the tone of a friendly guide throughout. The book is itself a gesture of healing.

Marilyn Ferguson
(Los Angeles)

Acknowledgements

There are many people to whom I am grateful for encouragement, support and help in bringing forth this book. While it would be impossible for me to mention them all by name, I can express my indebtedness to the following individuals:

Dr. David Manning White, my dear friend who insisted, long before I wrote the first word, that I had a book inside of me. David helped pull that book out of me by diligently reading through many revisions of the manuscript and giving me thoughtful advice and encouragement from his rich experience of many years as an author, publisher, professor, and humanitarian.

Sri Swami Satchidananda whose love and spiritual wisdom have nurtured me throughout the years.

Olga A. Worrall, a friend and teacher, from whom I learned the meaning of spiritual healing.

Steven Schatz, who helped me see that while psychotherapy deals with the mind, it is really a path of the heart. The portions of this book related to psychosynthesis come, in large measure, from the numerous conversations, counseling and teaching sessions that Steven shared with me.

Ashley Montagu, the "elder statesman of human touch," whose insights and writing have been a source of inspiration for me. I owe much of the section of this book on the relationship of touch to the physical and psychological development of human beings to his classic work *Touching: The Human Significance of the Skin.*

Carol Hermanson, a research assistant who always managed to find gems and treasures within the walls of a library.

Claudia Jemmott, whose skills as a proofreader and encouragement as a friend helped immensely in the final stages of this project.

My many teachers and guides: A part of each of you has found a way into this book.

George and Susan Quasha and the staff of Station Hill Press, for their commitment to bringing out a book of the highest quality.

Most of all, to the many patients—fellow travelers on this healing journey—whose lives I have been privileged to touch and who, in return, have touched me deeply as well.

Note About the Case Studies

The case studies presented in this book come from many different sources. In all instances I have changed names and altered certain non-essential facts to protect the confidentiality of the individuals involved. When faced with several similar cases, I have chosen to present a single composite study combining elements of each case.

1

Where Healing Waters Meet

Our encounter began as a routine office visit. Linda, age 32, lay on a table before me complaining of lower back pain. My examination revealed nothing unusual until I reached her right leg. There a searing pain shot from hip to toe. With one hand resting below each knee I proceeded to test the flexibility of her hip joints. I slowly rotated her legs out, but as I moved them she screamed.

"Stop, you're hurting me! Stop it! Stop it!"

I was startled. Her entire body visibly shook with the force of her insistence, yet I knew my touch was far too gentle to hurt her. Then she began to cry—softly at first and finally wave after wave of deep sobbing. Eventually, a tiny voice emerged from the midst of her anguish.

"He tried to rape me," she wept, "he tried to rape me."

"Who tried to rape you?" I asked.

"My father," she whispered, "I was only eleven and he tried to rape me."

Linda was once again swept away by her emotions. Through a tearful release she continued to let out the pain of that traumatic event. "What is going on?" I asked myself. Clearly my need to further examine her was superseded by her need to release this burden. I simply held her hand through the conclusion of this ordeal. Twenty minutes had passed when she looked up at me through red eyes and apologized for crying in my office.

"I came to see you for my back," she said, "not for this."

"There's no need to apologize," I assured her, "we can continue the exam tomorrow."

But to my surprise most of her leg pain was gone by the time she arose from the table. Linda thanked me for allowing her to release the emotions surrounding this event, although she also admitted being puzzled at why those feelings surfaced now. After all, she informed me, she had been in psychotherapy for many years to handle this childhood sexual abuse. I suggested that she consider seeing a therapist again; meanwhile, I would continue to work with her to correct the problems related to her back pain.

I was caught off guard, amazed by the lingering intensity of an event that occurred 20 years earlier; unsure of why my touch had evoked such a powerful emotional release; and surprised at the profound effect this release had on her physical condition. I was also a little scared. My clinical training had taught me to work with the body—the mind was unfamiliar territory.

For weeks afterward this experience haunted me. Questions turned over and over in my mind. Why were Linda's emotions so closely tied to her physical body? Could her emotional state have precipitated her physical condition? Or did her physical condition recall a past traumatic event? How did touch bring about such deep emotional release? Would other people react in a similar way? Could this response be used therapeutically?

I began to pay attention to the many ways that people responded to touch. In most people touch induced a variety of bodily changes—decreased pain, increased muscular relaxation, decreased stress and tension. These were expected clinical findings. But my patients also reported other occurrences when touched: a feeling of leaving their body; vivid mental imagery; changes in their perception of time; or spontaneous insights into the emotional, psychological or spiritual issues underlying their physical pain or illness. While not as dramatic as my session with Linda, these accounts continued to pique my interest.

Outside of manual therapy (manipulation, massage, traction, reflex stimulation), traditional medical literature made only scant reference to the use of touch therapeutically. Some healing disciplines specifically discouraged the use of touch. In psychology and psychiatry, for example, touch between therapist and client was prohibited for fear of contaminating the progress of therapy. I even read one report from a medical society to its members advising them not to hug their patients for fear of a malpractice suit.

Obviously this interest in touching had a lot to do with the relationship between mind and body, since the human psyche figured in almost all the effects of touching reported by my patients. Psychosomatic medicine is a fairly well-established discipline, and many sources can be consulted. But here too I was disappointed. Compared to the many references on the healing effect of the *mind on the body*, there are hardly any on the healing effect of the *body on the mind*. And, it was this latter relationship that I observed when people were touched.

Still attempting to understand how touch affected people beyond their physical body, I had a personal encounter with this very process while attending a workshop on the therapeutic use of touch. Here each participant had the opportunity to be the client of four other hands-on therapists simultaneously. One therapist facilitated the session by determining where the assistants placed their hands. The facilitator also guided the client through whatever personal issues (mental, emotional, or spiritual) emerged during the session. The roles of facilitator, assistant and client rotated throughout this week-long workshop.

During my last rotation as a client, the group was guided by the facilitator to place their hands at various locations on my body. Within minutes I began to experience some unpleasant childhood memories. Images of my parents and my sister flashed before me. Hidden feelings seemed to rise to the surface, and my body tensed as I recalled these early events. The facilitator asked me to voice some of the feelings which were present for me, and I did. There were even some tears brought on by childhood memories of being held by my mother. Eventually the stressful effects of these memories subsided and my body relaxed. The facilitator was ready to conclude my session, but there was a vague sense of unease throughout the group that my work was not yet complete.

"It's not over yet," I remember someone saying, "there's more to do."

My eyes were still closed and I could hear the other members talking in subdued tones. They all decided to place their hands in one location on my right abdomen, slightly lower than my rib cage. Their pressure was firm, but not painful, and I offered little resistance to them. The facilitator asked me to stay in touch with whatever feelings emerged during this time. Actually this was hard for me to do because I felt that I had discharged as much as I could during the childhood memories. Frankly, I did not know what other feelings could come. We remained in a stand-off for what seemed like a half hour—their hands pressing my abdomen as I wondered what possible content could surface.

But a storm was brewing deep within my psyche, I could vaguely feel its rising tide. It was the unrelenting nature of the group's touch that eventually caught up with me. I began to feel trapped; I wanted to escape but I couldn't. I felt suffocated, strangled and held down by them, although intellectually I knew none of this was true. One voice inside of me kept saying, "Relax Clyde, be cool." But events were taking a course of their own.

"They're going to kill me," I thought.

"That's a crazy idea," I told myself.

It was too late now. With the thought of being killed I tensed my abdomen for the first time, and that tension opened a floodgate of images and emotions. Instantly I was back on Bronx streets where I grew up, a twelve year-old black boy being chased by a gang of white boys. It was a game of hide-and-go-seek that turned sour. I was the last person sought by a group of about a dozen peers—they were all white, I was black.

I still remembered their faces in vivid detail, I even called out their names, "Ray, Duffy, Mike, Nick," and I felt the sting of their racial epithets which pierced me like sharp arrows.

"Let's get him," they all yelled.

They had found my hiding place and the entire gang of kids lunged toward me. My entire being was seized by an insurmountable terror. I leaped up and started to run, and I ran, and ran, and ran, faster and further than I remember ever having run. Somewhere deep inside I knew it wasn't a game any longer.

"You bastards," I yelled as I lay on the table, "you dirty bastards."

I was no longer in control—I was reliving a psychohistorical drama. It felt as though I was running for every other black man who had ever been chased by a crazed, vengeful mob. I never turned around, even when they gave up chasing, I just kept running. I hopped on a subway and rode for awhile, my body still shaking with fear. I jumped off the train several stops later and continued to run. I was no longer even sure what I was running from but I knew I couldn't stop. Years later I continued to run, only in my dreams rather than on the streets. The gang of kids often appeared as a Nazi army chasing me, a French partisan, through the streets of Paris. Sometimes they were a Japanese army in hot pursuit of me, an American GI in World War II. Regardless of the form of the dream, I was always running, and I always awoke with that same feeling of terror and fear. "I hate you," I screamed, "I hate you, I hate you."

At this point I remember my body lurching off the table and my fists striking out at the vision of those screaming faces that had become dogs nipping and barking at me. Meanwhile, the rest of the group had their hands full restraining me. My body was shaking and tears were streaming down my face. The facilitator took over at this point and helped me slowly work through and release much of the terror, fear and rage I had hidden in my body these many years. I imagined a release valve located in my left shoulder. Mentally opening it was the way I released my terror and fear—the technique worked well. The tension in my body began to subside, and I felt a wave of relaxation sweep over me. When I opened my eyes I realized that I was again surrounded by a sea of white faces—only this time they felt warm, supporting and loving.

I began to understand what Linda, my patient who had been sexually abused as a child, underwent when I touched her. I literally had no conscious registration that this particular event was so deeply pressed into my psyche. But when touched in the right manner the event was spontaneously recalled, and the psychological content related to it emerged. I did not say much afterwards: What words could contain such an experience? I walked on the beach for about an hour after this intense session, glad to have confronted an issue of such profound and long-lasting effect, one so far removed from my conscious mind.

Interestingly, before this workshop I too had been in psychotherapy. In fact I had even talked about this very event with my therapist, but in a distant, bemused and coolly intellectual way. However, when this same event was approached from my body first, I finally *got in touch with* a set of deeply held emotions surrounding my experience. Human touch reached deeper than my body bringing me face to face with the very core of my being and my deepest feelings and thoughts. It was a moving and personally healing experience, whose impact is still with me. It was a turning point from which I emerged fundamentally changed.

Our body remembers even when our conscious mind forgets. It stores our traumas and triumphs; our happiness and sadness; our anger and elation; our joy and sorrow; our guilt and grief; our fears and hopes; our instinct and intuition; our lowest drives and highest ambitions; our past, our present and our potential. While we look to the mind to understand these aspects of being human, the mind only gives us one part. Our bodies are essential to being human as well.

It was now clear that touch therapeutically reached far beyond the body. Just how far it reached became apparent once I incorporated some new techniques in my practice. Right from the start the results were profound. A good example was Walter, a forty-year-old endocrinologist I treated for lower back pain. After nearly a year of unsuccessful treatment through conventional medicine, Walter's daughter pleaded with him to seek nontraditional therapy for his nagging back pain. As a medical doctor, he was obviously skeptical of seeing a chiropractor. However, after an initial examination, x-rays, and a thorough grilling about my medical knowledge, Walter agreed to undergo a period of treatment.

The first session was unremarkable. I used my standard array of techniques for treating lower back pain: manipulation, traction, and reflex stimulation. Walter left feeling extremely relaxed and remarked that his lower back pain had eased. At the next session I decided to include something new, although I was apprehensive about his reaction as a medical doctor. So in a very matter-of-fact voice I asked Walter if he would help me understand why his back pain occurred and reoccurred periodically throughout his life. With his agreement, I invited him to relax and focus his attention on the point in his lower back where I was applying gentle traction.

"What's that like?" I asked.

"That's interesting," he observed, "I see a straight black line when I focus there."

"Stay with that image," I suggested, "and see where it leads."

Walter continued to focus on his lower back, and I continued to apply traction and gently manipulate that area. Suddenly, he blurted out, "It's moving, the line has become a wave and it's moving. This is really strange," he added.

By now I was applying very light pressure over his upper chest and back. After several minutes, the waving motion he sensed initially in his lower back seemed to extend up his spine to my hands. When I moved to the base of his skull the wave followed and his entire body began to gently undulate beneath my touch.

"Unbelievable," he remarked, "my whole body feels like it's floating, waving back and forth in a very tranquil sea."

When the session was over, Walter just wanted to stay in this ocean of the mind. He finally did arise and along with his clothes put on a critical, scientific demeanor more befitting of a medical doctor.

"What just happened?" he demanded to know.

"I'm not really sure," I offered. "How do you feel now?"

"I feel great," Walter said, somewhat surprised, "but I don't understand what that waving line was all about. And the only time I've ever felt a similar feeling of floating was in my dreams, but I was still awake on the table. I was still aware of your voice and everything your hands were doing to my body."

As I left the room, I heard him murmur,

"I've got to think about this, I've got to think more about this."

By our next session, Walter had given his experience some thought and he was eager to tell me about it.

"That line was my spine," he reported. "As a straight line it represented a stressed and tense spine. As a wavy line, it signified a spine in the process of relaxing and letting go."

Walter's eyes widened with excitement as he told about using the wave image during the week whenever he felt his body tensing. It had helped him stay relaxed and greatly lessened his back pain. He was also eager to pursue this combination of physical and mental therapy further.

"Let's do more of this," he suggested, "this is important for me."

This session was to prove even more rewarding. We began as before: I asked him to relax while I gently applied traction and manipulated his lower back. Only this time I asked him to focus on his lower back as though it were a place. Five minutes of silence had elapsed when I inquired where he was.

"I'm in a cave," he said, "a cave with multi-colored walls."

Walter walked around this inner cave, touched the walls and remarked how little light there was inside. When asked if there were a way for him to leave he paused for a minute or so and informed me that there was a hole in the floor of the cave.

"I'm going to go through it," he said, "I'm going through it."

For Walter, going through the cave floor was like Alice going through the looking glass. His experience immediately intensified and with short staccato bursts he reported what was taking place.

"I don't believe it," he blurted out, "I'm flying, I'm flying."

He then lapsed into silence for nearly twenty minutes. Meanwhile I continued working my way up his spine using light touch and traction. His body moved continuously—sometimes gently and other times wildly. Every now and then he would punctuate the silence with an exclamation.

"This is incredible, just incredible!"

My hands supported his upper chest and upper back as his inner journey was about to conclude. His body stopped moving, his breathing changed, and he uttered a sigh.

"I'm at the entry to the cave again," he said, "but I'm not sure that I want to go back in."

The session concluded five minutes later with Walter still sitting outside the cave pondering whether he should go in. He was really in no condition to talk about his experience now, he just lay on the table in a calm, deeply relaxed and pensive state. When I saw him next, he was very clear about the meaning of this session.

"I was out of my body," he said with amazement. "I've heard about experiences like this, but I never really gave them much credence. Yet, I truly felt out of my body. I could see myself lying on your table and I could see you but I was hovering overhead."

"The cave represented my life now," he offered in a sad tone. "I've lost a lot in the years since entering medical school. I love what I'm doing but I'm constantly under stress. Moreover, I've given up things which were very dear to me like painting, music and reading."

"The hole in the cave floor was the passageway back to my real self," he observed, "and the out-of-body experience was an opportunity for me to feel reconnected with my soul. My ambivalence about re-entering the cave was a true expression of my conflict over continuing my life feeling stressed and spiritually unconnected."

Walter then went on to inform me that after these two sessions he had made up his mind to reclaim those parts of himself that were set aside for his career. He had already started painting and reading and was setting aside time to play his violin again. Walter also came from a non-Western culture with deep spiritual roots. Though he had often heard the older folks talking about their spiritual practices, he had never paid much attention. After our two sessions, those familiar conversations took on a different meaning for him.

"Now I know what my ancestors meant by connecting with one's Spirit," he stated, "this is just the beginning of that process for me."

Through sessions like these, the far-reaching effects of touch became clearer. That touch could be used to elicit the emotional and psychological issues beneath physical pain was an important discovery. But an even deeper finding was that touch helped to reconnect people with meaning and purpose in their lives. As in Walter's case, this was often an especially moving, spiritual experience. The quality of my time spent with patients underwent a dramatic change as a result of using touch to reach beyond the body. Where I formerly enjoyed using hands-on therapy to bring about relaxation and physical comfort, I now was aware of a tremendous inner world that could be reached through touch.

Touch opened doors into the psyche, doors through which one could be guided to discover the deeper ground beneath overt physical signs and symptoms. Upon reaching this deeper ground, lives were changed in profound and powerful ways. The nature of my practice as a healing professional also underwent considerable change. Trained as a specialist in hands-on therapy (the word chiropractic was derived from two Greek words *praktikos* meaning *done by*; and *cheiro* meaning *hand*), I felt myself

in a strange land somewhere between manual therapy and psychotherapy; a border zone between body and mind. Far from barren, this
landscape was fertile with promise and possibility.

In some respects my situation mirrored the times. For the last two
decades have seen an increasing convergence of body and mind
therapies. These new therapies are often labelled *psychosomatic* (psyche =
mind; soma = body) or *psychophysical* medicine. As both names imply,
these approaches to healing deal with the effect of the mind on the body.
With them tremendous strides have been made in understanding mental
influences on body systems ranging from the muscular to the immune
system. This has lead to treatment procedures that exploit this connection
between mind and body—biofeedback for stress-related disorders and
mental techniques to enhance the immune response are two good examples of this process.

The role of the mind in healing the body is a fascinating subject which
is steadily gaining in importance even within traditional medical practice.
Mentally influencing the human immune system, for example, is an
exciting new field given the name *psychoneuroimmunology* (literally the
effect of the mind through the nervous system on the immune system).
Until recently it was believed that the immune system operated
autonomously, responding on its own to the presence of unwanted agents
in the human body. When all works well the immune system neutralizes
these agents rendering them harmless to the person. In many instances
of disease, however, the immune system is overwhelmed or compromised in some way that makes this natural protection from disease
ineffective. Cancer and AIDS are two conditions where the immune
system is overpowered.

Early studies by Simonton and Actherberg showed evidence that
people suffering from a life-threatening condition like cancer could often
reverse their disease process by using mental imagery to work with the
immune system. They were taught to "see in their mind's eye" the process
they wished to take place in their body. Images of armies overwhelming
a foreign invader, big fish eating little fish, and fighter planes dive-bomb-
ing a target were used by these individuals to symbolize a vigorous,
strong immune system response to the presence of disease. Studies
showed that remissions occurred in many who faithfully practiced such
techniques.

While this suggested the ability to influence immune system response
through mental imagery, it was not definitive. Then a series of animal
studies showed that the level of circulating white blood cells (the major

components of the immune system) could be conditioned in the same way that Pavlov's dogs were conditioned to salivate when a bell was rung. Follow-up human studies confirmed this ability to influence the function of the immune system.

In one study a group of experimental subjects were exposed to a substance which attacks the immune system without causing a life-threatening crisis. When given the suggestion under hypnosis that their white blood cells were like "powerful sharks" attacking "weak germs," they were able to increase the level of white blood cells needed to neutralize the foreign substance.

Fig. 1.1: An illustration of the mental imagery used by subjects who enhanced the activity of their immune system while under hypnosis.

Another study looked at the relationship between depression and the immune system. Severely depressed individuals also showed depressed immune systems when measured by the level of white blood cells produced in response to exposure to an experimental foreign substance. But as these individuals recovered from their depression, so did their immune system response. Thus the level of depression was found to be related to the level of immune system response and vice versa. For reasons such as these, many psychologically oriented therapists have grown to understand the importance of the mind in healing the body.

But there is another side to this convergence, the side of the somatically oriented therapist. By somatic therapist I mean all those therapists whose primary treatment method is with the human body. There are a wide array of disciplines represented in this group. The most familiar somatic therapies are represented by the professions of chiropractic, osteopathy, physiatry (a branch of medicine), nursing, physical therapy and massage therapy. Actually many others also employ a hands-on approach to treatment: occupational therapy, Rolfing, polarity therapy, structural integration, functional integration (the Feldenkrais method), Hakomi, Trager, psychophysical integration, Alexander, Hellerwork, applied kinesiology, to name some of the non-mainstream disciplines. Then there is an entirely different group of somatic therapists that do not take a direct hands-on approach but do work with the body: exercise therapists, dance therapists, yoga and movement therapists would be examples of this group.

Since somatic therapists approach the mind-body convergence from the body their viewpoint is different from psychotherapists who approach this convergence from the mind. So somatic therapists would be interested in the effect the body has on healing the mind. However not all somatic therapists actually have this interest. In fact, there are many more psychotherapists interested in the effects of the mind on the body than somatic therapists interested in the effects of the body on the mind. Thus, from a therapeutic standpoint, the mind-body convergence tends to be a little one-sided. Yet, as a somatic therapist interested in the mind, I find myself in the middle of this affair.

I have witnessed the body providing tremendous access to the mind through touch. There is something unique about touching that moves therapy beyond talking, the traditional route in psychology. Perhaps it is that long before we learned to talk we knew to touch. As humans we were created, formed and birthed through the contact of skin. Touch is our first language. Before we could utter a word, hear a sound, see an image, smell a scent or taste a flavor, we could communicate through touch. In the womb, our barely formed body responded to the world through the only sensory system open to it, the sense of touch. Many times I have laid my hand on the abdomen of an expectant mother and felt her baby move closer to, or perhaps away from, my touch.

Even for months after birth, touch continued be our most important tool in apprehending the world. As newborns there was little distinction between body and mind. What was experienced in the body was recorded by the mind, what was recorded by the mind was stored in the body. Eventually sight and sound gained the upper hand but an axiom of human development reminds us that the most important body systems are those formed earliest in life. Through touch our body still interacts with the world as it did when we were unborn and newborn. Like the circuitry of a modern day computer, touch provides us with direct, high-speed access to the recordings of the mind and the storehouse of the body.

Touch also creates a powerful therapeutic alliance, so vital to the healing process. Reaching out to touch someone is a lasting symbol of what it means to be human, and a universal sign of healing. For millions of years we have been brought into the world, and ushered out of it, through the arms of others. Witness the beginning and end of life—a mother cradling a newborn or Michelangelo's sculpture of the Pietà—and feel the similar message they convey of love, compassion and healing through touch.

Touch is our one reciprocal sense. We cannot touch another without being touched ourself. It is this quality of touching which forges such a strong therapeutic bond. Healing is so often attempted at a distance—across a desk, over the counter, or through the dials of an instrument. Thus we side-step the human factor. However when we touch, the human factor is unavoidable—in fact, it becomes the central aspect of healing.

For some practitioners touching poses a dilemma. Psychotherapists, for example, since the time of Freud, have been strongly advised not to touch their clients, for fear of bringing to the surface unconscious sexual issues between the two and thereby derailing the therapeutic process. No doubt this is one reason the body was so long neglected in mainstream psychotherapy. But risk is no reason to ignore an important therapeutic method. It may simply necessitate an increased awareness of the potential dangers, and the development of means of coping with them if they emerge.

Any somatic therapist can attest to the often magical quality of sustained touch. It has an entrancing power not only for the client but also for the therapist. Touch promotes a state of engagement between therapist and client, a key factor in successful therapy whether somatic or psychological. What's amazing is that touch brings about this therapeutic rapport so easily.

❖

Jean was a 30 year-old film director whose long hours with heavy film equipment were jeopardized by a knifing pain between her shoulder blades. She had responded well to two previous sessions with me. I noticed during this session that she quickly slipped into a state of deep relaxation reminiscent of the half-sleep/half-waking state that many people experience as they fall asleep. Her muscles twitched several times, she breathed a deep sigh of relief and her entire body relaxed into the table. I observed her body making this transition while my hands were grasping her feet, gently rotating her legs in and out.

The next thing I knew, my hands were on her head and I heard my voice, saying softly to her,

"Bring your awareness back to your breathing, and when you feel ready, stretch, take several deep breaths and open your eyes."

I looked over at my clock and struggled to account for the thirty minutes that had just elapsed. I vaguely remembered moving my hands to different areas of Jean's body. I also recalled engaging her in a dialogue, inviting her to use imagery in areas of her body where my hands were. But I had no recollection of what I said or how I had gotten to her head from her feet. "Thank you," she said at the conclusion, "this session had a lot of meaning for me."

I chuckled silently, although I was also slightly embarrassed. I too had fallen into a half-sleep/half-waking state similar to Jean's and it was not my first time. In fact, I have heard the sheepish admissions of many somatic therapists that they too have had at least one similar experience. While it is embarrassing to appear to be sleeping during therapy, there may actually be a reason why this happens when a therapist uses touch.

A body of knowledge has accumulated on this half-way condition called a *hypnagogic state* (different from hypnotic). It is noted for dramatic changes in brain wave activity, psychosomatic healing and ready access to the unconscious mind—in short, the barriers between mind and body are relaxed. What the mind ponders, the body enacts. What the body experiences, the mind absorbs. It is not surprising, then, that touch can evoke a state that engages two people in a healing process beyond the bounds of conventional therapy.

Exploring this new frontier of healing through touch is exciting. Early on, the greatest trouble I had was answering the simple question posed time and time again.

"This is very exciting work, Doc, what do you call it?"

For a while, not having a name was just fine. Then one day I read the work of an Italian psychiatrist, Roberto Assagioli. I was immediately struck with the similarity between his notions of healing through the mind and my ideas about healing through the body. Assagioli called his therapy *psychosynthesis*; I coined the term *somatosynthesis* to describe my work.

Somatosynthesis more than any other term, reflects the essence of this therapy. First, the name *somatosynthesis* is derived from two Latin words: *somato*, the conjunctive form of *soma* which means *body* and *synthesis*, defined as the integration of separate elements into a unified whole. Synthesis also implies a particular method of realizing this whole. Classically, a synthesis represents the unification of two opposite positions. Starting with a given assumption (the *thesis*) and its polar opposite (the *antithesis*), a higher order unification of the two (the *synthesis*) is derived. Body and mind are two such opposite elements.

As a somatic practitioner, my basic assumption is the importance of the body to the healing process (the thesis). Opposed to this view is the importance of the mind (the antithesis). Synthesis results in the area of convergence between the two, and this is precisely the therapeutic context of my work. Where some therapies approach this convergence from the mind, somatosynthesis approaches it from the body. In so doing, touch becomes the important force in achieving this synthesis of body and mind.

Synthesis stands opposed to analysis. Analysis, derived from the Greek, means *to separate, or break apart, a whole into its constituent parts again* (*ana-* = again; *lysis* = separate or break apart). Thus in psychotherapy Assagioli proposed the notion of psychosynthesis in response to early Freudian psychoanalysis. He felt that psychoanalysis placed too much emphasis on sorting out each element of the psyche; identifying the diseased elements and attempting to treat them. There are no isolated human problems, said Assagioli.

Traditional methods of healing the body are also analytically based: a physical symptom becomes the indicator of an underlying disease process; the disease is searched for and differentiated from diseases causing similar symptoms; and the isolated disease is treated. This is the theoretical foundation of modern medical diagnosis and treatment.

If there is a problem with this analytical approach to healing, it is that the individual is left fragmented. One of my favorite stories about analytical health care concerns a patient I saw in the early years of my practice. Anne was a middle-aged woman who came to see me after having been to the local university clinic complaining of stomach pains. To my surprise she informed me that she had received a thorough, "holistic" diagnostic work-up while at the clinic. When I asked her to tell me about it, she said.

> First, I saw my general practitioner. He wasn't really certain what the problem was, so he referred me to an internist. The internist felt I really needed to see a gastroenterologist. The gastroenterologist was similarly puzzled, so he suggested I consult a cardiologist. After examining my heart, the cardiologist couldn't find a problem but thought it might be hormonal, so he referred me to an endocrinologist. The endocrinologist found nothing definitive but to be on the safe side, he suggested I see my gynecologist. The gynecologist pronounced me free of problems as far as he could tell and referred me to a psychiatrist. The psychiatrist assured me there was nothing wrong mentally. "Perhaps you should wait until the pain gets worse," he said, "then I'm sure someone can tell you what's wrong."

Approached this way, healing becomes a matter of parcelling out pieces of our body and mind to separate specialists. I am not suggesting that analysis should be struck from the healing arts, but when we only treat a person as isolated fragments we lose all sense of the whole.

Contrast Anne's case with that of another patient whom I saw for complaints of lower abdominal pain. Jenny, a 40 year-old computer programmer, had consulted a gynecologist, an internist and a psychologist for her problem. Recently married for the first time, Jenny and her new husband were excited about trying to have children even though they would both be older parents. She wanted to make certain that her abdominal pain would not interfere with that possibility.

After a week of appointments with these other specialists, Jenny saw me. All of her examinations were normal but she still had the abdominal pain. She lay on my treatment table while I supported her with one hand underneath her lower back and my other hand directly over top, resting lightly on her lower abdomen. I had her relax, focus on her breathing, and bring her awareness to the area of her abdomen underneath my hand.

"There's something there," she said, "it's like a mass there in my abdomen."

I could also feel a presence underneath my hand. But after several minutes of sustained light touch, this area seemed to relax and whatever was beneath my hand appeared to melt away. Jenny also remarked how she felt the mass disappear. Next I moved my hands to her upper chest area and once again supported her on bottom and top. When I asked her to become more aware of this area, she began to voice her anxiety over having a child so late in her life. The moment she did she also noticed a return of her abdominal pain.

"It feels related," she said, "it is like that area in my abdomen is storing my anxiety about becoming pregnant."

She paused for a moment, and then, with a sudden flash of insight, realized that the worst pain coincided with talking to her husband about children. So, I returned my hands back to their previous position and again felt a raised area under my top hand. Once again, I invited Jenny to focus her awareness in the lower abdomen.

"It feels dark and fearful there now," she reported. "I feel like I have a lot of fear around having a baby."

I let my hand follow her abdomen as it began to relax again.

"Let's not leave this area so quickly this time," I suggested. "As you continue to focus here, be aware of whatever images emerge."

After five minutes of silence, Jenny began describing a house she saw in her mind.

"There's a little girl walking out of the house," she said, "my gosh, it's me."

That realization brought about a flood of memories and emotions from her childhood. The most overwhelming emotion Jenny had was one of not feeling supported and loved by her parents.

"I never felt good enough, and I never felt wanted by them," she claimed. "I put off getting married and having children because my memories of that time life in my life were so painful. Thinking about having children now brings back all the pain of my own childhood."

Jenny began to cry and her emotional release seemed to carry her even deeper into the pain she was experiencing.

"This pain in my abdomen is not just the fear of having a child," she acknowledged, "it's the pain and anger and fear I've stored in my body since being a child myself."

Having finally been put in touch with the psychological ground beneath her physical pain, Jenny breathed a deep sigh of relief. Her abdominal pain subsided and she concluded her session by saying, "I want to heal the child inside of me now, before I have a child of my own."

The difference between the cases of Anne and Jenny represent the difference between analysis and synthesis. In Anne's case an attempt was made to narrow the focus to find the problem. For Jenny, we broadened the focus to clarify the real issues—the body became a vehicle to the mind. This is a basic assumption of somatosynthesis: that one can find a larger, non-physical framework within which to understand and treat physical signs and symptoms. You might like to test the truth of this statement on yourself with the following exercise.

Somatic Memory

The best way to do this exercise is to have someone else lead you through it. Otherwise, read through the steps several times on your own until you can perform each step from memory.

1. Begin by finding a comfortable position to relax in. If you're sitting, have your spine erect and both feet flat on the floor. If you're lying down spread both legs apart slightly and have your arms spread several inches away from your sides. Take a moment to focus on your breathing. Without trying to control your breath, just observe the inhalations and exhalations, allowing them to lengthen naturally. Draw your awareness within, as though you could look within your body.

2. Select an area of your body to work with. Any area of your body will suffice, but you may want to chose an area which has some significance. It could be an area in pain or one that you previously injured. It could be an area of special importance to you—your legs if you are a dancer, your arms if you are a carpenter. Or it could simply be an area of your body which you normally pay little attention to.

3. Touch, or have someone else touch, that area. If possible, have a trusted acquaintance touch the area you selected. If this is not possible, touch the area yourself. If the area is not accessible to your touch, then focus your awareness on that area.

4. Recall the somatic history of that area. Instead of answering the following questions out loud, give yourself plenty of time to allow the answers to emerge in your mind.

    (a) When is the most recent time you remember being aware of this area? What was that awareness like for you? (Pleasurable, painful, loving, fearful, joyful, angry, etc.)

(b) Going back in time, at what points do you remember being aware of this area? See how far back you can go in your life. When do you remember first being aware of this area? At each point in your life, what was that awareness like for you?

(c) What images come to mind with increased awareness of this area? What are those images like for you?

(d) If this area of your body had a voice, what would it say to you? What would it be like to hear that?

(e) How important is this area of your body to you? What is it like to realize the importance of this area to you?

(f) What new awareness do you now have of this area of your body? How might you incorporate this new awareness into your life?

5. Slowly bring your awareness back to your breathing, and when you feel ready, stretch your body, take a couple of deep breaths and open your eyes.

Touch recalls somatic memory, an important component of the somatosynthesis process. Many people experience a similar recall through smell. Perhaps you can remember smelling a newly bloomed flower or a freshly cut lawn, and the scent produced an instantaneous flashback to a prior time in your life when that smell was present. Often such flashbacks are rich in visual and emotional detail. Touch has the power to recall events recorded by the body. Early life events fall into this category and therefore are often accessible through touch. Touch, after all, is the main sense that programs our brain from the early stages of pregnancy until several years after birth. Before we have well-developed mental structures, we experience the world through our bodies, and this occurs because we touch. Later on, touch can recall those early events.

❖

Elaine was a woman in her late thirties whom I saw for complaints of pain in her right shoulder. During our first somatosynthesis session, I placed both hands lightly on her shoulder, one underneath and one on top. There was obvious muscular tension in this area, but there was also the aura of another presence as well.

"This may sound strange," I offered, "but your shoulder feels as though there is a sharp object lodged in it, a knife or an arrow maybe."

My statement was one of those intuitive flashes that over the years I have come to accept as often providing therapeutically useful information. I asked Elaine to relax and bring her attention to this area. After five or six minutes of silence, she informed me that it was not a knife or an arrow.

"It's more like a spear," she exclaimed, "like a spear entered my shoulder."

As she further relaxed and allowed her mind to let in the images surrounding this area of her body, she related a story that happened to her when she was two-years old.

"I overheard my mother talking to my father," she recalled; "she said that she never wanted to be pregnant with me in the first place. I was really hurt when I heard that statement and I feel that I absorbed that statement in this shoulder." This realization by Elaine lead us further into her relationship with her parents and her feelings of being unwanted. In a manner similar to the case cited previously, this little two-year old child needed to be healed before the adult could be healed. So I physically tugged at Elaine's shoulder as if I were actually removing a spear. Symbolically removing the spear from the shoulder of the two-year-old ultimately resulted in releasing the pain from the shoulder of the adult. Afterwards Elaine was able to move her shoulder without pain.

It is not only early life experiences which are stored somatically; almost all illness or injury has a somatic component regardless of when in life they occur. An automobile accident is a good example of this. Painful neck muscle spasm is a common occurrence after a whiplash injury. One reason the neck muscles go into spasm is preventive. They tighten up to avert further injury. The problem here is that long after the accident is over the spasm remains. In a sense the spasm is a somatic memory of the accident. But more than just muscle tightness is stored as a result of the trauma.

Many emotions surface in those few moments before the impact of an accident, especially if a person is forewarned and waiting for this inevitable trauma to occur. All of the feelings present at the time of the accident are then stored in the body along with the physical trauma. In this case, healing requires not just releasing physical pain but releasing emotional pain within the body as well. Here too touch plays a role.

Casey's mother called our office to make an appointment for her son who had just wrecked his car while trying to brake on a wet, slippery road. The car skidded and eventually hit a tree. Fortunately, Casey, who was seventeen, had his seat belt on. He received only minor cuts and insisted he was fine.

"The soreness in my neck went away after a few days," he informed me confidently, "I feel great now."

It was clear to me that Casey was really here because his mother had insisted. During our first treatment session, I held his head in my hands and gently rotated his neck to the right, then to the left. Moving toward the right was no problem for Casey, he had nearly normal range of motion. But going left, his neck moved only a few inches before freezing. I held Casey's head at this emotional point, being careful not to force him beyond where his body moved naturally. As I did he broke into a cold sweat and, without urging, began to tell me what was going through his mind.

"I was really scared when I lost control of the car," he admitted. "I thought I was going to be killed. There was nothing I could do, nothing, I felt totally helpless."

I had moved Casey's neck into a position that closely approximated its position at some point of the accident—most likely the position in which his neck muscles went into spasm. Locked into his neck, then, was not only the spasm of muscles but his fear surrounding the accident. Holding his neck in this position somatically recalled the physical and psychological events of that accident.

Casey's neck had reached a point I call the *emotional point*, after the derivation of the word *emotion*. Emotion is a combined form of two Greek words, *ex-* meaning *out of* and *motion* meaning movement. So emotion literally means "out of movement." Since Casey could not move his neck beyond this point, his body was by definition emotional.

While holding Casey at his emotional point, I specifically encouraged his thoughts and feelings related to the accident. As he shared them with me, his neck muscles began to relax and his head rotated further and further to the left. After ten minutes like this, his spasms had reduced and he had nearly normal range of motion in his neck. Why is it important to release both the physical and psychological aspects of an injury like this?

First, either condition is serious enough by itself. And, secondly, either condition alone can recreate the other. Releasing only the muscle spasm leaves the underlying fear, which may well recreate the original muscle spasm. Similarly, releasing the fear alone, leaves a painful spasm which has every potential to recreate the original fear. Unresolved psychological issues can create physical problems, and unresolved physical problems can create psychological issues. This is the reason that so many people tell me that they have been in psychotherapy for years, only to find out that when their body is touched the original psychological issues surface again. In each of us, body and mind are thoroughly interwoven and are effectively treated together. In somatosynthesis we attempt to combine both physical and psychological methods of intervention. This can be done successfully because the human somatosensory system possesses the unique ability to store and recall images.

Our somatosensory system has two important, interrelated functions. It allows us to be aware of our physical being and, it makes possible perception through touch. The somatosensory system originates from nerve receptors located in the body and includes our sense of pressure (light and deep), temperature, pain, joint position and muscle tension.

Normally we think of storing and recalling sensory images as a function of the mind and not the body. Our senses filter signals from the world around us that our brains then use to construct and store images of that world. Vision and hearing are the two most familiar means of imaging— electromagnetic signals trigger the production of visual images, while acoustical signals trigger the production of auditory images. But the eyes themselves do not store and recall visual images, nor do the ears store and recall sound; the brain does.

On the other hand, body tissue, from which our sense of touch arises, is uniquely capable of creating, storing and recalling a variety of images. While the images created through touching are processed and stored in the brain, these images, along with those created by our other senses are also stored and recalled from the body.

Somatic tissue functions as a secondary storage facility for the brain. An automobile accident shows us how this takes place. The sound of screeching tires, the sight of an upcoming tree, the touch of an out of control steering wheel are the sensory cues which cause us to hold our bodies tight and to experience fear in the few moments before impact.

After impact, the continuing spasms and lingering fear are, in effect, stored images of these original cues. Here muscle spasm is a form of somatic memory arising from three different sources—seeing, hearing and touching.

Even fear, a psychological by-product of the accident, is not just stored mentally but physically as well. The same neurochemical receptors associated with the registration of emotions by the brain have been found at various locations in the body. Neuroscientist Candace Pert found that *neuropeptides*, the biochemicals associated with these receptor sites, formed a communication link between the brain, the immune system and our emotions. These emotion-related chemical receptors are concentrated at the body's sites for touch. Thus the neuropeptide system can be affected through touch, and emotions can be stored and recalled through the body. These unprecedented findings lead Pert to conclude that "emotions are not just in the brain, they're in the body."

Somatic memory and somatic recall, two frequently overlooked aspects of our somatosensory system, contribute much to the therapeutic application of somatosynthesis. Through somatic memory, our bodies store sensory and psychological data. We can gain access to this stored information through somatic recall—a process activated through touch. There is also a third attribute of our somatosensory system which figures into somatosynthesis: the multi-sensory nature of perception through the body, called synesthesia.

Synesthesia is the ability to produce a sensation in one sensory modality when another modality is stimulated. While it is present in all of our sensory systems, synesthesia is most pronounced through our system of touch. For example, the stimulation of the skin has a well-known ability to produce visual and auditory images of detail comparable to what we normally perceive through our eyes or ears.

In fact this has lead to the construction of some interesting equipment for the blind and deaf. Paul Bach-y-Rita affixed a twenty-by-twenty square array of small plungers on the skin of a blind person. The bank of vibrating plungers was connected to a television camera. Whatever image the camera was trained on registered in the plungers based on pressure corresponding to brightness—the brighter the image, the harder the plunger pressed into the skin. Thus as the brightness of the scene in front of the camera varied some plungers touched the skin and others did not. With a modest amount of training, people who were blind from birth were able to visually image, then describe objects in the world around them.

Bach-y-Rita's equipment, together with a sample of the image "felt" and "seen" by a blind person, is shown in figure 1.2.

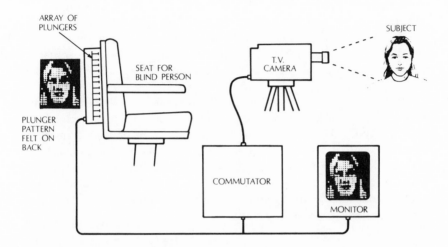

Fig. 1.2: An illustration of the TVSS (tactile visual substitution system) used by Bach-y-Rita to produce images from a television camera on the skin of blind persons. (Drawn after Bach-y-Rita, 1972.)

Similar experiments have converted speech to an array of vibrating plungers, enabling deaf individuals to "hear" the sound of the human voice through their skin. This remarkable cross-over effect is possible because the brain stores sensory information over a wide area, not just those regions normally associated with a given type of sensation. Sensory information coming through the skin apparently has an exceptionally large area of distribution in the brain.

In somatosynthesis we make use of the synesthetic qualities of touch. In a case study cited earlier, I simulated pulling a spear out of the shoulder of a patient. Moving my hand, and therefore her skin, in the same manner I would if I were actually pulling out a spear creates a somatosensory image rich in tactile and visual detail. From what is known in the field of therapeutic imagery, the response of brain and nervous system to the image of an event, is the same as the response to the actual occurrence of that event.

Typically, however, therapeutic imagery involves applying mental visualizations to physical problems: if one has a tight muscle, the imagery of a relaxed muscle would be called forth; if one has cold extremities, imagery connoting warmth would be used; and, if one has a malignant growth, the imagery of marshalling the forces of the immune system to fight the growth would be employed.

The beneficial effects of this kind of imagery have been substantiated and are now utilized in treating a wide variety of disorders. While somatosynthesis makes a similar use of imagery, an important twist is added—the body itself, is brought into the imagery process. Somatic imagery physically attempts to produce a desired therapeutic effect in the body.

Somatic imagery is synesthetic and, therefore, it enhances mental imagery by providing additional tactile, visual, auditory and other sensory inputs. Finally, somatic imagery is a means of accessing whatever content is stored in the body. Thus allowing the imaginal process of pulling out a spear to work its way to conclusion is an effective means of treating both the physical and psychological elements represented by the spear. Easily applied therapeutically, somatic imagery can have dramatic results.

❖

Irene was a graduate student in her late twenties who came to my office with complaints of severe pain and tightness between her shoulder blades.

"It happened suddenly," she informed me. "I woke up this morning and was unable to move my head or neck."

I asked her to lie comfortably on her back while I verbally guided her through the relaxation of her body. After several minutes of quiet relaxation I slipped one hand under her shoulder blades and rested one hand on top of her breastbone. The tightness was unmistakable, the muscles were taut, her shoulder blades seemed pulled together. Actually, she felt as though she were wearing a straight-jacket. I shared this perception with Irene who immediately seized upon its relevance in her life.

"You bet I feel like I have a straight-jacket on," she exclaimed. "I have pressure from my thesis adviser to complete my dissertation, my caseload at work has just increased, my husband feels like I spend no time with him, and I feel like I haven't been relaxed for weeks."

We both agreed that in the absence of having a straight-jacket, she would be freer to handle these complex, life problems. I simply asked Irene to help me remove the jacket. We determined that the straight jacket was fastened in the back with thin strips of material pulled tightly through two metal rings, tied securely in a knot. To undo the jacket, she sat up and faced away from me. I began to loosen the jacket at the uppermost fastener located slightly above her shoulder blades, in the middle of her back where her neck joined her shoulders. I meticulously simulated on Irene's skin the process of untying a knot, pulling the fastening material back through the rings and loosening the jacket. I went through this same process at each of the six fasteners on the straight jacket. Meanwhile I enlisted her help by having her visualize exactly what I was doing. Once I finished undoing the fasteners, I had Irene stretch her arms out and we slowly pulled the jacket off one arm, then the other.

"It's gone," she blurted out, "the jacket's gone, and so is the pain between my shoulder blades. As you pulled the jacket off, I could feel the pain and tightness leave."

Often, the common language we use to describe physical disorders lends itself to somatic imagery. A "knifing pain" suggests pulling out the knife; feeling "knotted up" hints at untying the knots; "twisting" an ankle or a knee implies unwinding the twisted joint; a "locked up" hip or lower back holds out the possibility of finding the key to "unlock" that area; "jamming" a joint together alludes to prying the joint apart; a "gripping pain" points to releasing the grip; and a "tight muscle" marks the needs to loosen, or even unscrew, the area in question.

Somatic imagery, somatic memory and somatic recall are the body's doorways to the mind—doorways opened through touch, enabling us to examine and change the physical and psychological components of our being. This is the essence of somatosynthesis, a healing process that gives birth to a very special type of therapist and an equally special relationship between therapist and client. No longer just a body therapist, the somatosynthesis practitioner actively explores the psychological elements behind physical symptoms. Not just a psychotherapist either, the somatosynthesis practitioner is able to ground the expression of psychological issues in the physical body.

Human touch is largely responsible for this exceptional role of the somatosynthesis practitioner, and touch also fuels the relationship between practitioner and client. The connection of therapist and client through touch is symbolic of healing—two apparently separate entities joined as one. It is the *reciprocal nature of touch* that affords this feeling of oneness better than any other sense.

Given this special relationship between therapist and client in somatosynthesis, the normal descriptive terms for healing relationships seem very limited: doctor/patient, practitioner/client, therapist/client, healer/healee—all suggest a one-sided affair in which one party is active and giving, the other party passive and receiving; only one party has the power. So in somatosynthesis we refer to the healing relationship between a *traveler* and a *guide*, terms that more closely reflect the healing process that unfolds.

Metaphorically speaking, a traveler engages a guide at the outset of a journey. The guide does not simply point out the path for the traveler and say "the mountain is there, I'll explain how to climb it" or "the path is difficult but I'm sure you can make it." The guide is not removed from the actual journey, but truly is an integral part of the journey. Both traveler and guide ascend the same mountain; both traveler and guide walk like paths; both traveler and guide face corresponding hazards; both traveler and guide discover the journey's rewards.

If there is a difference between traveler and guide, it is that the guide has walked the path, climbed the mountain, faced the hazards, and discovered the benefits before. This is very different from most healing/helping therapies where the guide is more like a god—someone who says to the traveler, "do this, or do that, but do not involve me directly in your journey."

In somatosynthesis, the guide cannot help being directly involved with the traveler—the use of touch insures this. So the somatosynthesis process becomes as much a healing journey for the guide as it is for the traveler.

In the following chapters we will examine this healing journey called somatosynthesis. To provide a background for the use of touch in somatosynthesis, we will trace the history of human touch as a healing agent from prehistoric to modern times; and we will explore the role of touch in the physical and psychological development of human beings from conception to adulthood.

To understand how to use somatosynthesis, we will consider the various physical and psychological techniques that make up this process. Many of these techniques are best done with traveler and guide, but some are also suitable for solo journeys of travelers alone.

In many respects the journey we are about to embark on is a recapitulation of my own healing journey—personally and professionally. I began to confront the mind as I worked with the body. Somatosynthesis, then, was my attempt to come to terms with this transition beyond the realm of treating symptoms and practicing structural health care. The more I explored this new frontier of reaching the mind through the body, the more I learned and the more I applied to myself as well. So somatosynthesis also became a tool of personal healing. Now, as your guide to somatosynthesis, I invite you to join me on this healing journey.

2

Primordial Connections

Ancient Roots

I reached back across millennia. Down this long, black chamber I peered millions of years backward in time to touch this primitive creature. My first attempt ended in retreat. It moved away quickly, and I pulled back too. But I tried again to touch it, this time very lightly. Tiny arms reached out, and its body moved toward me. It worked. We had acknowledged each other's presence and re-established our ancient connection through touch. With the help of a microscope, a morsel of food, and a needle-thin probe I had encountered *Amoeba proteus*.

Amoebae are among the oldest life forms on earth. When touched by an object, an amoeba will extend arm-like appendages of its protoplasm, called *pseudopods*. If the object is edible, the pseudopods will embrace, then engulf it. If the object is not edible, pseudopods will form on the opposite side and assist the amoeba in hastily moving away. The world of these primitive, one-celled creatures, lacking brain or nervous system, is organized almost entirely around touch.

Long before the emergence of early humans, long before our most distant ancestors walked the planet, touch had begun to fashion and synthesize life on earth. The role of touch in the process of life—the root of somatosynthesis—has its origins at the most primitive level of Nature.

Amoebae, along with many other protozoans, exhibit this avoidance/approach behavior in response to touch. Called *thigmotropism* (from the Latin *thigmo* meaning to touch and *tropism* meaning orientation), it is defined as the orientation, or movement, of an organism in response to touch. For the amoebae, orientation to touch is a simple matter of approach or avoidance, establishing a fundamental relationship in Nature between touching and movement, between body and behavior, between soma and psyche.

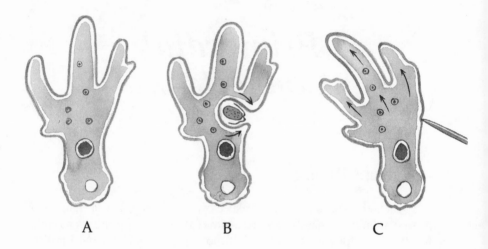

Fig. 2.1: An Amoeba Proteus demonstrating thigmotropism: (A) Neutral position; (B) Extending pseudopods to move towards and engulf a smaller organism that has touched it; and, (C) Extending pseudopods to move away from a needle probe.

In fact thigmotropism is present in almost every form of life. Throughout the animal kingdom, from single cells to human beings, touch influences function and behavior in a manner reminiscent of the amoeba. Cows, for example, when touched on their rumps will swing their hindquarters in the direction of the touch. Touched, in another location, they will move away. A pet will often roll-over to place a favorite part of their body in a position to be rubbed or scratched.

Humans are equally thigmotropic. Touch is a major source of pleasure and pain for us. Since we too often seek pleasure and avoid pain, our behavior is little different from the amoeba. Ours is the same approach/avoidance response to touch only expressed in a more complex fashion.

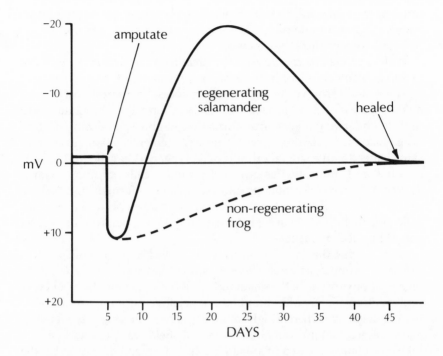

Fig. 2.2: The electrical fields of a salamander and frog when both are amputated at the shoulder. Notice how the salamander's electrical field becomes positive five days after amputation, then swings sharply negative for most of the regeneration period. The frog's electrical field also becomes positive at five days, but never shifts to a negatively charged field. The frog is unable to regenerate the amputated limb. (Drawn after Becker and Marino, 1982.)

Touch is a potent force in the genesis of life. Often referred to as the "mother of the senses," touch is clearly the most primordial sense of living things. Embryologically, it is also the first sense to come into being. All other senses—sight, sound, taste and smell—are derived from the sense of touch. While touch is fundamental to life it is also fundamental to healing. One profoundly moving account of Nature's insistence on touch in the healing process comes from the study of limb regeneration in salamanders. In experimentation spanning 25 years, Robert O. Becker, M.D.; along with his colleagues at the State University of New York in Buffalo, inadvertently demonstrated that touch plays a significant role in the regeneration of missing body parts. Salamanders were studied because of their natural ability to regenerate large portions of their body. Ninety percent of a salamander's body, including its eyes and portions of its brain, are capable of regeneration.

With the inherent complexity of recreating a missing portion of the body, regeneration is by far the most comprehensive example of healing in nature. Becker showed that this healing process has two distinct phases: *dedifferentiation* and *redifferentiation*. Cells around the amputation site initially underwent reverse-transformation. Highly specialized cells that once functioned as bones, nerves, muscles, ligaments, blood vessels and skin changed into a single, primitive cell type. Becker called this dedifferentiation. Ultimately, this group of primitive cells began a forward-transformation redifferentiating into a completely reformed limb. Nature seemed to reach backward to go forward, accessing a primitive memory contained in the body in order to heal. Touch, it turns out, was an integral part of this healing process.

After amputating a salamander's limb, Becker discovered a well-defined electromagnetic field that surrounded and apparently guided the regeneration process. In the salamander this direct current (DC) field was positive immediately after amputation, negative once reverse-transformation began and increasingly more positive as healing (regeneration and redifferentiation) continued. When this field was present around a limb amputation site in a salamander, a fully-formed limb regrew. If the electromagnetic field was disrupted, regeneration failed to take place.

For comparison Becker studied the electromagnetic field around the amputation site in rats and frogs—animals that do not naturally regenerate severed limbs. DC fields were present but they were markedly different from the salamander's field. They never achieved the negative polarity found in the salamander, no dedifferentiation took place and therefore no redifferentiation or regeneration occurred (see figure 2.2).

Becker then hypothesized that artificially creating the salamander's electromagnetic field around the amputation site in a frog might induce regeneration—a hunch which proved correct. After amputating the arm of a frog, Becker used electrical equipment to create and control a DC field. The equipment caused the electromagnetic field around the frog to mimic the electromagnetic field normally found in a salamander. With the salamander's electromagnetic field created by Becker's laboratory equipment, complete limb regeneration took place in normally non-regenerating frogs and rats.

When Becker set about discerning the mechanism that controlled the creation of this electromagnetic field, and thereby the regeneration process, he uncovered a peculiar relationship between nerve and skin cells at the amputation site. Before regeneration begins, a proliferation of skin cells formed a "cap" over the amputation site. Severed nerve endings then grew into this group of skin cells, forming a junction known as the neuroepidermal junction (*neuro* meaning nerve, *epidermal* meaning skin) or NEJ. But the neuroepidermal junction is really nothing more than a primitive system of touch—nerves connected to skin. It is a way of literally putting the healing organism in touch with itself and in touch with its environment.

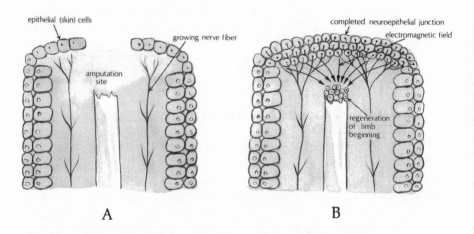

Fig. 2.3: The creation of a healing electromagnetic field at the site of amputation. In (A) the skin cells are just beginning to form a cap over the amputation site and nerves are starting to grow towards them. In (B) nerve cells have made contact with the skin cells completing the formation of the neuroepithelial junction (NEJ) which is a primitive system of touch. The NEJ then creates the electromagnetic field (shown as arrows) which directs the growth of the regenerating limb. (Drawn after Becker, 1982.)

It was the electrical field produced from this primitive system of touch that caused dedifferentiation then regeneration to occur. Becker proved this by disrupting the formation of the NEJ in a salamander. Now after amputation an abnormal electromagnetic field was present and regeneration did not take place.

Next Becker turned to non-regenerating rats in whom he artificially created NEJs. He surgically implanted severed nerve stubs into the animal's skin around the amputation site, then sewed the skin closed. No equipment was used to produce an electromagnetic field, but the surgically created NEJs worked! The rat's healing process now mirrored the salamander's: the polarity became negative, dedifferentiation took place, and a fully-formed limb was regenerated.

Nature seeks touch to heal. Touch is the first system to be formed in the case of regeneration. It then activates a healing process totally transforming the organism, ultimately leading to complete regeneration and regrowth of its physical body. Regeneration is the most extreme example of an organism's capacity for healing and the intimate relationship of touch to this healing process suggests a similar role for touch in other, less extreme instances of healing.

"The healer's job has always been to release something not understood," notes Becker, "to remove obstructions ... between the sick patient and the force of life driving obscurely toward wholeness." And touch is our most ancient healing tool used to release this ill-defined "something," thereby facilitating this journey toward healing and wholeness.

Human Touch: The Healing Matrix

Eons ago, on the African steppe, we were a newborn race, first encountering the meaning of life: a hunter injured during the hunt; a mother's cries during delivery of her child; an old one who breathes no more. How did we respond to these challenges of death, birth, pain and suffering? Scared, our first impulse I am sure was to run. But we soon discovered that the omnipresent forces of life were inescapable. So instead of fleeing we reached out for meaning and understanding. We literally reached out to embrace our human condition: touching our injured comrade; holding the mother during birth; and cradling the old one as the last breath left.

No doubt such events touched even early humans deeply. And to bring meaning to the experience of being human we, in turn, reached out to touch these events. In this way, touch connected our body, which experiences life, with our psyche, which reaches out for meaning in life.

Touch is so fundamental to our human experience that touching to heal may actually be an instinctual rather than a learned response. We know that the human nervous system exhibits a powerful reflex in response to pain. Called the *nociceptive reflex*, it causes us to draw away from painful stimuli (*noci* from the Latin *nocere* meaning to injure). For example, if you prick yourself with a pin or place your finger on a hot stove top, you immediately respond by violently jerking your arm and hand away. This

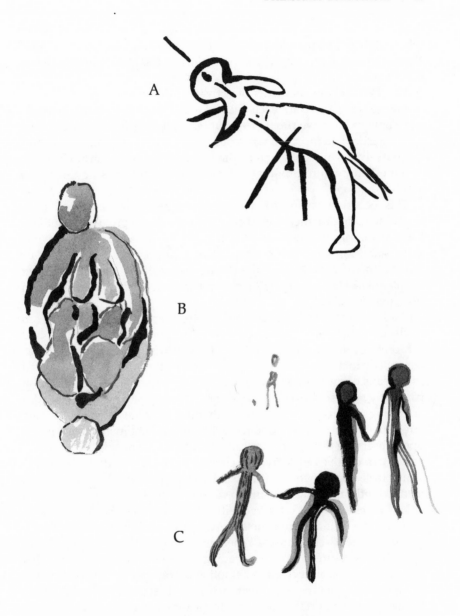

Fig. 2.4: Encounters with life and death depicted in the art of primitive human beings: (A) Stone Age European cave drawing of a wounded person; (B) Stone Age European cave drawing of a birth scene; and, (C) African rock art painting of people holding hands.

reflex action occurs in two stages. Our nerve pathways for touch transmit a pain signal to our brain which then sends a message to our muscles to pull the arm away.

However, within moments of activating this nociceptive reflex our instinctual response is to reach out and touch the affected area. If we hit our elbow or knee, we rub it. If we cut ourselves, we hold the area. If we have intestinal cramps, we wrap our arms around our midsection and hug ourselves. This behavior is not limited to humans but can be observed in almost any injured animal, which immediately licks or caresses a wounded area.

This secondary response to injury I have labelled the *curaceptive* reflex (from the Latin *cura* meaning to care). Like the nociceptive reflex it too is based primarily on the sense of touch and involves the brain, nervous system and muscles. The nociceptive and curaceptive reflexes link us directly to the amoeba. For these reflexes are easily seen as complex adaptations of the simple avoidance and approach behavior exhibited in primitive life forms.

These embedded reflexes also bond us to other human beings. One can easily envisage early humans transferring both the nociceptive and curaceptive reflex from self to other. If I desire to have someone avoid me, why not do to them what I myself avoid. Along these lines, touch evolved as a means of protection and combat. And, if someone else is hurt or in pain, why not also do to them what comes naturally to me. Thus the idea of healing and helping others through touch may have evolved. At any rate, a lot of what we know about the healing use of human touch is based upon observing the natural, untrained responses of people.

The curaceptive reflex gives us clues to a person's needs. We're accustomed to seeing someone with a headache lay their head in their hands, inadvertently applying pressure to various locations on the skull. Stimulation of these points is often very effective in relieving the discomfort. A typical response to a charleyhorse—a painful muscular spasm—is to firmly massage the affected muscle. When cut we frequently grasp the area and apply firm pressure to stop the bleeding. It is an instinctual response that functions as a tourniquet. Under emotional stress people will often place one hand on top of the other over their mid-chest (near the heart). It is a means of self-comfort that helps discharge the effects of stress.

Instinctual behavior eventually became accepted practice. Kleanthes, in his book *How Ancient Healing Governs Modern Therapeutics*, called them "hand-curatives" and found that every major human civilization practiced some form of healing through touch. He points to anthropological evidence that originally these methods were "instinctively practiced." Ultimately, he suggests, these early somatic methods evolved into modern practices like surgery and manipulative therapy.

Ancient art and artifacts from around the world support this view. They give evidence that early humans used their hands to heal and minister to others. Archeological findings of trephined skulls many thousands of years old offer further substantiation. Trephination is the process of drilling or puncturing holes in the skull. Primitive man performed this surgery, we think, in the case of severe headaches, epilepsy and mental disorders. In fact the word surgery is actually derived from the Greek *chirurgery* (*cheir* hand + *ergon* work) which means to work by hand. So surgery, one of modern medicine's most important therapeutic methods, can actually be traced to ancient healing practices based on human touch.

Refinement of primitive behavior is characteristic of our evolution as a race. The earliest evidence of this refinement in the use of touch for healing comes from Eastern civilizations, particularly China. Acupuncture, moxibustion, massage, and pulse diagnosis—the foundation of traditional Chinese medicine—are all based upon touch.

Tradition holds that acupuncture was developed through the efforts of the "Yellow Emperor," Huang Ti, during the period 2698-2598 B.C. Most historians of Chinese medicine feel that acupuncture was a refinement of more primitive measures of using touch for healing. Chu, for example, writes that acupuncture most likely evolved from primitive practices of using pressure to alleviate the pain of injury. Pressure was first applied by hand, then by stones whose shape was gradually refined to make the application of pressure to a single location easier. Ultimately the use of pointed flints and bamboo was adopted by the early Chinese. Archaeological evidence of flint needles in China dates back as far as 7000 B.C. As technology changed, so did the instruments of pressure. With the advent of the Iron Age, needles made of iron, steel or precious metals were used. In their *History of Chinese Medicine*, Wong and Wu saw massage developing in a similar way. As a medical practice it "evolved," they note, "from the instinctive action [curaceptive reflex] of rubbing, stroking and kneading to soothe an injured or stiff limb."

R. H. Major reports that massage pre-dated acupuncture. He notes that it was mentioned in the earliest Chinese medical works and enjoyed two periods of prominence, first in early Chinese history (2600 B.C.) and then again during the T'ang Dynasty (619—906 A.D.) when it was elevated to a science and became one of the seven branches of Chinese medicine.

According to Chow, the massage techniques of An-Mo (pressing and rubbing) and Tui-Na (thrusting and rolling) were described in medical texts of the Han dynasty (207 B.C.—220 A.D.) and taught in special institutes of the T'ang Dynasty. An intricate set of hand movements, the eight Kua, were used over specific body areas related to various organs. Practitioners were thus able to influence the function of the corresponding organs.

Moxibustion, or moxa, involves the use of combustible cones of *artemisia moxa* or *common mugwort*. These cones are placed in prescribed patterns at certain points on the skin and then lit. As the cones smoulder, blisters are raised and act as an irritant or stimulant through the skin. Even moxibustion is apparently a refinement of earlier healing practices. Prehistoric humans may have heated the stones used to stimulate the skin, attempting to enhance the overall effect.

If acupuncture, moxibustion and massage formed the basis of traditional Chinese therapy, examination of the pulse became the preferred method of diagnosis. When using the pulse for diagnosis, three fingers were placed along the wrist. By varying the depth of pressure, checking the pulse on both right and left sides of the body and noting the quality of the pulse, Chinese diagnosticians were able to learn the condition of various body systems.

Diagnosis through touch, when held up against modern methods seems quite primitive. Richard Selzer, a physician-essayist, wrote of one such rare encounter between pulse diagnosis and modern medicine that took place in 1975. Yeshi Dhonden, a Tibetan monk and personal physician to the Dalai Lama, made rounds in a hospital where Selzer was a surgeon.

In an almost ritualistic manner, Yeshi Dhonden spent nearly one-half hour examining a patient by simply monitoring her pulse. When he was through, he returned to a conference room to share his findings with a group of medical doctors. In a poetic way the Tibetan doctor rendered his diagnosis. There are eddies and vortices in the flow of the patient's blood. Winds coursing through her heart even before she was born, blowing open a deep gate that must never be opened. The waters of life cascade like waterfalls, "knocking loose the land and flooding her breath." A medical professor stammered for the 'real' diagnosis and the host of the rounds, the one physician who actually knew, answered, "Congenital heart disease. Interventricular septal defect, with resultant heart failure."

To the amazement of Selzer, and the other doctors present, Yeshi Dhonden had found through his touch alone the precise cause of the

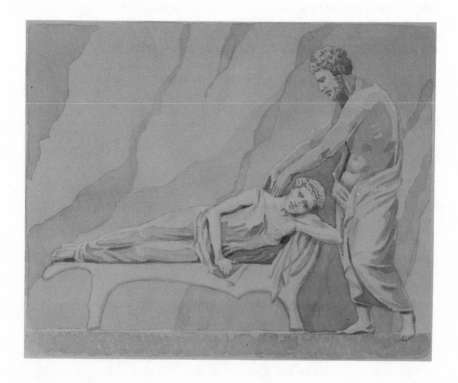

Fig. 2.5: Aesculapius administering healing touch to a girl. (Drawn after the original Greek relief sculpture.)

woman's troubles. His touch had penetrated as deeply as the most sophisticated probes of Western medical science.

In myth and fact, the history of Western medicine is closely linked with healing through touch. In Greco-Roman civilization healing by touch was the province of Aesculapius, a physician elevated to the rank of a demigod. Aesculapius, who had two daughters Hygeia and Panacea, is said to have been the son of Apollo and Coronis.

The cult of Aesculapius, also called the Divine Physician or Gentle Healer, began in Greece about 420 B.C. Aesculapian healing practices were carried out at more than 200 temples, known as Aesculapieia, where physician-priests were seen as conduits of this diety's divine healing power. They employed laying-on of hands as one means of transferring this healing power to patients. According to historian W. A. Jayne, Aesculapian priests applied their right hands to the patient in a fully opened position or with the thumb, index and middle finger open and the other fingers closed. The left hand was considered malevolent and never used in laying-on hands.

At times, the direct touch of Aesculapius was sought through a practice called temple-sleep, or incubation. Patients were first "purified" through fasting, bathing and massage. They were then allowed to enter the temple and sleep in the inner sanctum. During sleep they awaited a dream-like visitation by Aesculapius, often in the company of Hygeia and Panacea, who touched the afflicted area, performed an operation or gave special instructions. The patient would usually awaken, fully restored to health, and the healing miracle would be recorded on a votive stone tablet. Scores of votive tablets have been excavated at Aesculapieia throughout Greece and Crete. Inscribed are healings ranging from blindness to paralysis. By Greco-Roman times, at least, exploiting the healing relationship between body and mind through touch was accepted practice.

Early Physicians

Hippocrates, generally regarded as the "Father of Medicine" in Western civilization, was a member of the Asclepiad, a guild of lay-physicians who ascribed to the precepts of Aesculapian healing. The Hippocratic Oath, used as an ethical standard by physicians to this day, begins with the following allegiance to the Gods: "I swear by Apollo the physician, by Aesculapius, Hygeia, and Panacea... to keep according to my ability and my judgement the following Oath...."

In Hippocrates' view, healing resulted from the power of nature whose effects were produced through the release of vital forces (vis medicatrix naturae). The purpose of the physician, according to the father of medicine, was to aid nature in its healing process. Hippocrates was well aware of the value of human touch in assisting nature. In speech and writing he used the term *chiron* when referring to practitioners skilled in the use of manual methods to restore health. He emphasized the use of friction, the Greek term for massage and was one of the first practitioners to differentiate between the effects of specific types of massage. According to Hippocrates, vigorous massage tightened weak body tissues whereas soft relaxed them. Lengthy massage decreased tissue mass, while moderately long massage increased tissue mass.

Hippocrates was also aware of the role of the spine in health. Sounding very much like a modern day chiropractor, Hippocrates urged physicians to look to the spine as the basis of ill-health. His description of the relationship between areas of spinal misalignment and dysfunction of specific organs is amazingly accurate by modern standards. Hippocrates advocated manual manipulation to correct spinal misalignments. His recommended hand positions and specific instructions on the direction in which manipulative pressure should be applied are still heeded by today's practitioners.

Hippocrates' students and successors enlarged upon his therapeutic methods. Ascelpiades, a noted physician after Hippocrates, favored massage over all the Hippocratic methods. Celsus, also a successor of Hippocrates, cautioned physicians to look beyond the specific site of illness or injury in their use of massage. "Much more often," he wrote, "some other part is to be massaged than that which is the seat of pain...." Thus, the practice of *reflexology* (stimulating one area to effect another) was introduced into Greco-Roman medical practice. In fact, the idea of reflex stimulation was similar to traditional Chinese acupuncture where needles are inserted at points often far removed from the site of pain or disease.

Galen, who lived nearly 500 years after Hippocrates, used the same methods of manual medicine to restore health. According to author Chester Wilk, Galen was given the title "Prince of Physicians" after he manipulated the neck vertebrae of a prominent Roman scholar, Eudemus, and corrected the paralysis of his right hand.

The advanced anatomical knowledge of Greco-Roman physicians made an important contribution to the therapeutic use of human touch. Before the time of Aesculapius and Hippocrates, possession by "devils and evil spirits" was a popular theory of disease. Healing practices were focussed on driving these evil spirits out of the body. Massage, for example, was supposed to literally push out the evil spirits. For that reason, most massage strokes were *centrifugal*—starting near the middle of the body and moving out toward the periphery. With the advent of the "humoral theory" of disease the basis for this practice changed. The humoral doctrine held that "stagnant humors" in the body were responsible for disease. One of the early advocates of this theory was the Islamic medical scholar Ibn Sina, known in the western world as Avicenna. During the 11th century A.D., Ibn Sina authored a monumental treatise, *The Canon of Medicine*, drawing upon medical knowledge from Eastern and Western sources. Though the circulation of blood had not been discovered in the

West, Ibn Sina advocated *centripetal* massage, directed from the periphery toward the heart. This he felt would facilitate the movement of stagnant humors—a thesis which is correct based on modern anatomical and physiological knowledge.

"Thy shouldst lay thy hand upon it," reads a medical text written 1500 years before Christ, in Egypt. This instruction was given to the physician of a wounded patient. We glimpse at such ancient Egyptian healing practices through the records left by scribes of those days. Much of Egyptian medical knowledge was preserved in hieroglyphics on the leaves of the papyrus tree. Called the *Medical Papyri*, these texts reveal that "laying-on hands" was practiced by ancient Egyptian physicians, often in concert with other methods of healing.

In the *Berlin Medical Papyrus*, instructions for healing children were accompanied with the following recitation:

> "My hands are on this child, and the hands of Isis [a goddess of healing] are on him, as she puts her hands on her son Horus."

This incantation is based on the Egyptian myth of Isis and Osiris. Isis, an important Egyptian goddess, had two brothers Osiris and Seth. Seth killed and dismembered Osiris, whose body was reconstituted by Isis. Afterwards, Isis conceived a son, Horus, by Osiris. Therefore the hand of Isis symbolized healing to ancient Egyptians. Isis was also considered to be a protector and healer of children because she was the mother of the god Horus. Isis is often pictured holding the boy child Horus in a pose reminiscent of the gripping image of the *Madonna*, a powerful symbol of the healing bond of touch between mother and child.

Another important Egyptian medical figure was Wenen-nefer, described in Egyptian papyri as "Chief of Priests, Chief of Magicians, Chief Physician to the King; who everyday reads the books, who treats the sick, who lays his hand on them, whereby he knows them; gifted in the examination by hand."

Guido Majno, in *The Healing Hand*, seemed surprised at how often touching a patient or an injured area was found in the *Smith Medical Papyrus*. It suggested that Egyptian physicians afforded the practice an "intrinsic value" in the care of the sick and wounded. "The comfort of physical touch," Majno mused, "reaches deep down, to ancestral depths far older than mankind."

Fig. 2.6: Egyptian figures administering massage to the feet and hands. This appears to be a painting showing the early use of reflex stimulation.

The Royal Touch

Special power was accorded those who practiced healing through touch, particularly when it was linked to spiritual customs and beliefs. For this reason many individuals felt that merely proclaiming their belief in the spiritual dimension of healing was enough to establish their privileged right to heal others through touch. There is much more to spiritual healing than simple proclamation of belief. Historically, however, ruling monarchs were famous for usurping the power to heal through touch. Even today it may be said that some evangelical and charismatic "healers" are guilty of the same practice.

Vespasian, Roman emperor from 70 to 79 AD, was angered when a blind man asked to receive his touch. But before the man could be driven away, Vespasian's ministers, who sensed the power which the Emperor would accrue if successful, encouraged him to try. Vespasian consented, laid his hand upon this man and he was supposedly cured of blindness. Others touched by this emperor-healer were reportedly cured of lameness.

Adrian, another Roman emperor, healed dropsy through the touch of his fingertips, according to the ancient writer Spartianus. Pyrrhus, the Grecian king, used his foot instead of his hand, wrote Plutarch. He would pass his great toe over the bodies of people lying on their backs to treat intestinal complaints and disorders of the spleen. And Egill, the Icelandic hero, was reportedly healed of his battle wounds by King Olaf.

It was called the "Royal Touch" in the courts of England and France. The Holy Oil used to anoint monarchs at their coronations was said to have conveyed to them the power to heal through touch. From the ninth to the eighteenth century, kings and queens of England and France regularly exercised this power. In fact it was disputed whether French or English monarchs were first to use the royal touch. Historical evidence points to Robert the Pious, 970-1031, as the first French monarch to heal through touch. On the English side, apparently Edward the Confessor, 1042-1066, initiated the practice. At first the royal touch was applied in all instances of disease and ill-health. Ultimately it was limited to the treatment of one condition only—the "King's Evil."

The "King's Evil" was the name given to *scrofula*, a now rare form of tuberculosis spread by cattle. It primarily affects the lymph nodes of the neck causing them to swell and become pustulant. Left untreated, this bacterial infection often spread to the face causing open purulent sores and disfigurement. Scrofula was common in Europe from the Middle Ages through the seventeenth century, although the term was often a catchall diagnosis for many unknown conditions affecting the head and neck.

"Most pious Edward wrought the miracle of cure," wrote Shakespeare, as he set this affliction, and the healing touch of Edward the Confessor to verse in *Macbeth*.

In one scene a doctor says:

> There are a crew of wretched souls
> That stay his cure; their malady convinces
> The great assay of art; but at his touch
> Such sanctity hath Heaven given his hand
> They presently amend.

Macduff then asks Malcolm what disease the doctor is referring to and Malcolm replies:

> 'Tis called the Evil;
> A most miraculous work in this good King;

Which often since my here remain in England;
I have seen him do. How he solicits Heaven
Himself best knows; but strangely visited people,
All swoln and ulcerous, pitiful to the eye,
The mere despair of surgery, he cures,
Hanging a golden stamp about their necks,
Put on with holy prayer; and 'tis spoken
To the succeeding royalty he leaves
The healing benediction.

After being touched, the English supplicant received a gold coin from the monarch—the 'golden stamp' in Shakespeare's verse. Originally this coin was the *Angel-noble*, struck with the figure of St. Michael slaying a dragon: a symbol of Divine intervention against disease. Later known as a "touch-piece," the coin was pierced, strung with white ribbon and worn around the neck as an amulet to ward off the return of disease.

Christianity was the religious basis of the royal touch. Since monarchs were presumed to be divinely chosen, they inherited along with their office other divine gifts such as the power to heal. Healing through the "sacred hand" of a monarch was considered a miracle comparable to those of the saints of the Catholic Church. The comparison between Jesus healing leprosy through touch and a King healing scrofula through touch is unmistakable. A stained glass mural in the abbey of Mont St. Michel depicted the anointing of French kings in one section and their subsequent journey among the sick to administer healing through touch. This mural was set side by side with those recalling the miracles and deeds of other Catholic saints. No doubt English and French rulers enjoyed and used this comparison to their advantage. It afforded them a popular religious domain outside the established control of the church.

Typically the royal touch was administered by simple touching, stroking or making the sign of the cross over a victim's sore. In the French court it was also accompanied by the benediction, *Le Roi te touche, Dieu te guerisse* (the King touches, God heals). The English royalty had elaborate services and a special liturgy for the royal touch. Under the reign of Charles II, this healing service was included into the *Book of Common Prayer*, made available by the Church to the general public.

For the English, healing through touch was even taken as proof of rightful ascendancy to the throne. In the battle for sovereignty between Edward IV and Henry VI, Sir John Fortescue, a devoted follower of Henry VI, wrote in the years between 1461 and 1463, that anyone witnessing Henry VI's administration of the royal touch would be assured that "this monarch's undoubted title to the throne is thus confirmed by divine approval." Partisans of the House of York, supporters of Edward IV as king, would have none of this and countered that their man truly possessed this miraculous gift.

After the Catholic reign of Mary Tudor (1558), the English court reverted back to Protestantism under Elizabeth I, but Rome proclaimed that Queen Elizabeth, by reason of her excommunication from the Catholic Church, did not possess the gift of healing. Not so, said Richard Wiseman, a noted surgeon and medical historian. The Queen's "gift was not taken away upon our departure from the Church of Rome." Queen Elizabeth preserved and practiced this royal tradition although, for the first time, a number of voices in opposition were heard. It was not just the Vatican that condemned this practice by the Protestant monarchs of England but also members of a radical Protestant sect, the Puritans, who had taken a stance against the royal touch—a practice they labelled superstitious.

The English Civil Wars toppled the regime of Charles I. Yet even in prison and ultimately on his way to the gallows Charles I was beseeched by sick people longing to be touched. Charles I was not the only King to be asked to administer the royal touch while in captivity. A century earlier, while held captive in Spain, French King Francis I treated the Spanish public for scrofula, prompting the following verse in his honor:

> Behold how the king cures the scrofulous with a
> single gesture of his hand;
> Though captive, he has not lost the favours from
> on High.

At the conclusion of the English Civil Wars in 1656, Charles I was beheaded, and Oliver Cromwell took office as Lord Protector of the British Commonwealth, in place of a ruling monarch. There were reports, though obviously circulated by loyalists to the throne, that he too tried to administer the royal touch. One English chronicler writes, "that method had been tried by the late usurper Cromwell, but without success."

With the Restoration of 1660, and a return to the monarchy of Charles II, son of the beheaded Charles I, the royal miracle quickly regained its former stature. Charles II was a popular healer. Records kept by the king's physician, John Browne, show that during the twenty-five years of his reign he touched 4,000 to 6,000 sufferers a year for a total in excess of 100,000 persons. According to Browne, those who came before him hailed not only from the British Isles but also from various parts of Europe (Germany, France, Holland) and even from the American colonies.

But even from its inception not all were convinced of the royal touch. The Catholic Church, in particular, disliked the practice because it appropriated power and authority from the Church and placed a living monarch in a category usually afforded a saint. "The Holy Church praises them [the monarchs practicing the royal touch]," said Pope Gregory VII, as early as 1081, "but does not invest them with the glory of any such miracles."

Doctors of the period, though they referred afflicted patients to the king, questioned the methods by which reported healings took place. Yet investigations made by skeptical English physicians and church officials often turned up evidence that healings had taken place. This was the first time that modern medical science, though still in its infancy, attempted to confront such an ancient healing practice.

In 1732 William Beckett, a respected surgeon and investigator of the royal touch concluded that cures did result from the King's touch. He also provided one of the first scientific rationalizations of this healing phenomenon. The excitement of being in the King's presence was so great, according to Beckett, that it caused an increased rate of blood flow and thereby effected a cure. By hypothesizing a relationship between body and mind through touch, Beckett's speculation was actually quite advanced for its time.

Of course not everyone was miraculously healed. From inquiries similar to Beckett's we learn that some were cured of scrofula after once receiving the monarch's touch, while others sought the "sacred hand" again. Reports from credible witnesses attest to the effectiveness of the royal hand against scrofula although the period of recovery varied from individual to individual.

Both the English and French monarchs ended this practice in the early nineteenth century. It died for many reasons, not the least was a faltering belief in the exalted status of monarchs. "There are no longer any hands virtuous enough to heal the scrofula," declared Chateaubriand before Charles X's decision to revive the practice.

The intellectual climate of the seventeenth and eighteenth centuries was also predisposed against the notion of royal healing through touch. With the dawning of the Age of Reason, explanation of phenomena that did not appeal to accepted modes of reason were scoffed upon. Descartes had written his *Meditations* in 1641, and Newton had written his *Principia* in 1687. These seminal works laid down a logical, rational basis of proof that became the touchstone of scientific inquiry for the next three hundred years. However, those opposed to the royal touch were very selective and discerning in their arguments.

Since most scientists and philosophers of this period needed to be careful that their intellectual endeavors did not offend the Church, they often went to great lengths to separate their criticism of this royal miracle from criticism of miracles in general. Miracles occurring within the context of the Church were acceptable, but miracles performed by a monarch were not. What an interesting turn of events. Once this practice afforded monarchs a privileged position outside the scope of the Church; now, standing apart from the religious mainstream was a liability at the hands of detractors.

Many rode an intellectual middle ground on this issue. While agreeing that a monarch's touch was not miraculous in the religious sense, they did ascribe healing powers to the ruler's hand. Some even attempted to discern a rational basis for the phenomenon, appealing to astrology, herbal remedies taken by the monarch, the medicinal power of the ruler's saliva, or the genetics of the royal lineage. The most sophisticated explanations, like William Beckett's, proposed that psychological factors influenced the recovery from illness.

Finally people other than ruling monarchs began to practice healing through touch, and this also hastened its decline as an exclusive right of royalty. The English were not very tolerant of those laying claim to a gift reserved for kings and queens. So when Valentine Greatrakes, an Irish nobleman, declared that he too possessed the ability to heal through touch, it caused quite a commotion in the court of Charles II. The "Irish Stroker," as he was called, had an audience from around the world and claimed cures when Charles II had failed. Reportedly able to cure more than just scrofula, Greatrakes was invited by the King to demonstrate his ability on a noblewoman suffering from headaches. Greatrakes attempted to heal this woman by "laying-on hands" in the presence of Charles II, but to no avail—a failure which cost him his reputation and career.

In France they were called *septennaires* or *touchoux* (from the French word for touch), in Spain *setes* or *saludors*, in England the *seventh-son* or *seventh-daughter*. Throughout Europe, there was, and still is, a belief that the seventh child of an unbroken string of children of the same sex was a born healer, *panseux de secret* (possessor of the secret). Reference to this belief can be traced back to the European sixteenth and seventeenth century although the lore appears to have even more ancient roots in the metaphysical doctrines of Greece, Rome, Egypt and the East. Laying-on hands was the traditional method of these seventh-son healers. As with the royal touch of monarchs, initially these seventh-sons administered to sufferers of any number of conditions. It was primarily in England and France that some, like the ruling monarchs, limited their practice to the healing of scrofula. However, in Spain, many *saludors* were supposedly endowed with a special gift for treating rabies and other animal bites through touch.

The English monarchy, as mentioned earlier, viewed these seventh-sons as competitors and dealt harshly with them. It was a crime in England to lay on hands for the treatment of scrofula. The French were more lenient in their attitude towards the seventh-sons. In fact, a close relationship was established between the *septennaires* and St. Marcoul of Corbeny, often described as the patron saint of healing scrofula in France. It was to St. Marcoul that the French monarchy also looked for religious legitimacy of their divine healing gift. From the fourteenth century onwards, almost every French monarch stopped at the abbey in Corbeny to pay homage to the saint and hold a service for healing the sick. But the monks of Corbeny also welcomed the seventh-sons who then adopted St. Marcoul as their patron saint.

The healing touch of seventh-sons outlasted the "sacred hands" of French and British monarchs. A famous healer, the so-called seventh-son of Vovette, practiced successfully well into the middle of the nineteenth century. This seventh-son legacy forms the basis of a fascinating European shamanistic tradition almost entirely overlooked by writers on the subject. Remnants of this tradition of the seventh-son are still found throughout Europe and within non-European cultures as well.

Touch, Healing and Spirituality

Spiritual philosophy was as important as medical philosophy to these early practitioners. In varying degrees, cultures around the world based their practice of healing around spiritual notions and incorporated touch into this relationship. Whether in ancient China, India, Egypt, Greece, or Rome, health was assumed to reflect the relationship between man and God—good health implying a harmonious relationship, ill health implying a discordant relationship. Healing was therefore a process of reestablishing this balanced connection between man and God.

This is the original meaning of the word *holy*—a divine union between man and God. In fact, *holy* is actually derived from an Old English word *hael*, which also gave rise to the words *hale* (as in 'hale and hardy'), *health*, *heal*, and *whole*. Health, therefore, had an original spiritual connotation, as a state of being whole (holy), and healing was the process of establishing wholeness (holiness).

Interestingly *disease* (dis-ease), which implies the opposite of health, is derived from two Latin words, the prefix *dis*, meaning not, and *ease*, which comes from the Latin *adiaces* meaning adjacent or touching. Dis-ease literally means nonadjacent, separate or not touching. When we don't touch and are not touched ourselves, we are not whole. So the relationship between touching and healing is implicitly contained in our language.

Traditionally healing the relationship between man and a transcendent reality (call it Nature or God) has been a spiritual pursuit. Not surprisingly, 'laying-on hands' was first performed by priests and rulers—those most directly involved in the spiritual matters of ancient civilizations. Healing was a force of Nature (or God) and these spiritual leaders were conduits for its beneficent use by humankind. Symbolically and literally, they mediated this healing relationship between man and this transcendent reality through touch.

In the Hindu practice of *shaktipat diksha*, for example, touch plays a central role in establishing this spiritual union between man and God. *Diksha* means initiation, and *shaktipat* refers to various methods by which a Hindu priest initiates an aspirant's spiritual awakening. In *Sparsha diksha*, or initiation through touch, the priest touches the initiate at selected points on the body: traditionally, between the eyebrows, over the heart, or at the base of the spine. This touch arouses a latent divine energy within the initiate which, when fully awakened, brings spiritual enlightenment. There are written accounts of such spiritual awakening. Gopi Krishna writes of his experience in 1937:

> Suddenly, with a roar like that of a waterfall, I felt a stream of liquid light entering my brain through the spinal cord. The illumination grew brighter and brighter, the roaring louder, I experienced a rocking sensation and then felt myself slipping out of my body, entirely enveloped in a halo of light.

A similar theme—reestablishing the connection between man and God through touch—is echoed in the healings attributed to Jesus. The Bible records many healings through touch ranging from blindness and leprosy to spinal malformation and epilepsy. In each case, touch was a means of linking the afflicted person with God (spiritual healing), thereby facilitating the healing of the body (physical healing). St. Luke 13: 11-14 tells the story of a woman healed of a spinal deformation:

> And there was a woman who had had a spirit of infirmity for eighteen years; she was bent over and could not fully straighten herself. And when Jesus saw her, he called her and said to her, 'Woman, you are freed from your infirmity.' And he laid his hands upon her, and immediately she was made straight, and she praised God.

Reference is frequently made to Jesus experiencing 'virtue leaving him' as a result of healing. More modern translations of the Bible substitute the word *power* for *virtue* as in this passage from St. Luke 6: 17-19, "And all the crowd sought to touch him, for power came forth from him and healed them all." For "virtue" not only means "moral excellence," it also means the "inherent power to accomplish a given effect." Jesus passed this gift of healing to his disciples. In St. Mark 16: 18, he says of them, "They shall lay hands on the sick and they shall recover."

The Universality of Healing Through Touch

The healing use of human touch is a part of the history of humankind not only in cultures like China, Tibet, India, Greece, Rome, Egypt and Europe where written records survive to tell a fascinating story but in every culture around the world. The island cultures of the South Pacific, tribes throughout Africa, Eskimo peoples, aboriginal Australians, traditional societies of Central and South America and Native Americans all incorporated human touch in their healing practices. The difficulty is that in this age of modern, technological medicine it is hard to take the notion of touching and healing seriously. At best, a skeptic might conclude, as did William Beckett in 1732, that human touch is a placebo, effective not of its own accord but because those who receive it want it to work. At worst the practice might simply be viewed as charlatanism. Even monarchs who performed the royal touch—from Vespasian to Queen Anne—had difficulty accepting its effectiveness. William III called the practice "a silly superstition" and performed the rite only once. He offered those who came before him a cautious blessing, "God give you better health and more sense."

Perhaps it is easier to dismiss the healing use of human touch with the advice of King William III than to accept this practice today. Yet, the long history and universality of this tradition suggests more than mere ritualistic superstition. Here is a classic encounter between modern science and ancient tradition where, at first glance, reason would appear to rule over ritual.

Modern Medicine versus Ancient Healing Practice

This stand-off between modern medicine and ancient healing practice can also produce the unexpected results I witnessed one summer in San Diego. It was 1979 and by accident I stumbled into a talk being given by a spiritual healer to a group of several hundred medical doctors.

Olga Worrall, the healer, reminded me of a favorite aunt. She was a prim and proper woman in her seventies who for 50 years practiced "laying-on hands" at a Methodist Church in Baltimore, Maryland. Throughout her life she never accepted any payment for her services. She was studied by scientists, referred to professionally by medical doctors, and loved by thousands whose lives she affected. At this meeting she was speaking about a research project involving her, on display at Harvard University Medical School. Toward the end of her lecture she turned to the medical audience and matter-of-factly asked, "By the way, would you like to see how a session goes?"

Olga then motioned for a young medical doctor to come down onto the podium as a subject for "laying-on hands." He had a quizzical look on his face but he sat very still. She walked behind him, gently placing one hand at the base of his neck and the other on top of his head. She described what she was doing in a very unpretentious way.

"I'm going into neutral," she said, "coasting just like a car and allowing whatever will happen to take place. I'm not trying to make anything happen one way or the other, I'm just acting as a channel for this healing energy."

After several minutes she removed her hands and whispered something to this young doctor. He left the podium and she went on to conclude her talk. It was all rather strange. From outward appearances, nothing had happened. The doctor said nothing upon leaving the stage. However, as we filed out of the auditorium, I noticed this young physician sitting on the grass under a nearby tree. His white coat and name tag were still in place, but his head was in his hands and he was sobbing, softly.

Something had taken place! In the brief time Olga had her hands on this young man, she was able to reach him—her touch easing his pain. Here now was someone lost upon terrain he was supposed to have known well. What a tender outcome for this encounter between ancient and modern healer. "Laying-on hands" had affected him profoundly, and it was very difficult to rationalize this experience with his traditional medical training.

Three years later I was again back in San Diego with Olga in another unlikely setting. Instead of watching, I participated; instead of receiving, I administered "laying-on hands" along with 14 other individuals under Olga's tutelage. This was not a religious service, it was a conference on health, yet there were almost 2000 conferees who came before us.

There was very little formality to this event. Olga insisted on that. Each of us stood behind a chair as conferees came to us and sat down. Olga instructed us to place both hands on the head or shoulders of the person in front of us, for no more than 20 or 30 seconds. After that we could share some words of concern and compassion with them, then we were ready for the next person.

It was like a choreographed ballet: people flowed in front of me, I reached out to touch them, they left, and someone else took their place. It happened so fast, there was no time for ordinary contact; no time to ask a name, let alone to remember a face. But we managed to see all those people in less than an hour.

Looking back on this experience I can imagine what Charles II or Louis XIV must have felt when administering the royal touch to thousands of people. Perhaps I can also understand Vespasian's hesitation at "laying-on hands." At first I was a little scared too. What was I doing up there in front of all those people? And how was it helping?

Two months later my telephone rang with some answers to these questions. The female caller asked if I were the person who had done "laying-on hands" at the San Diego conference. I said I was and she replied, "Good! It's taken me two months to track you down."

She went on to tell me that she had suffered with neck pain for the last twenty years. She had seen various specialists but to no avail.

"After you touched me that day," she recounted, "my neck pain disappeared and hasn't returned since. I was just calling to thank you."

I thanked her for going out of her way to find me and, after placing the receiver down, I was overcome with a strange urge to cry and laugh at the same time—partly out of joy and partly because I felt overwhelmed. Like the young medical doctor I had seen several years before, some familiar parameters of my world had just been shaken.

High Tech, High Touch

Ironically the rapid growth of technological medicine has also sparked renewed interest in older healing traditions like spiritual healing. John Naisbitt dubbed these countervailing trends, "High Tech/High Touch." As health-care grew technologically (high tech), Naisbitt noted, the "human factor" became less important. Countering this trend, he observed the emergence of more human-oriented, health-care practices (high touch).

There are many examples of high touch balancing high tech. Home births or "birthing rooms" often replace traditional hospital room deliveries. Hospices, places that humanely care for dying patients, replace sophisticated life-support measures. And people seek health-care that involves the most human-oriented practice of all—human touch.

Western interest in acupuncture, the growing acceptance of chiropractic and osteopathic methods of manipulative therapy, the increased use of massage and the inclusion of laying-on hands healing services in church ministries are signs that human touch is being reintroduced into Western healing practices.

Massage, for example, once a cornerstone of healing in Greco-Roman times was largely neglected until the early nineteenth century. Ironically, a French translation of an ancient Chinese book, *The Kung-Fu of the Tao-Tse*, restimulated modern interest in massage. Per Henrik Ling of Sweden, considered the father of massage in the West, based his system of Swedish massage on the ancient Chinese practices described in this book. *Effleurage* and *petrissage, friction* and *vibration*, French translations of the Chinese techniques of *An-Mo* and *Tui-Na*, form the basis of modern day massage.

Chiropractic and osteopathy, which also emerged during the nineteenth century, can claim a similarly ancient heritage. Osteopathy was founded by Andrew Still in America shortly after the Civil War. It was Still's belief that misalignment of the joints of the body impeded the circulation of blood and lymphatic fluids, which in turn contributed to disease and poor health. Manual manipulation to re-align the joints, Still concluded, would re-establish a normal fluid flow, thereby enhancing the body's ability to combat disease and remain healthy. Poor circulation of body fluids is a modern term for "stagnant humors," held to be the cause of disease by Hippocrates, Avicenna and many of the ancient practitioners mentioned earlier.

Chiropractic owes its beginning to Daniel David Palmer, also in the later half of the nineteenth century. Palmer felt that misalignment of the joints of the body, particularly the vertebral joints of the spine, interfered with the flow of nerve impulses between the brain and peripheral organs. Since the control of the body was established through the nervous system, Palmer reasoned that interference with this control system would lead to incoordination and disease.

In a manner analogous to Andrew Still's hypothesis, Palmer proposed that manually manipulating the spine to reduce these misalignments (called vertebral subluxations by Palmer) would correct nerve interference and remove this cause of disease. Palmer's concepts of the spine's relationship to disease hark back to Hippocrates, while spinal manipulation has been used for thousands of years in cultures around the world.

Chiropractic, osteopathy, acupuncture and massage are examples of the healing use of human touch that have attained a high degree of popular support in recent years, albeit limited acceptance within the traditional medical community. At the same time, the creation of a new class of health practitioners has also taken place. Referred to as *somatic therapists* they are an eclectic group, borrowing methods from more established disciplines like chiropractic, osteopathy, massage, physical therapy, and acupuncture or creating their own novel methods of using human touch for healing. This new field, as noted previously, includes a wide variety of techniques based on human touch for diagnosis and therapy—a collection of "hands-on" methods ranging from mechanical manipulation of muscles and bones to modulation of the electromagnetic fields associated with the human body.

Touching to Heal the Mind

The use of touch to heal the body is well-established in the history of human civilization. Tracing the historical role of touch in healing the mind is a more difficult task. In part this is because the distinction between body and mind was not nearly as important in earlier civilizations as it is today. Were we able to peer into the minds of our earliest ancestors, I think we would find the motivation to touch for healing (the curaceptive response) was as much psychological as physiological. To comfort someone in physical pain may not only ease that pain, but also reduce the psychological tension the pain causes in the comfort-giver.

When you observe someone crying or hurt, there is often an immediate response to reach out and touch that person. Your touch may bring comfort and even relief to that afflicted individual. But it will also ease the psychological stress you felt in witnessing the plight of another. In a sense we act as each other's lightning rods, grounding the build-up of psychological and physical pain through human touch. Herein lies the seeds of using touch to heal the human mind.

In reviewing the history of touch, we noted that in the evolution of human civilization touch also was used to connect human beings with a divine reality that surpassed ordinary physical existence. Healing was closely aligned with religious and spiritual beliefs, and touch was a means of accessing this domain of the human spirit. Mind, spirit and soul were intimately related as the derivation of the word *psyche* so clearly demonstrates. Human touch, therefore, has long been a way of bridging the gap between the physical, psychological and spiritual realms of being.

In modern times, however, this tradition of touch has been lost. Today psychology is viewed primarily as a mental science which resists the inclusion of touch and the human body into the healing process. This is ironic since even modern day psychology has its roots in the study of the human body. Freud's original hypothesis was that the human mind followed the development of the body. As the body developed through several stages of erogenous fixation (oral, anal, genital), the mind was stimulated to focus on the physiological needs of each stage. But psychoanalysis developed along strictly mental lines, Freud never incorporated any form of human contact in his clinical work. In classical psychoanalysis the patient lay on a couch while the therapist sat out of sight, and out of touch. Only the sound of each other's voice connected the two.

Some of Freud's contemporaries pursued the role of the body in psychology with more vigor than Freud. Most notably, Alfred Adler, Georg Groddeck and Wilhelm Reich espoused the importance of the body in psychotherapy. In 1911, Adler reasoned that psychological disturbance was often the result of underlying physical dysfunction. The mind, according to Adler, attempted to compensate for the body's deficits and in so doing, psychological distortions arose.

Groddeck proposed the opposite view in 1923. He suggested that physical symptoms were the unconscious expression of underlying psychological forces, particularly psychosexual tension. Groddeck also wrote about, and prescribed, therapeutic massage for his patients. But while recognizing the body's role in the mind's welfare, neither he nor Adler directly incorporated any form of body therapy during their clinical treatment of a patient.

It was Wilhelm Reich, however, who first made contact with the body during psychotherapy. Reich began as a mainstream Freudian analyst in the early 1900s. In a sense, Reich took Freud's original hypothesis to its logical extreme. For Reich, the psychosexual imperative was the fundamental drive of human beings. Frustration of this drive, according to Reich, manifested itself as a variety of tension states which he classified as either "character armoring" (psychological tension) or "muscular armoring" (physical tension).

Reich did not accept Groddeck's proposition that physical dysfunction was the result of psychological forces (i.e. that muscular armoring was caused by character armoring). Nor did he subscribe to Adler's position that psychological dysfunction was dependent upon underlying physical conditions. Essentially, Reich synthesized both positions through the simple but profound insight that "muscular attitudes [bodily states] and character attitudes [psychological states] have the same function.... They can replace one another and be influenced by one another. Basically, they cannot be separated."

Reich adapted this concept of "functional identity" of body and mind to his clinical work. When he encountered difficult psychological resistance (character armoring) in a patient, he moved to the corresponding areas of physical tension (muscular armoring) in the body and used various forms of somatic therapy (i.e. massage, deep pressure, exercise) to correct the underlying physical distortions. Not only did this help correct physical tension but it also resulted in a loosening of the patient's psychological resistance. Similarly, if Reich was unable to affect a change in the tension of a patient's body through somatic therapy, he resorted to working with the psychological issues beneath that tension. By helping a patient deal with those psychological issues he was then able to loosen the tension expressed in a patient's body.

Although much of Reich's later work was controversial, his novel insights into the functional identity of body and mind inspired a generation of psychotherapists, often known as *neo-Reichian* therapists, who followed him. Alexander Lowen, for example, was one of Reich's students who went on to adapt Reich's work to a system of combined body and psychotherapy known as *bioenergetics*.

Most of the modern history of using touch and the physical body to work with the human psyche was written by a handful of creative psychotherapists who freed themselves from the confines of classical psychoanalytic practice. Historically, however, very little contribution to healing the mind through the body has come from somatic therapists.

Philosophically, at least, one small offering in this area is found within the history of chiropractic. Daniel David Palmer, the founder of modern day chiropractic, conceived this field on the premise of a *Universal Intelligence* manifesting uniquely in each individual as an *Innate Intelligence* that governs the individual's life and health. This innate intelligence was communicated from the human brain through the nervous system and out to the organs and tissues of the body. Any interference with the communication of innate intelligence from brain to body resulted in dysfunction and disease.

Palmer saw the task of the chiropractor as identifying and correcting interference to the flow of innate intelligence through the nervous system. Such interference, he reasoned, was most likely produced by the misalignment (subluxation) of opposing spinal vertebrae. For it was between the vertebrae that nerves exited from the spinal cord on their way to communicate with muscles, organs and other somatic tissue.

Thus Palmer envisioned the chiropractor not only correcting the structural alignment of the body, but also restoring the communication of innate intelligence from mind to body. Most modern day chiropractors eschew the notion of universal and innate intelligence because the terms sound archaic and unscientific. But if the word *unconscious* is substituted for *intelligence*, and the word *collective* used in place of *universal*, Palmer's notions take on a different and useful meaning. Bearing in mind this swap of words, consider the following statement made by Georg Groddeck, who, along with Adler, Freud, and Reich, lived during the same period as Palmer.

> I came by chance upon the idea that in addition to the unconscious of the thinking brain, there is an analogous unconscious of the other organs, cells, tissues, etc., and that through the intimate connection of these separate unconscious units with the organism as a whole, a beneficial influence may be directed upon the individual units by means of the analysis of the brain unconscious.

Groddeck mirrors Palmer. The only difference being that Groddeck sought to influence the unconscious communication between mind and body through treatment of the mind, while Palmer sought to influence this communication through attending to the body. Unfortunately Palmer's philosophical ideas have been obscured in the development of modern chiropractic. So today chiropractic is primarily a technical specialty which treats the body by manipulating the spine and pays little attention to the mind.

But regardless of one's philosophical orientation, few somatic therapists can avoid encountering the human psyche. Like my experience of having a patient relive sexual abuse during an examination, almost every somatic therapist has worked with at least one person who exhibited an emotional or psychological response to being touched. A sigh, a whimper, a tearful outpouring; a feeling of inner peace, euphoria, well-being or even depression: this is what the somatic therapist who cares to listen hears from those who are touched. These responses are the empirical evidence, at least, that touch reaches, and heals, the mind as well as the body.

And it is from this empirical evidence that the somatosynthesis work was born, to better understand how to use the access to the psyche provided by human touch. The relationship between human touch and healing both body and mind is as old as life itself. Now we need simply to reassert this primordial connection for its intended purposes—healing and helping ourselves and others.

3

Bonds and Bounds of Touch

Human touch is an important mediator between the realm of Soma (the body and material reality) and the realm of Psyche (the mind and non-material reality). This importance is reflected not only in the historical account of healing through touch, but also in the role of touch in the physical and psychological development of human beings. However the prominent position of human touch in the healing practices of earlier civilizations is no longer reflected in modern society. And even the significance of human touch in the growth and development of human beings, from birth to death, is overlooked shortly after infancy.

Surprisingly touch itself has much to do with this neglect. For human touch, it turns out, is not only the healer but also the destroyer. Touch creates bonds, but it also creates bounds. Touch joins, but it also separates. Touch brings together, but it also breaks apart. Thus in examining this paradoxical nature of touch we see both the problems and the promises of this essential mediator of human experience.

Child's Play

Trust Me? It was a game we played as adolescents. In groups of two, usually of the opposite sex, we explored the limits of touching the human body. After placing a hand on your partner you would ask, "trust me?"—

"yes" allowed you to continue, "no" gave the other person a turn. Areas once touched then became off-limits to further touch.

Like the opening moves of chess, easily accessible areas like the feet, lower legs, hands, arms, shoulders and head were touched in rapid succession, at which point the game became a contest of daring. All moves were now done with the slow, careful deliberation of two grand masters facing off over a chessboard. A hand would loom over an area as though it were about to place a chess piece into play. A potentially embarrassing moment might be adroitly avoided with a quick "No!" before the hand actually landed. Onlookers and known pre-game attraction between the players heightened the intrigue. "Would she be bold enough to touch him there? Would he actually let her?"

Delicate decisions had to be made in order not to appear too aggressive or too reticent, especially in front of friends. The game was finally over when both players declared they no longer had any body areas where they trusted being touched. Winning and losing never seemed that important; in a sense both players always won. The player who touched most was lauded about as much as the one who allowed the most touching. Amid cheers of "Go for it!" crowds would gather around and proclaim their favorites: "mousey," someone afraid to touch; "frigid," someone afraid to be touched; "good hands" and "hangin' loose," those engaged in sustained play within accepted limits; and, "gross," anyone who overtly transgressed the game's unspoken boundaries.

This was one way we explored our budding sexuality. The potential of entrapping your partner into permitting touch in a "forbidden" area was an enticing part of the game. But a deeper cultural message was buried within this game: skin is the boundary between self and others—a boundary crossed by touch only in proscribed ways. We mapped out the extent of our "body boundaries" and defended them in playful competition. We played out sexual roles related to touch. Most often, men were the touchers, "mousey" or "good-hands," and women were the objects of touch, "frigid" or "hangin' loose." In short, we enacted a ritual of touch and reinforced the "skin deep" barriers erected between people: cultural barriers that dictate when, where and why it is permissible to touch.

Not all cultures embrace the same prohibitions against touch. Stanley Jourard, sitting in cafes around the world, counted the number of times people engaged in casual conversation touched each other during a one hour period. In San Juan, Puerto Rico, he found that touching occurred an average of 180 times an hour; in Paris, 110; in London, 0; and in Gainesville, Florida, 2.

Ashley Montagu developed a continuum of tactility. On the low end, he placed people of Germanic and Anglo-Saxon origin—cultures which touch little. (Americans of Anglo-Saxon descent were ranked slightly higher than their British ancestors). The middle position was occupied by Scandinavians and the high end, those cultures which readily embraced touching, was held down by people of Latin, Mediterranean and Third World ancestry.

Cultural attitudes about touch have profound social and behavioral effects, as I discovered one fall. I was a freshman at Wesleyan University in Middletown, Connecticut, excited about beginning college and anxious to make a good first impression on my schoolmates. I had also just returned from spending a summer in the West African country of Ghana. Much to my surprise, strolling down the main promenade of the campus, I met a Ghanaian student. After hurriedly introducing myself and my summer's sojourn, I reached out to shake his hand. This was not an ordinary handshake: by now it was an automatic response learned during my first few days in Africa and nurtured throughout my summer's stay.

After grasping each other's outstretched hand in the usual fashion we pulled away slowly, then let our palms slide back across each other. Then each caught the other's middle finger between his middle finger and thumb. Next we snapped middle fingers and thumbs sharply, interlocked our little fingers, and went walking away down the campus promenade. Thus the simple handshake was elevated to the level of a majestic ritual of touch.

Unfortunately one culture's ritual is another culture's ridicule. My initial hopes were shattered rather abruptly when this first impression quickly became infamous. Two young men rubbing hands, then holding little fingers and swinging arm-in-arm, was perfectly acceptable in Ghana, but in New England it was quite another story. Needless to say, we were the talk of the campus for several days and the subject of many indelicate jokes and rumors. Although I can look back now and chuckle, it took me a long time to live down the repercussions of that handshake. Touchability, the ability to touch or be touched, cannot be taken for granted. We have a strong sense of when, where, why, and how our bodies may be touched. In the same way, we understand the accessibility of another person's body to our touch. Although touchability may vary slightly from person to person, it is based on strict social and cultural norms. This norm in Western culture is often limited: we have more don'ts than do's about touching.

Sidney Jourard was the first researcher to systematically investigate touchability. He developed the *Body Accessibility Questionnaire* to record how frequently people touched others and were touched by others. Jourard divided the body into 24 regions "suggested by beef-charts on which butchers delineate the various steaks and chops." Four target groups were used for his 1966 study: mother, father, same sex friend, and opposite sex friend. Male and female students recorded whether they had touched or been touched in any of the demarcated regions by a member of the target group within the last year.

From this study Jourard drew several major conclusions. Within the family male and female children are equally touched by their mother. However, mothers touch their male children in more areas than males touch their mothers. Females, on the other hand, touch their mothers in more places than males. Females also touch their fathers in more areas than males do, and fathers touch more body regions on their daughters than on their sons. The study confirms that the most extensive physical contact is sexual, for opposite-sexed friends touched more than any other group.

Then in 1976, researcher Lawrence Rosenfeld repeated Jourard's study. Some changes in touchability had occurred over these ten years, but mainly for opposite-sexed friends. A greater portion of the body was available for cross-sex touching. Women reported being touched more by men from their thighs to their shoulders, while men reported being touched more by women in the pelvic region and the upper chest area. Little or no changes were shown in same-sex touching or touching among family members.

Rating Body Accessibility to Touch

Perhaps you would like to rate your accessibility to human touch. A modified version of the *Body Accessibility Questionnaire* appears in the appendix. If you would like to give the questionnaire to someone else, photocopy the page before filling in your answers. This version of the questionnaire maps out ten body regions. There are two target groups to this study: (1) friend (or mate) of the opposite sex; and, (2) friend (or mate) of the same sex. Underneath the diagrams of the body is a chart with the regions listed by number down the left side and the two target groups listed across the top. For each target group there is a separate column headed "Touched" (meaning *you have touched* that person) or "Been Touched" (meaning that *you have been touched* by that person).

The questionnaire is filled out by completing the two columns under each target group. In the box corresponding to a given body area you are to rate how often you have touched this person (under the column labelled "Touched") or how often you have been touched by this person (under the column labelled "Been Touched"), in the last 12 months. You should use the numbers 1, 2, 3, 4, or 5 to rate the frequency of touch as follows:

1. you never touch this part.
   you never have this part touched.

2. you seldom touch this part.
   you seldom have this part touched.

3. you sometimes touch this part.
   you sometimes have this part touched.

4. you frequently touch this part.
   you frequently have this part touched.

5.you always touch this part.
   you always have this part touched.

Now compute an average score for each column by adding the numbers in the column, dividing by 10 and rounding up to the highest integer. Place this average score in the last box of the column on the row labelled "Average Score."

Once you have completed the questionnaire and tabulated your scores, there are several ways to analyze the results. For all columns labelled "Touched" you can rate your average score according to the following chart:

AVERAGE SCORE	RATING
1—2	Restricted contact with others
3	Limited contact with others
4—5	Unrestricted contact with others

In effect, this is a measure of how readily you contact others through touch.

For the columns labelled "Been Touched" a similar rating scheme applies:

AVERAGE SCORE	RATING
1—2	Restricted accessibility to others
3	Limited accessibility to others
4—5	Unrestricted accessibility to others

These ratings reflect how readily you allow others to make contact with you through touch.

On average, how do you compare across the target groups? Are your average scores consistent or is there much variability? Take a look at selected body areas and compare them across the target groups. Can you explain why some areas show a high incidence of touching behavior while others are low? Do your scores between touching and being touched vary much? Are you a person who gives and therefore touches more readily than receives, or are you more inclined to receive than give? As the questionnaire shows, we have mapped out our human real estate, demarcated the boundaries of various regions, and defended them from outside intrusion. Thus we have separated ourselves from ourselves as well as from others. It is this tactile isolation that makes it so difficult to find a place for human touch in human health.

The Touch Taboo

When Jourard initiated his study of touching, he was particularly interested about the touching habits of health care professionals. What he found when he walked through hospital corridors, counting the number of times hospital staff touched patients, was surprising. The only time doctors touched patients was to take a pulse or examine them, never even for comfort or reassurance. Nurses fared only slightly better, touching occasionally for comfort but primarily to dispense medication.

Maintaining the distance between doctor and patient seems to be a well-established medical practice. (Of course, it is only in modern times that this is the case, recall that in ancient Egypt medical doctors were given explicit instructions to touch their patients.) There are many reasons why health professionals keep their distance from patients, and avoid touching like the proverbial plague. Separation lends an air of unquestionable authority. What patient hasn't encountered a physician sitting confidently behind a desk, dispensing medical information on a "need to know" basis, like a judge administering law from the bench.

Even a physician's uniform is a way of saying "I don't touch!" The legendary white coat had its origins during the eighteenth century when Western medicine was just discovering the importance of aseptic treatment. Before this time many patients died simply because of poor sanitary conditions in hospitals. White allowed a surgeon to determine how dirty his garment had become and dispose of it for a new, clean one. At one point, surgeons were actually judged on how bloody their coats were— the bloodier the surgeon's coat, the more operations he had performed and presumably the better he was.

Like cowboys wearing white or black hats in a Western movie, a white coat is also a symbolic way of separating the good guys from the bad guys, the clean from the dirty, the doctor from the patient. I often wondered why we doctors change from street clothes to a white coat only to sit behind a desk and consult with patients for eight hours. Surely there can be no confusion of identity. The sign on the door and the diplomas cluttering our walls are enough to establish our identity.

When I first got into practice I felt that all the years of sweat and tears in school had earned me the right to wear a white coat. Perhaps in a dissection lab or operating room it's needed, but why here? No dirt was ever deposited upon me by a patient, not even any blood. Continuing this practice unconsciously reinforces the original ideas behind the white coat. The patient is dirty, the doctor is clean, and by donning my white coat I signal patients that I don't want to touch them because I don't want their dirt. It is a bizarre paradox. My white coat provides a psychological barrier protecting me from the one person I am sworn to help. What are we afraid of? Might we be contaminated with this person's humanity?

There is also a feeling that when we touch we contaminate the healing process. This is because we view modern medicine as a scientific experiment rather than a human encounter. As a doctor I am the experimenter, my patient is the experimental subject, and healing is the grand experiment. As in any scientific experiment, the experimenter is by design removed from the experiment. I can give instructions, manipulate the experimental environment, but above all I must play the role of the objective observer. Personal involvement would violate the scientific method and bias the experimental results.

Understandably the scientist who performs an experiment will employ someone else to actually collect the experimental data in order to guard against bias. The doctor administering an experimental drug will not be told whether the pill is a placebo or the actual drug to avoid a gesture, facial expression or unconscious body signal that would clue the patient to the real nature of the treatment.

Medical practice adopts this model: prescriptions may be written, therapy administered, instructions given, body parts even removed, but the doctor is supposed to remain distant from the patient to preserve professional objectivity. Loss of objectivity supposedly biases the doctor's ability as a healer. There are even medical myths to guard against this loss of objectivity.

For example, doctors often refuse to treat their families because they are "too close" to be objective. Doctors make poor patients themselves because they are "too close" to the same medical procedures they may need for their own healing. And doctors must not become "attached" to their patients for fear of lost objectivity. Touching crosses this boundary of objectivity and therefore must be avoided.

There is a certain irony about this touch taboo in the helping professions. Mark Hubble and his colleagues at Harding Hospital in Worthington, Ohio compared the responses of clients who were touched (by a specially trained group of psychotherapists) to those who were not. The significant finding was that clients who were touched gave their therapist a more expert rating than the rating given by those who were not touched. Preceding Hubble's study, Joyce Pattison completed a complementary study which showed that trained observers judged clients who had been touched as moving into deeper levels of self-exploration than untouched clients. The simple moral here is that everyone, therapists and clients, benefits from being touched.

But this touch-taboo is woven into our cultural and social fabric—from the games we play as adolescents to the models we have for healing/helping relationships. The problem is that, from conception through our earliest, formative years, touch was the most important part of our physical and mental well-being. Now, as adolescents and adults, touch is no longer there. In the schism between the touch-rich years of early life and our touch-poor later years lies the roots of many health problems. Here too lies the need to reestablish a place for touching in human health.

The Bonds of Touch

Within three weeks of conception we can touch. We have already formed a primitive nervous system which links skin cells to our rudimentary brain. Our nervous system develops so early because of its primary importance in creating and maintaining life. Brain and nerve cells along with our skin cells all arise from the same mass of precursor cells in the fetus, called the *ectoderm*. This common origin of our skin and nervous system underscores the importance of the skin to our development as well.

As life unfolds in the womb, our primitive skin cells differentiate and specialize even further. Our skin convolutes and enfolds to form the lining of our eyes, ears, nose and mouth—the sites which house our other senses. Sensory apparatus that actually allow us to see, hear, smell, and taste are also derived from the cells that first allow us to touch. Our other senses are simply more refined ways of touching. Little wonder that touch has been called "the mother of our senses."

But the skin's importance does not end with the creation of our senses. Throughout our fetal life the skin continues to provide a tough, waterproof barrier whose shape changes with our evolving human form. Within the skin the internal structures of our body grow and take shape. From the outside our skin is subject to many different stimuli in the womb. Chemical, temperature, and pressure changes continually bombard us. Through the pathways of touch, our skin transmits a record of these sensory encounters to the evolving human being. These stimuli contribute to growth at the fetal stage and prepare us for life outside the womb.

At birth we make an abrupt transition from water to air, from warmth to cold, from other-dependent to self-dependent. Once the umbilical cord has been cut, our frail being has but a short time for its life-support systems to switch on and operate in a self-sustaining manner. Touch plays a critical role in this process. Ashley Montagu, in his classic work *Touching: The Human Significance of the Skin*, was one of the first to call our attention to this relationship between touch and birthing, his insight stemming from previous research with animals.

With the exception of humans, newborn animals share a common fate meted out by their mothers. During the first few days of their lives—that critical transition between the womb and the world—they are continuously licked, cuddled, nuzzled, tickled, patted, and otherwise touched. On the surface, this appears to be part of their mother's attempt to groom and clean them. But Montagu hypothesized that these forms of touching served a more crucial function. They were, in his view, essential for the physical and behavioral development of the newborn.

Whether in regard to dogs, cats, rats, birds, monkeys, apes, goats, horses, dolphins, sheep, rabbits—almost any species—scientific research and practical experience had shown that if a newborn failed to receive enough touching its chances for survival were greatly reduced. Touch somehow eased the transition from the womb to the world.

Universally animal mothers lick their babies around the perineum— the area between the sexual organs and anus—to stimulate the elimination of waste products. Because newborn animals have underdeveloped systems of elimination, this stimulation prevents the baby's death from an accumulation of waste products. The relationship between perineal stimulation and elimination is found throughout the animal kingdom and is known as the *cloacal* reflex.

But skin stimulation helps newborns in many other ways as well. Some animals, like sheep and lambs, need to be licked in order to stand, to find their mother's teats, and to develop an active sucking reflex. Here touch stimulates the development of complex reflexes involving the brain, nervous system and muscles.

Gentled rats (those handled and stroked gently by humans) fare considerably better than their ungentled counterparts. Touching results in greater body weight and brain size, less fear, and increased resistance to stress and disease. It appears that touch increases hormonal and immunological activity in gentled rats—a significant finding which illustrates the positive effect of touching on those body systems responsible for an organism's health.

Touch was so important to rhesus monkeys that they valued it more than eating. In a classic experiment done by Harlow, infant rhesus monkeys raised in the laboratory were given a choice of two surrogate mothers. One mother was made of soft terry-cloth and lit from behind with a light bulb for warmth. The other mother was made of wire mesh, but was outfitted with a nipple to provide milk. Contrary to what we might expect, the rhesus babies chose the terry-cloth mother over the milk-giving wire mother. "Contact comfort," as Harlow called it, was as important as a full stomach.

But touching is reciprocal, and mothers also respond when they touch, or are touched by their infants. Touch triggers important changes in the mother's body like lactation and recovery from pregnancy. Here the mechanism in animals is similar to that in humans. Stimulation of the skin during breast-feeding initiates the secretion of prolactin, a hormone that regulates the production of maternal milk.

Nipple stimulation also causes contraction of the uterus which helps the mother expel the afterbirth and return the uterus to its normal size. If a newborn animal is removed from its mother before being licked, the mother has difficulty in bonding. Untouched newborns may be fed less or otherwise rejected by their mothers, and the mother may also suffer from a delayed recovery from her pregnancy. Self-touching is equally important to animals. Self-licking, like being licked by a mother, is not only a way to groom and clean, but also a method of stimulating the function of various body systems. For some species self-touching seems imperative for survival. For example, when pregnant rats were experimentally prevented from licking themselves, their mammary glands remained underdeveloped and their maternal behavior was so poor that their pups invariably died.

Weighing this body of evidence, Montagu concluded that newborn animals who are adequately touched have overall better health and an increased chance of survival. But what about human newborns? What makes up for the fact that most of us were not licked by our mothers? Montagu contended that there was a human activity which took the place of licking, it had to do with the birth process itself.

Human infants are born immature with months before being able to walk and years of dependence on others. A sharp contrast to other animals that walk within hours of birth and are self-dependent within months. In part this is because of the relatively short period of time we spend in the womb, about 267 days. Animals with longer gestation times produce more mature infants at birth. Therefore humans experience shorter *uterogestation* (growth and development in the uterus) and longer *exterogestation* (growth and development outside the uterus).

Human mothers also undergo an exceptionally long period of labor when compared to animals. And here was Montagu's clue. He conjectured that the forceful contractions of the uterus during labor served "much the same functions and end effects that licking of the newborn does in other animals."

What we experience during our birth are powerful uterine contractions that stimulate our nervous system through the skin. This cutaneous stimulation, in turn, activates body functions we need immediately upon entering life in the world. Here too nature reminds us that life is begun and sustained through touch. And again the research findings are in agreement.

Premature infants and those delivered via caesarean section don't receive this prolonged cutaneous stimulation. And their example serves to support Montagu's hypothesis. During the first year of life "preemies" show markedly higher rates of upper respiratory tract problems than full term babies. Later in life "preemies" have greater difficulty developing bladder and bowel control, muscular coordination, postural control, emotional and behavior control.

C-section babies, at the time of Montagu's original study, had a mortality rate two to three times higher than vaginally delivered infants. They fared poorly at very basic life-support functions like producing glucose, the body's major energy source, and were ten times more likely to suffer from a fatal respiratory disorder known as hyaline membrane disease. C-section babies were more anxious and emotionally disturbed than vaginally delivered babies.

Birthing is touching. And the pattern that emerges from these observations shows that when we are not touched during birth—from the lack of uterine contractions throughout labor—our health and well-being suffer. There is a greater risk of infection and incompetency of our nervous, respiratory, digestive and eliminative systems—the systems that sustain life.

Animal studies show that the lack of touch during birth can be offset by increased touching afterwards. The same holds true for us. When Tiffany Field, at the University of Miami Medical School, studied two groups of premature infants fed the same diet she found that "preemies" who were touched did much better than those who were not. Through delicate massage the premature babies gained more weight per day, were more alert, and had more mature nervous systems. They also left the hospital sooner than babies who were not massaged.

Similar findings have brought teddy bears into the cribs of premature babies in hospitals. Just the presence of a warm, cuddly object increases the recovery rate, and decreases the mortality rate of these infants.

Breast-feeding is another way our need for touch is met after birth. Beyond providing food, breast-feeding helps to develop key areas of our brain. Through sucking, our brain learns to control the complex actions of our lips and mouth—body parts we will eventually use to eat and talk. Simply locating our mother's breasts—first with our lips, later with our hands and eyes—has important consequences within the brain. Finding and following the stimulus provided by her breasts helps develop the *orienting* and *grasping* reflexes we will eventually use to stand erect, move fluidly, and interact successfully with our surroundings. Coordination of our lips and mouth is so crucial that as adults more than 50% of our brain area is devoted to sensory reception and muscular control of this area alone.

Breast-feeding is also an example of how touch enables our most essential relationship, the bond between mother and child. Touching aids the emotional and behavioral development of both mother and child through a process termed *psychocutaneous conditioning*. Normally, a mother touches her child in stages, moving from smaller areas of contact to larger ones; first using fingertips only, then palms, and finally her arms and entire portions of her body. When a mother is denied physical contact with her child immediately after birth, the bonding consummated through touch fails to occur.

Mothers don't mother well if they are separated from their child soon after birth. Instinctual maternal skills fail to emerge, and even when reunited these mothers tend to feel the child is more the doctor's or the nurse's than their own. Throughout the course of pregnancy and the ordeal of birth touch has defined the relationship between mother and child. Denying them physical access to each other immediately after birth abruptly breaks the continuity of this relationship with disastrous effects.

Just as in animals, human babies separated from their mothers struggle to survive. During the early twentieth century, the death rate for children under one year of age in American orphanages was nearly 100 percent. They were kept in sterile environments, fed by the clock from bottles and rarely picked up or held. While consistent with the current scientific and medical advice on caring for children, such treatment obviously lacked any human component.

Then Americans discovered that European facilities regularly held, massaged, picked up, cuddled, and otherwise "mothered" their infant wards. Though unconvinced of the importance of such "mothering," American institutions began the practice, and their death rates dropped sharply. Montagu has even suggested that S.I.D.S (sudden infant death syndrome) or "crib death" may be due, in part, to lack of tactile stimulation.

Touch is essential to our growth and development as human beings—from fetus to newborn to infant. "The infant's need for body contact is compelling," Montagu summarized. "If that need is not adequately satisfied, even though all other needs are adequately met, it will suffer."

Yet within a few short years after birth, perhaps ten at most, this compelling need for touch has dramatically changed. In its place are a host of boundaries and taboos, a set of rules and regulations governing the whos, whens, whys, and wheres of touching. Touch, which once brought us so close to others, now keeps us apart.

The Bounds of Touch

How does touch move so quickly from intimate contact to rigid constraint? And why? There are obvious developmental changes that occur. As we grow out of infancy, we rely more on sight and sound and less on touch. In this sense, to gain sight we loose touch with the world. We also develop sophisticated language skills allowing us to manipulate a world of symbols rather than objects themselves. As a child, to move a block from here to there, I manipulate the block by literally moving it with my hands. (Manipulate comes from the Latin *manus* meaning hand). Manipulation at this stage is largely a sensorimotor skill based on touch.

With the development of language skills and the substitution of symbols for objects, manipulation takes on a different meaning. It is no longer necessary to physically manipulate the world. I can cognitively and linguistically manipulate the world now. It is faster and much less work, for example, to mentally move a block from here to there or to write or speak about the movement of the block.

Not only can we manipulate symbolic representations of objects but we can also manipulate ideas in a similar fashion. We speak about "grasping" or "apprehending" an idea which, for an infant at least, occurs in the literal sense of both words. To understand the shape of a block, I would, as an infant, touch it. Yet as I grow older grasping occurs almost exclusively in a visual and mental domain. Now I would rather visually inspect the block and mentally determine its properties. Touch demands our active participation in life's experiences, while vision, language and our mental faculties allow us to passively observe. Both modes of experience are important, but for some reason we have forsaken the former for the later.

Sexuality is also related to the "touch barriers" we eventually erect. From birth our sexuality unfolds through touch. "The quality of physical intimacy between mother and child," wrote Alexander Lowen, "reflects the mother's feelings about the intimacy of sex." A child's tactile exploration of its own body eventually includes pleasurable, autoerotic stimulation. These early sexual experiences, combined with the social and cultural values passed on to the child, form the basis of our later sexual behavior.

Through touch a mother can communicate to her child positive and negative messages about sexuality. A woman uncomfortable with her body will have difficulty offering it to her nursing infant. The infant will experience this aversion and associate it with intimate contact. Every time a mother touches her child, Lowen observed, "[it] is an opportunity for the child to experience the pleasure of intimacy or to be repulsed by the shame and fear of it."

Myths and mores about sexuality abound in Western culture. Admonishing children not to touch themselves because "it's dirty" or because "nice girls don't do that" only teaches them to deny their sexuality—with potentially devastating consequences in later life. The "double standard" is another such myth. Pressure is put upon "real" men to be sexually active at an early age while "nice" women are encouraged to be virgins until marriage. Apart from the confusion it engenders, this double standard also invites men to view women as objects to be manipulated—to be touched at will—in a quest to uphold the masculine side of this standard. Adolescent games, like "Touch Me" further develop cultural barriers related to touching and sexual behavior.

The development of sexuality, perception, linguistics, and mental faculties are symptoms, not causes, of this transition from intimate contact to rigid constraint. While they assist us in creating and maintaining tactile boundaries, they are not enough to explain why we draw these boundaries to begin with.

To raise a boundary one must first distinguish between what lies inside and what lies outside its borders. Continents have been carved up, cities laid out, knowledge compartmentalized, diseases categorized, human affairs institutionalized by this very simple process: Draw a line, literally or figuratively, then decide what belongs inside and what belongs outside the line.

In fact, the history of civilization could be recounted on the basis of boundaries: who created them, why, and what happened once they were in place. Idealism versus realism, one nation fighting another, haves versus have-nots, "should I see an internist or a cardiologist?," classical versus modern physics, Democrats against Republicans, true-believers versus non-believers are just a fraction of the issues that could be addressed in this way. Boundary-making is an endemic process through which we separate, divide and fragment ourselves and our world.

The fascinating and paradoxical aspect of boundary-making is that it is ultimately based on touch! Our fundamental boundary is established through the skin. The touching behavior of infants helps them create this "skin boundary" which separates *self* from *not-self*: everything inside the skin becomes *self*, everything outside the skin is *not-self*. By touching myself and being touched by people and objects around me, "myself" comes to mean "within my skin."

An infant's identification, vague at birth, gradually becomes defined through this self/not-self boundary of the skin. "I am not mommy." I can use my senses to find mommy "out there," but mommy is not "in here, in my skin," I am. Likewise I am not this set of keys. I can manipulate the keys, and even put them in my mouth. The keys are cold, hard and have jagged edges, they make jingling sounds. Mommy is warm, soft and cuddly, and she makes cooing sounds. Mommy also has milk to give and the keys don't. So the keys can't be mommy. But the keys are not "in here" either, they're not inside my skin, I can touch the keys with my skin, so they must not be me. The keys are another thing in the world-out-there. If it's not-self it can be *mine* but it cannot be *me*—it's *my* mommy and *my* keys but it's not *me*.

From mommies to keys, it is not too hard to understand the emergence of the other boundaries we erect to separate and fragment our world. Having drawn this first self/not-self boundary at the skin, we further divide ourselves into *body* and *mind*. Ken Wilber illustrates the creation of this important inner boundary with a simple question: "Do you feel you *are* a body, or do you feel you *have* a body?" Most of us would answer that we *have* a body. We refer to *my* body in the same way we refer to *my* mommy or *my* keys or *my* book—something out there that we possess. Our body has become just another fragment in an already cluttered, fragmented world.

This was not always the case. As infants, we drew the self/not-self boundary line to include the body as "self." However, as we mature this boundary is gradually redefined by our developing mind—or ego. Ultimately, mind becomes the new boundary line between self and not-self. Since we feel our body is *not* contained within our mind, the body is now placed outside of "self."

"Biologically there is not the least foundation for this dissociation or split between the mind and the body," writes Wilber, "but psychologically it is epidemic. Indeed, the mind-body split...is a fundamental perspective of Western civilization."

Close your eyes for a moment, and ask yourself, "Where is the center of my being?" Try to feel where you would point in answer to this question. Many would describe a location within their skull, on the midline, forward of the ears, about level with the eyes. Now become aware of where your body is in relation to this center of being. A majority would simply say the body is "somewhere down there"—physically, somewhere below the skull; psychologically, somewhere below the mind and subordinate to it. It is as if we see ourselves as disembodied egos with a collection of appendages suspended beneath us like a puppet on the strings of a puppeteer.

Separated from "self," our body becomes just another fragment of the external world, subject to the same boundary-making activities as other objects in the "world-out-there." Like the map of a city or a butcher's chart, it can be divided, sub-divided and re-divided again based on any number of criteria. *Mind* is the map-maker, *body* is the territory. Many touch-taboos—the rules and regulations, the whos, whens, whys and wheres of touching—are simply boundaries the mind has imposed on the body.

The seeds of separation are sown within ourselves. The boundary line between self and not-self is the fundamental separation upon which all others are based. It is a boundary created through touch which ultimately renders us alienated from ourselves and isolated from others. But *boundary lines* are also *battle lines*, observes Wilber, and the many conflicts we face today, whether individually or as a world community, can be traced directly to the boundaries we have created ourselves.

War is the most compelling example of a boundary line turned into a battle line. Religious, racial, economic, political—whatever the motivation may be—a line is drawn, sides are chosen and a war begins. Fortunately not all social conflicts end in war, yet the process is similar: Draw a line, choose sides and mount a defense. Political power may replace fire power, goods and services may replace guns and bullets. The weapons may change, but not the strategy. How quickly we forget that without the boundary lines there would be nothing to battle over.

Health and disease pose similar problems for the individual. In fact, the primary system involved in maintaining the health of the human organism is also charged with defending the self/not-self boundary—the immune system. Like a sentry on guard at a military installation, the immune system identifies most substances that pass through the body. Identified as *self*, the substance can remain. Failing such identification, the immune system tags the substance *not-self* and marshals its considerable resources to "neutralize" this foreign body.

While the immune system works, we are provided with superb resistance to many unwanted foreign bodies. If the system fails we face potentially fatal consequences. Many current human health problems directly involve the immune system; hence, the boundary between self and not-self. Cancer and AIDS are two instances where the normal function of the immune system is compromised. New drugs are continually being sought to combat these diseases. Yet new research has also shown that the function of the immune system can be influenced through the mind.

Experimental subjects have been psychologically conditioned to raise and to lower the activity of their immune system, as mentioned in a previous chapter. This is a radical departure from conventional wisdom which draws a sharp boundary between body and mind—one is not supposed to influence the other. Mentally influencing the immune system challenges the validity of this boundary altogether. Without the body/mind boundary, the internal boundary of self versus not-self, there would be no conflict here either.

Globally and individually, human strife is rooted in common ground: the erection and defense of arbitrary boundaries separating self from not-self. Whether healing ourselves or healing the planet, the healing process is fundamentally the same as well. We have to bridge the separation and literally get back in *touch* with our *selves*. Touch, which played a major role in establishing this separation to begin with, can play an equally important role in healing it.

Boundary-making and the separation it engenders are not the inevitable destiny of humankind. In fact, boundary-making is not an essential part of many non-Western cultures. The reason we are so heavily invested in this process is only partially explained through the psychological development of the individual. The balance of the answer lies in the development of Western culture.

Historically, from Aristotle to Freud, Western culture has been fascinated and absorbed by analytical thinking. The ability to *analyze* (to break apart) is considered by many the greatest faculty of the human mind. "I think, therefore, I am," said Rene Descartes, the sixteenth century mathematician and philosopher whose writings heralded the modern scientific era. When I think, I exist as a conscious being, a thinking entity. It is a truth I can always rely on, observed Descartes.

But this self-evident truth, the cornerstone of Cartesian logic, also introduced the problem of *subjectivism* into Western thought. Subjectivism creates a knowledge boundary between *what I know* and *what I do not know* by claiming that I can know with certainty my conscious existence—myself and my thoughts. Knowledge of the existence of other minds or material objects, knowledge of anything outside of my mind and my existence is questionable at best.

Pushed to its extreme, this type of thinking creates what is called "the problem of the other." It is a notion that the *only* thing that really exists is my mind and its thoughts. Other people and the physical world in general are merely ideas conceived in my mind. Of what relevance is subjectivism and Cartesian logic to our understanding the importance of human touch? Consider the following familiar scenario.

Imagine that you are at a party among people you have never met. Even as you stand there talking with someone, Cartesian logic would have you question the existence of the other person. For all you know, you could be talking to a life-like apparition, so the reasoning goes, created perhaps with a three-dimensional hologram. Or maybe it is really a sophisticated android, designed by the special effects team of a Hollywood studio and made to look, talk, even feel like a person. You could never be sure. All you could be sure of is that it is you standing there, thinking thoughts and contemplating the reality that unfolds before you.

I am an island, an independent sphere of consciousness separated from other such independent spheres of consciousness; unable even to prove conclusively that anything outside of my consciousness exists. My subjective consciousness physically separates me from the natural world and socially isolates me from other human beings. Nature and others are external to me, fragments of a reality somewhere "out there," separate from the only reality I can ever be sure of—the reality of my consciousness, the contents of my thoughts. This is the Cartesian soliloquy. Yet before we dismiss these ideas as outdated, too cold or unfeeling, we should realize they are a part of our cultural heritage, more deeply embedded in our behavior and experience than we realize or care to admit.

Riding in a crowded subway car at rush hour, is a case in point. Growing up in New York City, I rode the subway frequently. I vividly remember being packed so tightly that the entire front of my body was touching one person and the entire back surface in contact with someone else. This is probably the most intense physical contact that one experiences outside of intimate contact with a lover or mate—and it can last for an hour or more. Yet, the average New Yorker does this on a daily basis with little or no thought for the web of humanity in which they are enmeshed. Expressionless stares, silence and a "grin and bear it" attitude all serve to create the illusion that no one else exists. In every other way, you are physically as close as people can be, yet you desperately pretend that you are alone.

This scenario is in sharp contrast to the "Mammy Lorries" of West Africa. In Ghana, where I rode them, the mammy lorries crisscross the country like a network of worker ants, providing basic transportation for even the remotest areas. "NEVER SAY DIE," read the hand painted slogan on one. "DON'T FEAR, BEWARE," another advertised. They were vintage British stock that could easily have carried troops in World War II or even World War I. Privately owned now, these rickety old contraptions were in constant danger of breaking down.

Lorries were designed to accommodate 12 to 15 people on simple wooden planks laid out across the passenger compartment and one or two others in the front seat with the driver. There were no time schedules—they came when they came. And there were no routes— they'd stop here one day and someplace else the next. There was really no comparison, riding a lorry made the subway seem tame. 25 or more passengers were not uncommon, and not just people—chickens, goats and dogs. The fuller the lorry, the more exciting it was to see if just one more person could climb on board. People sat on each other's laps, on the floor or just hung off the sides of the vehicle.

It was hot under the Africa sun and we were all sweaty, but still there was an instant feeling of camaraderie. I remember a conversation with three other people, pressed tightly against each other, in which none of us spoke the same language. It didn't seem to matter. Deeper within we all understood the comedy, the beauty and the shear fun of our situation. There were no boundaries, everyone joked, and laughed, and shared themselves as this web of humanity clattered down the road. It was easy to understand why they were called *mammy* lorries: They provided a warm, comfortable, supportive environment for all who rode them.

Why should it be different on a subway? In the West we seem more anxious to create and defend boundaries. To deny the existence of the others, the crowded subway passenger must draw the boundary between self and not-self. It cannot just be the simple skin boundary because the skin is in intimate contact with the "world out there." The self/not-self boundary must be drawn at the level of the mind. Once done, even though my body is in intimate contact with someone else, I can say with Cartesian certainty, "It's not me, because I'm in here, I exist in my mind. It's not mine because it's not my friend or my lover or my child. It's just my body bumping up against some thing in the 'world out there.' Therefore, since it's not me and not mine, it (this incidental contact) really doesn't matter."

In a sense, subway riders are living proof of the power of Cartesian thought. For the body, according to Descartes, was a part of the material world, composed solely of objects and things. Mind, however, belonged to the non-material realm of consciousness and thought. Between the two lay an inseparable gulf.

This separation between the realm of Soma and the realm of Psyche was absolute because, reasoned Descartes, physical objects could only be affected by other physical objects. One billiard ball moves only after being struck by another—the thoughts of the billiards player do not cause the ball to move. One clock gear turns only after coming in contact with the teeth of another turning gear—the clock's owner cannot cause this to happen through thought. Likewise mind cannot affect body, and vice versa, because they are of two different, incompatible essences. Paraphrasing an old English couplet:

What is mind? No body.
What is body? Never mind.

Descartes' influence cannot be overstated. His reasoning forms the basis of modern science and, thereby, of modern medicine. His insistence on the separation between mind and body explains, in part, why therapies which work with the convergence of these two realms are seen as such radical departures from the common wisdom.

Yet it is through this common wisdom that we have sorted through, divided up and mapped out ourselves and our world. Our efforts have been frequently rewarded. Fragmentation has brought with it tremendous technological change, enhancing our control over the forces of nature. But the victories are often bittersweet. By fragmenting our world and disregarding the fundamental wholeness of life we have created as many problems as we have solved. In attempting to control nature we have recurrently caused Nature to turn on us with an unerring and sometimes deadly aim.

The barriers to touch are deeply rooted. Touch is of the body, not of the mind. It falls on the wrong side of our internal boundary of self/not-self. In being touched, we ask the mind to acknowledge the body, to span the chasm, to relinquish the separation—we ask Psyche to embrace Soma. When bodies are viewed as material objects, they also fall on the wrong side of our external boundaries, into an inanimate, lifeless, mechanical world. Through touching, we defeat "the problem of the other" by feeling the pulse of another's life and acknowledging our common humanity. This is the healing that touch affords. Touch, our first step towards fragmentation, can also be our first step towards wholeness.

In taking this first step, we needn't go further than our own bodies. By reaching out and touching, we penetrate the boundary between self and other. The "problem of the other" is resolved through touch, as we experience the other as an extension of self. In opening up and being touched, we heal the separation between body and mind. "You have touched me deeply," no longer means just "you have touched the depths of my soul" but that "you have touched the depths of my body" as well.

In this chapter I've spoken about the problems that happen when boundaries are erected and defended. Of course not all boundary-making is damaging. Defining boundaries is also an important part of human development. As infants we create a "self/not-self" boundary to help ourselves separate from the undifferentiated world of maternal attachment. Eventually we develop a separate sense of self which becomes the basis for our individual ego. In fact problems arise when boundaries are not developed or respected.

Borderline personality disorders are found in individuals who do not develop an adequate sense of self as infants. They can be paralyzed by intense "emotional flooding" and fears of being engulfed by others. Sexual, physical and emotional abuse are examples of harmful violations of personal boundaries that strip away the sense of self. Traditional psychotherapy avoids the use of touch in treating boundary problems like these. But touch is the basis of our first boundary. It can be used to create or heal our boundaries when needed. And this use of human touch to heal the boundaries that separate us, creating the boundaries that define us, is the foundation of the somatosynthesis journey.

4

The Language of Touch

My day was not over yet. Peggy was in the second treatment room, the last person to be seen. It was 6: 00 o'clock on a Friday evening and I was tired, having been in the clinic since 9: 00 o'clock that morning. Although a part of me wanted to leave and go home right then, I turned the doorknob and entered the room where she was resting on the treatment table.

The atmosphere was like a temple—the lights were low, gentle music was playing and the air was heavy with the days's voices. I could still hear them: tense voices of pain; shrill voices of anguish; calm voices of relaxation; and, deep voices of healing—a truly human chorus. I paused for a moment, and silently asked to be placed in touch with a source of inner wisdom that would help me understand how to best help this person in my charge. I pledged my head, my heart and my hands in service of this goal. That being done, all my senses perked up, like radar antennae scanning a distant horizon for even the faintest signals.

"How are you?" I asked.

It was really an excuse, an opportunity to hear her voice and to examine it for how she really was.

"Fine," Peggy responded, "I still have some pain but it has moved from my lower back into my left chest, upper back and neck."

"Hmmm," I mused to myself, while listening to her meticulously describe her aches and pains. "I wonder if this is really about her back and neck pain?"

Instinctively I moved my hands toward her feet and activated my sense of touch. When I reached out to grasp her heels, my hands passed through what felt like a field of static electricity. I paused before touching her because the field seemed to surround her entire body.

"Focus, concentrate," I told myself, as I closed my eyes and turned my gaze inward.

An image of Peggy's body enshrouded in a bluish gray mist came into my mind. I could see points of intensely bright light—red-orange centers with a white surround—in her lower back on the right, her left shoulder blade, clavicle, her throat and the left side of her neck. In due course, I would discover the meaning of these highlighted areas, for now I filed their existence in my mind.

It was all right to grasp her feet now. I gently pulled both legs towards me, evaluating the response at her joints—ankles, knees, hips, pelvis, and spine. Her left leg moved easily, the right leg was restricted from a place in her pelvis and lower back. This is where our journey would begin. My left hand slipped under her pelvis, allowing the protruding bumps of her sacrum to press into my palm. My right hand rested lightly over her lower abdomen. I began to speak to myself as though I were going through a preflight checklist with an inner copilot.

"Check the breathing, muscle tone, eye twitching, and remember, relaxation first," I repeated mentally.

"Yes, of course," the copilot answered, "relaxation first."

I felt that Peggy was carrying the weight of her life this week, and her job as a bank executive officer with her. Her body was still tense, her eyes were fluttering open and closed, her breathing was slow but shallow. Concentrating on her lower back and pelvis between my hands, I offered her the opportunity to relax:

> Bring your awareness to your breathing and just observe your breath. Try not to control it, just let it deepen naturally. With each exhalation imagine that you are breathing out areas of stress, tension, discomfort and pain. With each inhalation imagine that you are breathing in a gentle wave of relaxation that crests at your head and flows softly down your body to your feet. Feel your relaxed body as it sinks into the table.

I paused for about two minutes, allowing her time to experience this relaxation. Then I continued:

Now, allow your mind to follow your body into relaxation. Feel that your mind is a leaf falling from the branch of a tree into a pond below. Watch the leaf as it gently floats through the air and comes to rest on the surface of this calm, quiet and clear pond. Let your mind find a calm, quiet and clear place to rest.

Again I was silent for several minutes, after which I resumed in a carefully paced tone:

As your body and mind relax and let go, allow your awareness to be drawn deeper within. Imagine that you could travel to a place we will call the center of your being. It could be located in the middle of your chest, in your abdomen, in the space between your eyes or at some other location. Wherever you feel the center of your being is, I invite you to draw your attention there. Notice a dim light that grows stronger and brighter. Watch this light as it illumines your entire body on the inside, from head to toes. Feel this light as it illumines your mind and your thoughts; your heart and your emotions; your entire being. Then, allow this light to radiate from you into the world.

All the while, I monitored Peggy's body between my hands. There was a profound change in her pelvis and lower back about midway through the relaxation. It felt like a superstructure collapsing under more weight than it was originally designed for. There was a shifting of the muscles from side to side, then a softening, widening and finally a sinking of the whole area—a phenomenon often referred to by somatic practitioners as a *soft tissue release*. This all happened within four or five minutes. From such a quick release, I doubted that her lower back and pelvis were to be the primary regions of our journey. So, like an operator consulting a radar screen, I glanced at the misty image of Peggy's body field that I held in my mind. Her left shoulder and neck were still glowing intensely. "That's the place to go," I thought. Locked onto a target area, I moved my hands to support her left upper chest—one underneath and one on top. I also invited Peggy's help, because from here on we'd have to work together.

"Slowly bring your awareness to the area between my hands," I suggested. "Just experience this part of your body without trying to control or analyze it."

She went into silence for five or six minutes before I intervened:

"What's it like for you to experience this area of your body?"

"There's a blue-gray band here," she said slowly. "It's holding me back. In fact my entire rib cage feels like a prison holding me in. And I can feel my entire spine respond to my awareness of this area. I can feel some pain now at the base of my spine."

"Just stay with your awareness of this area," I encouraged, convinced even more that this was the right location.

I noted her words: "band," "prison," "rib cage," "holding back." A tentative, perhaps illogical, hypothesis began to form: She has tension here to hold back some emotion or feeling. It may be connected to someone she loves, after all the heart could be seen as a prisoner of the rib cage. Maybe it's her husband. I stored this notion, subject to revision as the journey continued.

Then without prompting, Peggy blurted out:

"I feel a burning pain in my throat. It's like a fire that has moved from my upper back into my throat. I feel as though I want to say something but I can't. I always feel this way. It seems that everything I say is not right. This is especially true with my husband. Whether I speak from my head or my heart, what I say seems to come out wrong. So I'm afraid to say anything and I don't."

I knew we were on track. Her remarks had the right feeling about them. This is an intelligent, very intellectual, bank executive who could very well have difficulty expressing how she feels.

"Give a voice to these sensations in your body," I offered, "if that voice were talking what would it say?"

Peggy paused in silence for several minutes and then said softly, almost at the point of tears,

"It's calling out for help. It's calling out for help. I've never been very good at asking for help," she went on. "I seem to be able to give help to my husband and to others, but I can never ask for it myself. I find it really hard to communicate with him. We don't seem to understand each other. I also don't seem to be able to cry."

Peggy's body exerted a tremendous amount of energy to repress this rising emotional tide. She held her eyes tightly shut, trying desperately to fight back the tears. Her neck, shoulder and back muscles all rippled under my hands. If this were to come to a head, the repression needed to be resisted.

So instead of going with the movements of her body beneath my hands, I offered a gentle, but firm, barrier. Like a rolling river meeting an obstacle, I hoped her emotions would find another route of expression besides her body. I felt we were awfully close to the real issue but not quite there yet. The extent of her body's response actually caused me to doubt my original hypothesis. All this activity seemed too much to be solely about her husband. After all, I reasoned, they had only been married for seven months. Maybe their relationship contributed to Peggy's feelings, but I suspected that more than a lack of communication between wife and husband was involved. Still, it felt as though we were moving in the right direction.

"Peggy, imagine you're communicating ideally with your husband," I interjected, "what would that be like for you?"

There was a deep silence for five minutes broken finally with these words:

"I would feel loved and supported. I would be able to have that connection," she said wistfully, "I would be able to have that connection with him. I really want that connection, I really miss that connection, I really need that connection."

Lights popped in my head. It was obvious now that this was not really about her husband. I saw a little girl who wanted to be connected with her father. It was no longer a hunch. I knew this was the live issue even though she had never mentioned him in this session or before. It was that strange feeling of knowing you're right even without evidence. But it was also not my place to say this now. I felt she needed to come to that realization on her own. So, I decided to test my intuition:

"Peggy, allow yourself to be in touch with the first time you remember missing this connection?" I suggested.

She went into a period of troubled silence. As though she were locked in an inner battle to prevent herself from seeing something right before her eyes. Now I felt it was time to move my hands to her neck. To determine exactly where they should go, I gently probed her spine with my fingertips. Like a blind man reading braille, I felt the ridges and valleys created by her delicate bones. I stopped reading when my fingers encountered a mass of tightness at the base of her skull. It was as if Peggy had created a ring of tension here to prevent the feelings locked in her body from ascending to her mind. I supported her neck with my fingertips under her skull, offering her muscles an opportunity to relax, opening a channel between her body and her mind. I could feel her entire body moving back and forth like a large fish on the end of a line.

"Come on, say it if you can, say it if you can," I repeated to myself. "You can do it, Peggy, you can do it." I reminded myself of a cheerleader, urging the home team on in silence. Finally it came.

"It was with my father," she let out.

All right! My head was nodding up and down as if to tell a disbelieving audience watching these proceedings that I thoroughly agreed with what she said. I also knew that Peggy was a courageous traveler to have fought through her resistance to this issue so quickly. I did not know any of the details yet, but it was obvious from her body that this pattern of repression had been with her for years.

Having connected with her real issue, Peggy's hands went up to her face, to physically try to prevent herself from crying. She was too far downstream, however, and feelings that had been held so tight for so long were finally out of the cage.

"But I don't want this to be about him," she sobbed, "I don't want this to be about him. Why does this have to be with him? He left when I was seven. He walked out on me. Why is this affecting me now? Why is this affecting me when I'm thirty-five-years old? When I married my husband, everyone said I was marrying my father because my husband was twenty years older than I. But I don't think I'm really looking for a father in my husband, I just want that connection with him. I have tried so hard not to think about the connection with my real father, he left when I was seven. I have an uncle, he's a really nice man, we're really good friends and I can talk to him. But somehow it's really different. I don't know why he can't take the place of my father?"

The tension of coming face to face with these deeply held feelings was beginning to show. Peggy opened her eyes and started to talk about random and unrelated things: her job, her house, her pets. I let her go on for a while, she felt like a heavyweight fighter sitting in her corner between rounds. The tension also began moving her head turning it toward her left side. This time I followed her motions. Like a couple dancing, I let her head lead my hands. When it turned, I turned, when it stopped I stopped, when it moved in another direction, I followed.

With each choreographed step her head and neck muscles relaxed even further. Next, I supported her at her chest with a light, reassuring touch at the top of her breastbone. When that area released, I simulated opening her throat. With a few fingers on either side of her windpipe I stretched the area as though I were parting blades of grass looking for an object I had dropped. Now, with her body having released a majority of the stress associated with her repression, it felt like time to get back on track.

"Peggy," I whispered, "allow your awareness to return to your relationship with your father."

She closed her eyes and quickly found her father again:

"I don't remember very much about that relationship," she said. "It all seems so unconscious now but I know I have resentment, fear and anger. It has been easy to cover these feelings up intellectually, and I have tried hard to do that all my life."

She started crying again, this time with no effort to resist her tears. Tears came to my eyes as well, it was both hard and touching to see her finally allowing herself to feel this pain.

"I guess this is really good," she sobbed. "I've never allowed these feelings to surface. I suppose I need to."

At this point I was simply holding her head, supporting her to stay with the emotions she had just discovered. After several minutes, it was apparent that Peggy was starting to tire, and I had no desire to push her any further. We'd covered a lot of ground in this session, and it was time to put some closure on our journey so far. I invited her to slowly bring her awareness back to her breath.

"Let yourself be in touch with how you can incorporate this session's experience into your life," I asked.

She emerged from two or three silent minutes and surmised:

"Maybe I can take a little of this [being in touch with her feelings] at a time and begin to look at this relationship [with her father] and these feelings I have towards him. I would like to do that."

"Bring your awareness back to your breath, again," I offered. "You might wish to stretch, take some deep breaths and when you feel ready, open your eyes."

I slowly pulled away my hands and shortly thereafter, Peggy yawned, opened her eyes and looked at me. We stared at each other for a long moment, silently acknowledging where we'd been and what we'd come through. We were both filled with amazement and awe.

"I didn't know I kept all this in me for these many years," she said. "My body feels much better and more relaxed now. I don't have that pain in my chest and upper back."

I waited for Peggy to sit up, hugged her briefly and thanked her for her courage in this journey. Then I headed home.

Guiding a journey like this, I get the feeling of playing jazz, improvising on top of a well known tune. There is a clear sense of the key, the beat and the overall movement of the music without the knowledge of exactly which note will come next. The process unfolds through a mastery of basic skills combined with a strong feeling for what sounds right at any given moment—a creative blend of technique and intuition.

Somatosynthesis brings forth similar talents. A journey moves forward through the guide's sensitivity to the traveler. As for the musician, this sensitivity is based on a combination of technical skills and an awareness of 'what feels right' as the journey proceeds. This mastery of technique and intuition comes about as the guide learns to extend quite ordinary human capabilities beyond their normally accepted limits. For example, a guide learns to use touch to assess the physical and psychological state of another individual.

Palpation is the name given to human touch when it is used as a diagnostic tool. Through touch one can investigate many aspects of the body—its bones, joints, muscles, ligaments, organs, membranes, fluids, and even the energy radiated from its surface. Once a major part of medical diagnosis, palpation has become a dying art in mainstream health care, having given way to highly sophisticated, highly technological methods of surveying the body. But for somatic therapists palpation is a valued tool.

I vividly remember the first time I attempted to palpate the spine. It was my first day of classes at chiropractic college and we were simply instructed to count the number of vertebrae from the top to the bottom of the spine. That was it, no other information or guidance. Working in pairs, one student disrobed while the other palpated. It was intimidating to touch someone whom you barely knew, but it was overwhelming to also have to obtain specific information as a result of that touch.

Starting at the neck, I carefully ran my middle finger down my classmate's back, all the while mentally tabulating each ridge and valley I crossed. To double check I went back over the spine again, only this time counting from the bottom up. Sometimes I lost count and had to start all over again. Other times I debated for several minutes whether I really felt a valley between two vertebrae and rolled my finger back and forth across the same area. From top to bottom I counted 43, from bottom to top 41. I decided to err on the side of plenty and settled confidently on the first figure of 43—at least I would be close.

After relinquishing my body to my classmate for an equal amount of time, the instructor asked each student to report the results of their investigation. "Twenty," blurted one. "Thirty-six," another proudly proclaimed. "I only found fifteen," someone lamented. And on, and on it went. It seemed like each student found something different. A little shaken by all these diverse opinions, I hesitatingly offered my hard won count of 43.

"There are 24 movable and easily countable vertebrae," the instructor informed us. And with those few words, my first class in palpation was over.

Palpation finds wide-spread usage in chiropractic, and in the succeeding weeks of this class we studied the art and skill of this discipline. We learned to close our eyes and listen to our hands. We experienced the fundamental paradox of palpation that the lighter you touch the greater the information you receive. We heard tales of gifted, old docs who, upon shaking your hand, knew immediately where your problem lay. And we practiced, practiced and practiced some more.

My favorite exercise, used by students of palpation over the years, required a yellow pages telephone directory and a strand of human hair. A freshly plucked hair was placed under one page of the directory. With eyes closed you palpated the page attempting to find it. If your palpation was successful another page was added and another and another—something like the Princess and the Pea. Twelve pages marked my best attempt, but a really skilled palpator could locate a single hair under 20 pages or more.

Think of how many objects we touch without paying the slightest attention to what we could learn about them through our skin. Like reading braille, palpation is a way of gaining knowledge about the world. Once learned, palpation brings the body alive under your fingertips—bones dance, joints speak, organs reveal, muscles move, fluids flow, the entire body vibrates with life. And, where you do not feel this aliveness, problems are usually found.

Through palpation one also has the eerie experience of feeling as though you can see through eyes at the end of your fingers. With enough practice, the sensation of touch appears to produce visual images. When you palpate a part of the body, you not only 'feel it' but also have the sensation of 'seeing it,' even though the body part may actually exist several inches below the skin's surface. I have always supposed that this sensation of "seeing through one's fingers" is similar to what is experienced by blind individuals connected to Bach-y-Rita's skin-sight apparatus. It also demonstrates palpation as a form of *somatic imaging*.

With this form of somatic imaging however, touch creates an image of the traveler's body in the guide's mind. At one level, this allows the guide to picture the relationship between two opposing bones that form a joint or the tightness in a given muscle. Although once opened, this channel of information between traveler and guide can provide more refined knowledge, like a picture of energetic fields emanating from the body or impression of the deeper emotional, psychological or spiritual issues related to a given body area.

In this way the guide's touch accesses a domain beyond the physical boundaries of skin and body. The barrier created by the skin—that primordial demarcation between self and other—after all may be more a limitation of mind than a statement of fact.

The work of one Nobel laureate helps us understand how it is possible to touch beyond the apparent confines of our physical bodies. Georg von Bekesy, who received the 1961 Nobel Prize in Medicine, was a Hungarian-born American who originally set out to discover how the ear analyzes and transmits sound. But he faced a major obstacle in the size and inaccessible location of the human inner ear—composed of very small structures imbedded deep within the skull. Although he devised ingenious methods to overcome these limitations, his most unique contribution came when he realized that human skin could serve as a substitute for the human ear.

Bekesy reasoned that the skin and the ear shared one important feature in common: Both were vibration-sensitive membranes equipped with an extensive system of nerve fibers. This crucial insight, combined with the skin's enormous surface area, allowed him to perform hundreds of experiments on the skin and translate his findings into a better understanding of the ear. As a result, Bekesy left us better informed not only about hearing but also about touching.

In one of his many experiments, Bekesy studied the perception of stimuli applied to two different locations on the skin. He placed two vibrators on the tips of the index and middle finger, as shown in figure 4.1. The vibrators were tuned to the same *frequency* (each produced the same number of clicks per second) and *intensity* (the strength of vibration was the same at each finger).

First, Bekesy varied the time between the series of clicks applied to each finger. With the onset of the clicks spread out over time, the expected result occurred: The vibration was felt first at one finger, then the other. However, if the delay between the two fingers was diminished to roughly 1/1000 of a second (about the time it takes you to blink your eye), the two separate vibratory stimuli were perceived as one vibration, located in the finger that received the clicks first.

As Bekesy continued to decrease the time between applying the clicks to each finger, the sensation appeared to move into the region between both fingers; and, if the order of applying the stimuli was reversed, the sensation shifted to the opposite finger. Thus, from two separate stimuli

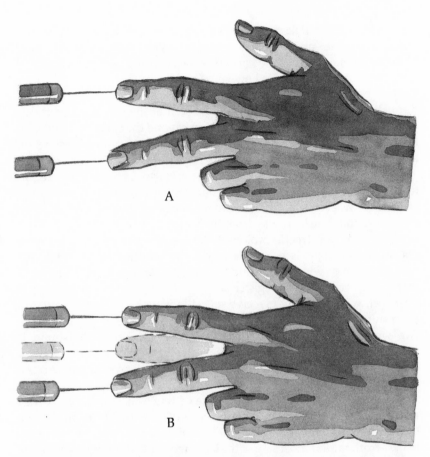

Fig. 4.1: Bekesy's experiment with vibrators. (A) shows how the experiment was conducted with two vibrators applied to the ends of the fingers. (B) shows how subjects perceived the vibrators as a single stimulus in the space between both fingers (dashed lines.) (Drawn after Bekesy, 1967.)

Bekesy produced the appearance of a single vibration that moved smoothly between both fingers of his subjects.

A more surprising result took place when both vibrators were turned on simultaneously. Again the subjects reported feeling a single point of vibration on their skins but it was located "out there," in the space between their fingers where there was no skin! Even with their fingers spread further apart, these subjects experienced the vibration in free space. It felt like their skin was being stimulated but at a point where there was no skin. Next Bekesy placed vibrators on each leg just above the knee—the same phenomenon occurred. When the vibrators were switched on, subjects, whose knees were separated by several inches, felt a skin sensation in the space between their knees!

Here Bekesy showed that under the right circumstances the sharp distinction between self and not-self created at the skin is blurred. We project and experience our physical being beyond the borders of our skin. It would be easy to dismiss this phenomenon as a perceptual illusion but, as it turns out, projection of perception is an ordinary sensory experience.

Visually we project images great distances away from the actual receptor cells of our eyes. The tree you see out the window really appears to be 100 feet away, even though each eye has focussed the image of that tree on your retina, 3 inches away from the optical center of your brain. Your perception of that tree is projected 100 feet away from your body. A distant train whistle is perceived as distant, not the few centimeters it takes to get from your inner ear to the temporal lobe of your brain where that sound is consciously registered.

In fact, we commonly perceive sound in ways remarkably similar to the results of Bekesy's skin experiments. The next time you sit in front of two well-balanced stereo speakers, ask yourself where the sound is coming from. You perceive the sound to come from the space between both speakers, although you know very well that the sound waves reach your ears from the speakers themselves.

We even routinely project our sense of touch. If you have a pencil nearby pick it up and hold it so the eraser end is furthest from your hand. Close your eyes and slowly run the pencil over the width of this open book—from the left most side of the left page to the right most side of the right page. Notice the roughness of page edges on your left, the smoothness of the left page itself, the depression in the middle of the book between both pages, the smoothness of the right page, and finally the rough page edges on the right. Also notice where you felt these changes in texture. You didn't feel them at the surface of your skin, you felt them at the end of the pencil. In other words, you projected your sense of touch to the end of the pencil.

Now flip the pencil over and write something, your name will do just fine. Observe the varying degrees and direction of pressure you exert in creating the lines, loops and squiggles that form the letters of your name. You sense this changing pressure at the tip of your pencil, not at your fingertips which are grasping the pencil. Try changing the pressure with which you grasp the pencil—you'll quickly discover that you can't write.

The pressure exerted to hold the pencil needs to be constant so you can extend your perception to pencil tip and thereby control the complex task of writing. A good craftsperson knows this instinctively. The woodworker's sense of touch extends to the teeth of a saw, a machinist's to the end of a wrench, a surgeon's to the edge of a scalpel, an artist's to the tip of a brush.

Bekesy also recognized the importance of sensory projection to palpation. While observing that the extensive use of X-rays (and now CAT, PET, and NMR scans) had all but eliminated the development of this skill, Bekesy noted that:

> [I]n earlier times a good practitioner did not feel a tumor as at his fingertips but he projected his vibratory and pressure sensations *into* the patient.

Skin is an arbitrary boundary between traveler and guide, a boundary crossed through projecting our sense of touch. Projection of sensation beyond our physical being, while seemingly uncommon, is something we routinely do to obtain knowledge about our everyday world. Through palpation we merely make this ordinarily unconscious process available to our conscious mind. And so, by further developing this ability to project touch, a guide effectively crosses that delicate boundary between self and other to explore, to learn and ultimately to help the traveler. In fact, paying attention to the normally unconscious aspects of touching gives the guide access to a rich supply of information about the traveler.

Touch and the Human Electromagnetic Field

While routinely palpating the spine of a patient with back pain, I.N. Toftness, a chiropractor from rural Wisconsin, noticed his fingertips encountered greater resistance when he moved them directly over problem areas. Toftness found a sensation of "drag" in these areas that he did not find elsewhere—like the difference between moving through sand and sliding on ice. It was a half-century ago when Toftness happened on this occurrence, and he spent the following years attempting to understand the phenomena.He came to believe that the human body emitted a signal indicating areas under abnormal stress, and he sought to design equipment to amplify and display that signal. His early equipment was quite primitive by today's technologically sophisticated standards and could not confirm the existence of this mystery signal. But Toftness persisted, and a breakthrough came in the early 1970s.

Toftness was placed in contact with an electronics research laboratory in Maryland that had access to a special electronics device known as an interferometer. This apparatus is used to determine the identity of unknown sources of electromagnetic energy. With a subject present in the lab, Toftness felt along the spine, stopping when he sensed an area of increased friction. The interferometer was then turned on and a plot of the various frequencies it detected was made. After a number of trials, a pattern emerged.

When Toftness detected an area of increased drag, the interferometer detected increased energy in the microwave region of the electromagnetic spectrum. It appeared that the human body was emitting detectable microwaves. At the time, there was no body of knowledge to support this conjecture. But simultaneously, a train of events had been set in motion, worlds apart from Toftness, which would ultimately coincide with and confirm the events taking place in that laboratory room.

As America's funding of the space program diminished following the success of the Apollo moon landing, NASA declassified much of its tightly held technological knowledge. Along with this declassified technology came NASA scientists eager to apply extraterrestrial know-how to terrestrial goals. In particular, the technology to design extremely sensitive microwave detectors became available and a space scientist, Jochem Edrich, sought to use this technology in medicine.

In the late 1800's physicist Max Planck discovered a principle known as *blackbody radiation*. It holds that any object above a temperature of *absolute zero* (-453 degrees fahrenheit) radiates energy throughout the electromagnetic spectrum. As preposterous as it may sound, this book or the pen you're holding in your hand is radiating electromagnetic energy right now. Since the human body is well above absolute zero, it too radiates energy throughout the electromagnetic spectrum.

A large portion of the energy radiated from the human body is in the microwave region of the electromagnetic spectrum. (Microwaves are sandwiched between the broadcast bands for FM radio and television, and the infrared frequencies.) However, the amount is still extremely small, only 10^{-10} Watts for each square centimeter of skin—one trillion times less energy than a 100 Watt light bulb! But NASA's technology had solved the problem of detecting such small amounts of energy, and Edrich had experience building such microwave radiometers (as devices to detect microwaves are called) for space. He was interested to see if they could detect phenomena emanating in the human body, and, in an astounding synchrony of events, Edrich was introduced to Toftness. From 1974 to 1980, Edrich constructed several radiometers for Toftness who used them to demonstrate that microwaves could be reliably detected emanating from the human body. I joined the Toftness research team in 1981 and participated in a series of experiments showing that these microwave patterns changed after applying sustained light pressure to the body. For years, Toftness had used light pressure to manipulate the body and had a wealth of clinical studies (pre- and post x-rays, subjective reports of patients and physical examination findings) to document his effectiveness with this method.

To this documentation he now added the ability to objectively monitor the human electromagnetic field and demonstrate its relationship to the physical condition of the human body. Typically the radiometer detected abnormally high or abnormally low microwave readings in problem areas of the body. After sustained light pressure, these peaks and valleys normalized—the high readings were reduced and the low readings were raised. Monitoring the electromagnetic field produced by the body is a unique form of diagnosis because it is truly non-invasive.

There is no radiation, as in CAT scans; and there is no need to subject a person to extremely high magnetic fields as in MRI, NMR or PET scans. Since the early days of microwave radiometry, the technology has advanced significantly, to the point that battery-powered units are now available, so sensitive that I have been able to measure a human electromagnetic field ten feet away.

The irony is that a complex technology like monitoring the human electromagnetic field would emanate from the simple act of touching. In 1982, while in the midst of experimentation with early versions of the radiometer, Toftness received a note from an interested doctor. Thumbing through *Dorland's Medical Dictionary*, a standard medical reference book, this doctor had discovered a curious word, *psauoscopy*. As defined in the medical dictionary, psauoscopy was a method of palpation in which the index finger was passed back and forth lightly over the margin of an abnormal area. "Over the pathological area the finger seems to encounter greater resistance...." How surprising. Toftness's phenomena of touch was once known and used, then discarded, only to be uncovered and flourish again.

When do guide and traveler, or any two people, actually touch? Is it when skin comes into physical contact with skin? Or is it long before, when the electromagnetic field of one interacts with the electromagnetic field of the other? The presence of a human electromagnetic field can be demonstrated instrumentally. And the field emanating from the body carries information about the body—just as the electromagnetic field emanating from a television station's transmitting antenna carries information broadcast by the station. From the reports of Toftness and many other somatic therapists this field can be felt even at a distance from the body. So we need to expand our notion of touch to encompass all the ways we communicate through the skin regardless of whether physical contact is involved, particularly when touch is used therapeutically.

Early humans held the idea that people could be connected through energy fields. Figure 4.2 is taken from a South African rock painting. For many years, European anthropologists interpreted this scene as portraying the capture of several women. The solid line connecting the figures was thought to be a rope or some other restraining device. Recently new meaning was given to this painting after interviewing local African villagers. These people had grown up with the cultural traditions expressed in the rock art. They reported that the line in the painting actually represented the "power field" linking the figures together. Similar lines of power appear in many rock paintings, particularly those depicting the visionary and healing practices of shamans.

When Dolores Krieger, a nursing professor at New York University, proposed a therapy she labelled "Therapeutic Touch," many considered it a misnomer because the technique failed to include physical contact. Krieger believed that people could be taught to sense the energy fields emanating from the human body with their hands held several inches above the skin. Imbalances in a person's health, according to Krieger, would appear as distortions in an otherwise homogeneous energy field. When distortions in the field were felt they could be corrected, Krieger hypothesized, through the interaction between the field of the healer and the field of the subject. This correction of the energy field would then aid the restoration of health. In more than a decade of research since 1976, Krieger and her graduate students have demonstrated the validity of these premises and the value of Therapeutic Touch as a healing method.

To touch diagnostically does not require physical contact. Even when we need to make physical contact to palpate, we face a dilemma. Seasoned palpators have long known that the best hand is a light hand—the lighter the touch, the more information can be obtained. This appears to be true even when we examine areas deep beneath the skin. The more force we

Fig. 4.2: Originally interpreted as women being held captive, this South African rock painting actually depicts three women linked via a "power field."

use to palpate, the more disruptive influence we create in the body and the less useful information we gather.

For example, suppose you had a severe stomach ache and I wished to palpate your stomach. Since your stomach lies beneath several layers of tissue (skin, fat, muscle), I would need to press very deeply to actually make physical contact with this organ. However, before I even got close to your stomach, this deep pressure would cause your abdominal muscles to tighten and you would most likely recoil from my touch in pain. In other words, I would be evaluating your defensive response to my intrusion rather than receiving useful information about your stomach.

Alternatively, I could simply rest my hand lightly over your stomach. Then, projecting my sense of touch and being receptive to the energy fields radiating from this organ, I could obtain a better picture of the stomach's true condition. So, when assessing a traveler, a guide attempts to use minimal intrusive force, to yield maximal information about the condition of a traveler.

Touch, Perception and Healing

Through Bekesy, Toftness and Krieger we can see the role of touch in healing is closely linked to the nature of sensory perception itself. What's it like "in here," this inner world which generates sensation through my skin when I touch? And what's it like "out there" beyond my skin, that outer world which gives rise to my experience of touch? With touch so important to our growth and development, and so central to the somatosynthesis healing process, let us investigate these questions further.

Reconsider Bekesy's findings: Vibrators simultaneously stimulating two fingers cause you to feel touched in the space between your fingers, where you have no skin. How do you explain this experience? Do you become a *rationalist* and talk about the vibrators which create your experience of touch? Or do you side with the *phenomenalist* and insist on the validity of your perception of touch regardless of its location? What is the essential feature of this sensory experience: the equipment which gives rise to your perception, or your perception which results from the equipment?

Similar questions arise when we palpate a body in the absence of elaborate equipment: What is it exactly that we come into contact with? And how does the sensation called "touch" occur? What we're really asking about is the nature of reality which gives rise to our perceptual experience, while simultaneously inquiring into the nature of our perceptions themselves. These questions are at the heart of any therapeutic process based on touch. And healing through touch is coupled to our answers.

There is a long history of human inquiry into such matters. In modern times physicists have undertaken study of the nature of reality—the world which gives rise to our perceptual experience. Psychologists, on the other hand, are concerned with the nature of perception itself.

"Modern physicists and modern perceptual psychologists," noted brain researcher Karl Pribram, "have converged onto a set of issues that neither can solve alone." To study the nature of reality which produces the world of appearances, the psychologist must turn to the physicist. And to understand one's perceptions while studying the nature of reality, the physicist must turn to the psychologist. How do physicist and psychologist respond to this challenge?

The physicist's question is deceptively simple: What is the nature of the world I touch, the outside my self? Close your eyes, reach out, touch anything within arm's distance and ask yourself this question. For thousands of years the obvious answer has been *things*. You, I and the physicist touch *things* in the world "out there." It's an easy answer and one that is supported, so it seems, by our everyday experience. I can touch, see, taste, smell and hear *things*. If *thing-ness* is the nature of reality, then the physicist's task is pretty straightforward: to discover what these things "out there" are made of. Of course common wisdom has it that things are made up of other things in a sort of hierarchical manner. Like a Chinese doll, big things are made up of smaller things which are made up of even smaller things, and so on. If only our physicist works hard enough, the reasoning goes, eventually he or she will "get to the bottom of things."

David Bohm, a protege of Albert Einstein, even suggested that most of physics could be viewed as a search for the ultimate "thing," the fundamental building block of the material world. In ancient times matter was supposedly composed of certain natural elements—water, air, fire, earth and wood. But later it was felt that there must be a more fundamental building block of matter, and the race was on.

Molecules were next considered to be the building blocks of matter, but it was soon discovered that they too were made up of more elemental things called *atoms*. However, the atom's tenure as fundamental building block was short lived. For atoms it turned out *were* divisible into *protons*, *neutrons* and *electrons*, thought to be the real building blocks. But they too had a short reign because *leptons, muons, baryons,* and a host of other sub-atomic particles were soon discovered. Eventually, even these sub-atomic particles were found to be impostors because *quarks* were found to be more basic building blocks of matter. But the number of quarks grew quickly and some even had *charm, color,* or *flavor* (the qualities assigned to quarks by physicists themselves!), so quarks were also dethroned. Undaunted, physicists next proposed the existence of *gluons* because something was necessary to hold quarks together. Gluons too were soon replaced by W-particles—elusive things theorized to exist, but never actually seen. When I last visited the "particle zoo" *ultra-weak strings* were in vogue as the fundamental building blocks of the material world.

Do you remember what it was like trying to pick up a piece of mercury from a broken thermometer? Each time you touched the mercury it broke up into smaller and smaller pieces. Beset with similar difficulties, physicists still proceed with an unshakable faith that they can really "get to the bottom of things." In the midst of this apparently unending paradox, Bohm made a simple suggestion. Physicists, he observed, have asked this same question about the ultimate building block for three thousand years. If nature keeps answering them paradoxically maybe it's the wrong question.

Bohm was not the first to make this proposal. While studying the nature of light, Einstein suggested something similar in his famous equation of matter and energy $E=mc^2$. Observed one way light appeared to be a particle of matter called a *photon*. Observed another way light appeared to be a *wave* of energy without the properties of matter. Could light be both a thing and a not-thing? Einstein showed that it really depended upon how the observation was made. But observation after all is a faculty of the mind. Nature seemed to say to physicists: How you perceive determines what you perceive.

Of course this proposition is a little troubling if you go looking for "objective" reality in the world "out there." To have objective reality requires subjects and objects; observers and things to observe; touchers and things to touch. Observer and observed are supposed to be separated, one is not supposed to affect the other. After Einstein this was no longer true, and some physicists recognized the profound implications that resulted.

Erwin Schroedinger, the founder of Quantum Mechanics, spoke eloquently for many physicists when he said:

> The same elements compose my mind and the world. This situation is the same for every mind and its world, in spite of the unfathomable "cross-references" between them. The world is given to me only once, not one existing and one perceived. Subject and object are only one. The barrier between them cannot be said to have broken down as a result of recent experience in the physical sciences, for *this barrier does not exist*.

What began for some as a study of the world "out there" (objective reality) lead to the world "in here" (mind), and ultimately to a conclusion that the two were inseparable. "The stuff of the universe is mind-stuff," said astrophysicist Arthur Eddington.

Reflect upon what this means in terms of touch. Once again close your eyes and reach out to touch something within arm's distance. What these physicists are saying is that you are not contacting some solid object "out there." Instead you are experiencing a phenomena of mind which we call "solid."

But before going further, shouldn't we let the psychologist ponder these issues of the mind? Here the psychologist's question is also deceptively simple: What is the nature of my perception, the world created "in here" when I touch?

Again reach out, and with closed eyes touch something while asking yourself: How does the image of what I'm touching come to be? The obvious answer, once more is *things*. Things happening "out there" cause things to happen "in here"; within the brain of the toucher. What happens "in here," the reasoning goes, is a reflection of what's taking place "out there."

Located at varying depths below your skin surface are millions of specialized nerve receptors. They go by curious names: Merkel cells, Pacinian corpuscles, Meissner corpuscles, bulbs of Krause, Ruffini terminals, and touch domes. What they share in common is a sensitivity to touch. When pushed, pulled or jostled these receptors fire impulses from your skin to your brain. Based on these impulses you then surmise that "touch" has occurred.

The common view is that each aspect of what we contact in the world "out there" is assigned a unique place within our brains. We then end up with a tactile picture of that outer world. There's a simple conversation piece that illustrates this idea. Several hundred straight pins are aligned in a rectangular box. When you hold your hand against the sharp edges of the pins, the blunt sides are pushed out to form an image of your hand. The movement of the pins corresponds to the features on the surface of your hand. For example, over the fleshy mound at the base of your thumb the pins would be pushed out further than over the flat area in the middle of your palm.

Similarly, when you touch something "out there," brain cells fire according to the features of what you're touching. When touching a person's hand, the cells responding to raised areas would fire a lot when you were over the fleshy mound at the base of the thumb. Those same cells would not fire as much over the middle of the palm.

Touch, sight, hearing, taste and smell are all presumed to occur in the same way. Brain cells are organized along the lines of a corporation, or the chain of command in an army. Lower level cells perform the most menial tasks: extracting basic features from the sensory environment. Several such lower level cells then converge on a single cell at the next higher level of command. This process continues until there is but one cell at the top of the heap. Like the CEO of a corporation or the field general of an army this single highest level cell pontificates the actions of the cells beneath it. In fact in the early days of this theory of perception it was called a "pontifical cell."

But this cellular theory of perception had its problems. For example, what happens in a stroke? An individual might lose brain tissue without losing a commensurate amount of memory. Just because you lose 10% of your brain substance in a stroke, Karl Pribram once observed, it doesn't mean that you remember only nine of the ten people living in your house. Your memory may be partially lost or somewhat fuzzy, but it doesn't simply fall away. If a pontifical were lost, then the perception it commands ought to be lost with it.

In response to this cellular theory of perception a group of researchers, lead by psychologist Karl Lashley, proposed a field theory based on interacting wave patterns in the brain. Psychology was beginning to resemble physics before Einstein with a split between a "particle" (cellular) and a "wave" (field) theory of perception.

Speaking about field theory, Lashley said in 1950 "I can best illustrate this conception by picturing the brain as the surface of a lake." He went on to describe how the normal background activity of the brain sent small ripples in all directions over the lake. Incoming stimuli he likened to the bow waves of a speeding boat, momentarily interacting with the continuous rise and fall of the background wave motion.

Lashley's views on perception were prophetic, although he never lived to see the proof. By the 1960's discoveries in brain research and optical image processing, paved the way for an elegant theory of perception based on wave forms. In 1958 Sir John Eccles, a distinguished neuroscientist, demonstrated how wave-like activity could take place in the brain, substantiating Lashley's poetic vision of "bow waves" on a lake. Several years later holography—then a novel technique for storing optical information—was described. Not only could there be waves on the lake but also they could carry a message.

Several researchers, most notably Lashley's one time associate Karl Pribram, combined these discoveries into a coherent hypothesis of perception and brain function. Through original research and the findings of others like Bekesy, Pribram demonstrated that the way the brain functioned in perception was as though it were creating a hologram.

The outline of Pribram's holographic model of brain function is straightforward. Incoming sensory information is first stored as wave patterns in our brain. From these stored wave patterns our brain then reconstructs the images we associate with our perception.

Back to our ongoing experiment: close your eyes and reach your hand out to touch something within arm's length. Maintain that touch as you consider the events taking place in your brain. The pressure you're exerting causes the nerve receptors beneath your skin to fire volley after volley of sensory impulses towards your brain. Meissner receptors rapidly adapt to the slightest change in pressure. Like the lines on a compass face, these receptor cells selectively respond to pressure applied along different angles. Some receptors respond to pressure exerted straight across the width of your palm; others are excited by longitudinal pressure applied in a direction parallel to your fingers; while still others are most sensitive to pressure directed on an angle somewhere between.

Merkel cells are also stimulated by your touch. Many such Merkel receptors are clustered together just below your skin surface to form a touch dome—a raised portion of skin invisible to the naked eye. These receptor cells fire sensory impulses according to how much pressure is being applied to them. Deeper beneath your skin Pacinian receptors are busy filtering out all but the most rapidly changing pressure stimuli, and thereby responding only to the purr of a steady vibration under your hand.

Meanwhile there is a whirlwind of activity in your brain. Every time a receptor fires it's as though a pebble has dropped into Lashley's lake. Each pebble contains different information encoded on the waves it produces. Eventually these waves of tactile information ripple throughout the brain's surface, interacting with each other and with the ongoing activity of the brain.

But how do interacting waves produce an image? To answer this question Pribram resorted to the hologram. A hologram records information by storing the unfocussed interaction of light waves from an object. This is completely unlike an ordinary photograph which records information by storing focussed points of light.

Imagine you're looking through the lens of your camera, about to take a picture of a tree. You slowly turn the focussing rim of the lens back and forth until the tree is in sharp focus. Click! You press the shutter release and capture the tree's image on film. You've produced an ordinary photograph. Each point on the tree is represented by a single point of light on the photograph.

Now imagine that instead of bringing the tree into focus you unfocus the camera lens so severely that you can't even recognize the tree. If you press the shutter release you'd then capture unfocussed light waves. This would be similar to producing a hologram. Each point on the tree is now represented by light waves on the film. All the waves from all the points interact with each other to form a complex wave pattern.

There's nothing on film except unfocussed light waves, you say, "Where's the image?" Let me stretch the analogy of the camera lens a little further to answer that question. Suppose I unfocussed the camera lens by turning the focussing ring ten times to the right. Can you envision a process that would then work in reverse? You'd have to look through a viewer with a similar lens that could be turned ten times back to the left. Each time you looked at that garbled image through this lens, voilá, out would pop your tree.

By the way, don't try to create a hologram using an unfocussed camera lens, it won't work. A lot more is needed to actually create one, but the essential details are contained in this simple analogy. This is the essence of holographic imaging: a process that records interacting wave forms, and a reverse process that reconstructs an image from those recorded waves. This, Pribram showed, is how the brain processes sensory information.

But let us return to our experiment which is still in progress. You had been reaching out to touch something, and I was describing what was happening in your brain. We had reached a point where waves of tactile information were spreading out over your brain's surface. In a manner similar to the way film emulsion records light, your brain cells now record this pattern of interacting wave forms. When it's time to form an image of what you're touching, your brain then runs the process in reverse.

From beginning to end it has just been a few milliseconds before you exclaim:

"Aha! I'm stroking my cat!"

So perception happens through constructing images from stored patterns in our brains. Psychology says that we construct images of what we touch, while physics says that we touch images which we construct. There is no separation between the process of perception and the objects of perception and our psychologist concludes: "in here" is one with "out there."

We must also conclude that touch is more than a means of accessing psychological events, for touch itself *is* a psychological event. Thus when we touch for the sake of healing we are not merely manipulating a body in the world "out there." Touch creates new patterns in the brain, enabling us to construct new images of ourselves. When we act on these images of wholeness provided through touch we embody the healing process.

Somatic Therapy and Somatosynthesis

Support for this relationship between touch and perception is found in the close relationship between the diagnostic and therapeutic uses of touch. When touch is involved, it is not uncommon to hear of diagnosis turning into therapy without the awareness of the guide or the traveler. I found myself in that awkward position with one traveler.

Paul was a young artist in his twenties, who had been suffering from a continual fever of 100 degrees for over a year. As a result he was chronically fatigued and exhausted. Thoroughly examined by traditional medical science, he came to see me out of frustration because there was neither a diagnosis given nor a treatment recommended by all the specialists he had consulted. Everyone shook their heads at his condition but no one had any answers. I had nothing definitive to tell him either, except to say that I would do a complete examination first and then determine how I might help.

My examination of Paul consisted mainly of palpation. I checked his spine, from coccyx to skull, for alignment, mobility and pain. I evaluated his muscles for strength, tension and tenderness. I palpated internal organs: liver, spleen, and kidneys. And I assessed the energy field surrounding his body. Afterwards I asked him to give me a day to review my findings, read the medical reports he had brought with him, and formulate a plan of action. We arranged a consultation for the following day to discuss these matters. When Paul came into my office the next day, he was beaming all over and vigorously shook my hand.

"Thanks. What a great treatment you gave me yesterday," he said. "My fever broke about an hour after leaving here. It's normal now and I feel much better. Can we do that again?"

I smiled and reassured him that I would try my best to continue helping him. I think I also smiled inside for the rest of that day, partly out of gratitude and partly out of amazement over what had taken place. I asked myself whether it was a *bona fide* treatment or a placebo effect induced through touch. Ultimately, I concluded that it really didn't matter. What did matter was that touch had helped this traveler on his healing journey.

❖

There are an unlimited number of ways for us to use touch therapeutically. Analogous to the spectrum of palpation, a spectrum of therapeutic touch also exists—from hard touch to soft touch; from heavy force to light force; from invasive pressure to gentle presence; from manipulation of the physical body to modulation of the human energy field. In the somatosynthesis work, we use all portions of this spectrum, although the emphasis is on the use of light, minimally intrusive touch.

The difficulty in suggesting the therapeutic use of light touch is a popular belief that "if a little is good, a lot must be better." For example, if I use an ounce of pressure to help relieve pain, then a pound would probably get the job done that much quicker, according to this common wisdom. However, in practice this is not necessarily the case.

A recent study of the effects of chiropractic spinal adjustment illustrates this point. Chiropractors are well-known for their vigorous, forceful manipulation of the spine to alter the position of vertebrae. Chung-Ha Suh, chairman of the Department of Biomechanics at the University of Colorado in Boulder, investigated spinal manipulation by taking motion picture x-rays of the spine as it was being adjusted by a chiropractor.

Called *cineradiography*, the technique allowed Suh to test a basic chiropractic assumption: that the spine actually changes position as a result of manipulation. Suh's findings were surprising. The spine did, in fact, move in the direction of a thrust given by a chiropractor. However, the film showed that once the thrust was over, the spine moved back to its original position—a result which appeared to contradict chiropractic beliefs.

But Suh continued to observe the spine and found that over time, it did move to and stay in the position it was directed to through manipulation. Suh concluded that manipulation did not result in the permanent movement of a bone from one place to another. Rather, manipulation was a force that stimulated the brain and nervous system. In turn, the nervous system exerted control over the body's muscles and joints, causing the permanent movement of a bone to take place. As it turns out, stimulating the brain and nervous system require much less force than moving a bone.

There is a point in the middle of each buttock which chiropractors call a *Logan Basic Contact Point*. Hugh B. Logan, was the doctor who first described its effect on the structural alignment of the spine in the 1930s and 1940s. (Feel where your body makes contact with the surface you're sitting on right now and you will be close to this point.)

Logan used pre- and post x-rays of the spine to demonstrate that gently holding this point could dramatically change the alignment of the spine. His treatment resulted in normalization of spinal alignment, reduction of spinal curvature (scoliosis), decreased pain, increased muscular relaxation and overall enhancement of health. How much pressure did he use? Close your eyes and use your thumb to gently press on your eyeballs through your closed eyelids. If the pressure is not comfortable for you, back off until it is. This was Logan's yardstick for the amount of force actually needed to move the spine.

Of course, we can use touch therapeutically for more than just realignment of the spine. For everything we can palpate, there is a corresponding application of touch to correct problems that are discovered—bones can be realigned, joints mobilized, organs repositioned, muscles relaxed, fluid flow enhanced, coordination between brain and body improved, and the energy field modulated.

There is also the use of touch to uncover the deeper psychological ground beneath physical problems—one of the main functions of the somatosynthesis work. My approach to therapeutic touch has always been to keep it simple, getting maximal results from a minimal number of techniques and procedures. In a typical somatosynthesis session, I find myself strategically touching just a few areas of the body. Once I've palpated to determine where to touch, there are three things I take into account: *depth, direction and duration*. How deep does my touch need to be? Should it be at the level of the energy field where no physical contact is involved, at the skin surface, where my hand is resting on the traveler, or pressing firmly into the traveler's body? In what direction should I apply force? Is it straight down, right, left, pulling, pushing, steady force, continuous movement, or some combination of these? Finally, how long should I apply this force? The traveler's body is always my guide in answering these questions.

With these *3 D's of Somatic Therapy* nearly any need for therapeutic touch can be met. Remembering that palpation and therapy are happening simultaneously, I can constantly monitor the effect of my touch on the traveler, without altering the position of my hands. For example, I might begin by working with the four major areas of cross-restriction in the body: the base of the pelvis, the base of the rib cage, the base of the neck and the base of the skull. These areas are often called *cross-restricting* because the orientation of the body's tissue is from front to back rather than from top to bottom. If you stand up and hold your arms at your side, you can see that most of the muscles in your body are arranged in an up-and-down (vertical) orientation. Your major blood vessels and nerve pathways also follow this orientation.

However, in some areas muscles, ligaments and other supporting tissues are arranged front-to-back (horizontal) rather than up-and-down. Where the normally vertical orientation of the body meets this horizontal orientation, a patchwork effect takes place and cross-restriction can result. Usually the horizontal tissue cross-restricts the vertical tissue of the body, thereby hampering normal muscle movement, fluid flow and nerve transmission. The body's normal energy flow can also be blocked, and these restricted areas often produce abnormal microwave output.

The practical result is that these areas of cross-restriction turn out to be the places that most of us experience and retain stress, tension and pain in our bodies. And they are also the areas often related to the deeper psychological issues beneath our physical signs and symptoms. A simple, straightforward approach to working with these cross-restrictions is to gently compress them from front to back.

Figure 4.3 is a pictorial representation of the major cross-restricting diaphragms of the body, along with the physical and psychological conditions related to these areas.

Beginning at the base of the spine, one finds a large area of potential cross-restriction called the *pelvic* or *urogenital* diaphragm. This diaphragm's normal function is to act as the floor of the abdomen and support the pelvic organs. It is attached to the inside rim of the pelvis on the front and sides, and to the sacrum and lower spine in back.

Restriction in this area is often related to lower back pain and dysfunction of the pelvic and urogenital organs. With the traveler lying face up, slipping one hand under the sacrum and resting another hand over the lower abdomen is an easy way of applying gentle compression to this area. In this case, your pressure is extremely light to begin with—merely the weight of your upper hand is enough. The traveler's body will respond by releasing the area between your hands. Any number of sensations can be felt as this release takes place. Frequently, you will feel the abdominal tissue soften, widen and sink beneath your hand—a

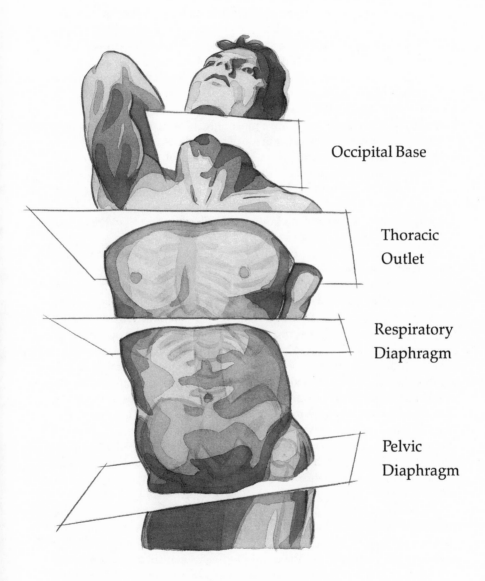

Occipital Base

Thoracic Outlet

Respiratory Diaphragm

Pelvic Diaphragm

Fig. 4.3: The location of the four major areas of cross-restricting soft tissue or diaphragms.

sensation not altogether different from the feeling one has upon sinking deeper and deeper into a water bed.

If you allow your hand to follow this first release and drop a little deeper into the abdominal soft tissue, multiple releases may follow. At the same time, your bottom hand will often detect movement in the spine. The sacrum may rock back and forth, the pelvis may move side to side and audible clicks may be heard in the spine as tension is released in this area and the body shifts itself into a more agreeable structural alignment.

Changes may happen in other areas of the body as well. The traveler's breathing often deepens and a sigh of relief is heard. The muscles of the pelvis or legs may jerk quickly as they release tension in a manner similar to what takes place as you fall off to sleep. The traveler may report sensations of warmth or tingling in the pelvic region and down the legs. The lower part of the traveler's body may feel unconnected to the upper part which is still tense.

And, the traveler may report reliving some past event associated with stress, trauma or pain in this area. All you are doing is providing a gentle compression, and then monitoring the body's response. When the release is completed, the pelvis will feel as though it has fallen into a deep silence.

The therapeutic benefits of releasing the pelvis in this way are many, ranging from the physical symptoms of this area to the associated psychological issues. I have seen marked improvement in lower back pain, bowel problems (constipation, diarrhea, hemorrhoids, irritable bowel syndrome, colitis), female sexual problems (pelvic inflammatory disease, cystitis, premenstrual tension, dysmenorrhea, endometriosis, vaginitis, dyspareunia), male sexual problems (congestive prostatitis, impotence, hernia), labor and delivery of children, and the overall stress referred to the pelvic region. Many of these physical symptoms have obvious psychological counterparts, often related to the traveler's sexuality. In releasing stress and tension in the pelvic region these deeper psychological and emotional issues can surface.

Ascending the body, the next higher area of cross-restriction is the *respiratory diaphragm*. This is a huge muscle that goes from the base of the rib cage in the front, to the upper part of the lumbar spine in the back. The most important function of the diaphragm is its control of breathing. As you inhale, the diaphragm contracts and drops down, creating a negative pressure in the upper chest and causing air to rush into the lungs. During exhalation, the diaphragm relaxes and moves upward forcing air out of the lungs.

Piercing through the respiratory diaphragm are very important tubal structures: the esophagus which transports food to the stomach, the abdominal aorta bringing blood into the pelvis from the heart, and the inferior vena cava returning blood from the pelvis to the heart. Important nerve centers, called *ganglia*, that control the function of intestinal organs are located close to the points of attachment of the diaphragm in the back. Restrictions in this can affect many functions within the body.

The respiratory diaphragm is released in the same way as the pelvic diaphragm. One hand is placed underneath, the other hand on top of the area and gentle compression is applied. The bottom hand is centered over the base of the rib cage behind, while the top hand rests lightly just below the base of the rib cage in front. As light force is applied you will experience the same phenomena as in the pelvic region. The upper abdominal soft tissue will release by softening, widening and sinking. The rib cage will often shift in one direction or another, the spine will move, breathing will become deeper, and intestinal gurgling will be heard. These are signs of decreased muscle tension, increased blood flow, and better neurological control of intestinal organs. In short, by releasing restrictions in this area, the body is given the opportunity to heal itself.

Fig. 4.4: Hand position for releasing the pelvic diaphragm.

Physical conditions that benefit from releasing the respiratory diaphragm have to do with the spine (middle and lower back), upper gastrointestinal tract (stomach, pancreas, small intestines, liver, gall bladder), abdominal organs (spleen, kidneys, adrenal glands), and, of course, breathing. In the process of releasing the respiratory diaphragm, it is easy to determine whether a traveler is a shallow or a deep breather.

When asked to take a deep breath, shallow breathers will frequently tighten their diaphragms and breathe by expanding only their upper chest. Releasing the respiratory diaphragm, then asking the traveler to breathe deeply by expanding their abdomen—pushing your top hand away—will counteract this tendency to take short, shallow breaths. A common response to stress is to adopt this shallow breathing pattern, one reason why people under stress have chronically tight diaphragms. The respiratory diaphragm and breathing are fundamental to good health. Chronic tightness in this diaphragm negatively effects many other body systems. So releasing the respiratory diaphragm and helping the traveler take deeper, fuller breathes can also be an important step in thwarting the harmful effects of stress. Furthermore, releasing this diaphragm can allow the traveler to "get in touch" with the sources of the stress affecting this area.

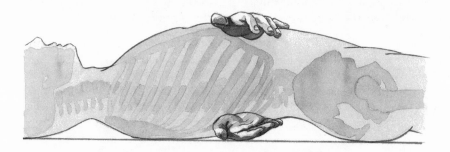

Fig. 4.5: Hand position for releasing the respiratory diaphragm.

Across the shoulders, at the base of the neck, there is no true diaphragm. But the tension pattern in this area makes it remarkably similar in function to a cross-restricting diaphragm. Anatomically it is called the *thoracic outlet* because important bundles of nerves, arteries, and veins pass from the neck out to the arms through a maze of soft tissue (muscles, joints, ligaments) and bone in this area. Nerves, arteries and, veins communicating between the brain and body also pass through this area. Restrictions in this area can entrap these nerves, arteries or veins resulting in tension and discomfort across the shoulders and upper chest, decreased mobility of the neck, diminished nerve or blood flow to the arms, consequent loss of coordination and function in the arms, and fluid congestion in the head.

The thoracic outlet is released in the same way as the pelvic and respiratory diaphragms. One hand is placed under the spine just below the junction of the neck and shoulders, the other hand rests lightly on the upper chest just below the collar bones. Gentle compression results and a softening, widening and sinking of this area occurs as it is released. You will often feel movement in the lower neck or upper back, the rib cage, the sternum (breast bone), clavicles (collar bones), and scapulae (shoulder blades), as the body shifts these structures into a stress-free alignment.

The organs most affected by this release are the heart, the lungs, the esophagus, the trachea (wind pipe), and bronchial tubes. These structures are frequently subject to the effects of emotional and psychological stress. Asthma, usually associated with emotional or psychological factors, produces muscle spasms in the bronchial tubes and smaller passageways of lungs. Love, fear, excitement, anxiety, tranquility, rage, grief, guilt, all of our human emotions effect our cardiovascular system and, therefore, our heart.

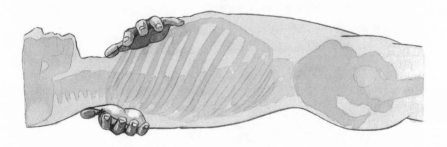

Fig. 4.6: Hand position for releasing the thoracic outlet area.

This is one reason we consider the heart to be the center of our emotional selves. You need only blush or feel panic-stricken to realize this. A change in heart rate and blood pressure typically accompanies your experience of a particular emotional state. As the emotion subsides, your body returns your heart rate and blood pressure back to normal. However, sometimes when emotion does not subside, and the cardiovascular system remains under chronic stress, restriction in the thoracic outlet occurs. Releasing this area helps remove the physical basis of this stress and opens the possibility of controlling the underlying emotional and psychological components as well.

One final area of cross-restriction is at the base of the skull—the *occipital base*. Like the thoracic outlet there is no true diaphragm here, but the muscles and ligaments attached to the base of the skull form a zone of cross-restriction. Tightness in this area is a frequent source of tension headaches and possible entrapment of key nerves and veins exiting from the brain. Restrictions in the occipital base region can cause fluid congestion within the skull and reduced nerve communication between brain and body. The occipital base area is a principal

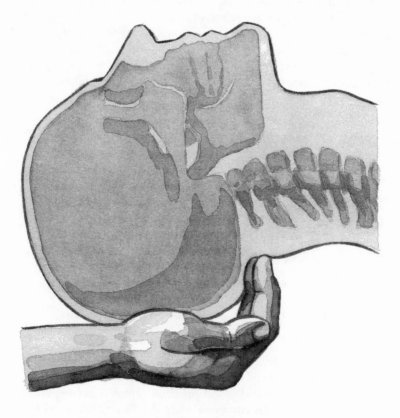

Fig. 4.7: Hand position for releasing the occipital base.

focus of somatic techniques like Upledger's *Craniosacral Therapy* or DeJarnette's *Sacro-Occipital Technique.*

On many people, this area is very tender to touch and must be released with patience and care. It is not possible to gently compress the occipital base from front to back, so one technique here is to slide the outside edge of your index finger along the length of the occipital base and allow the skull to drop back over your hand. The weight of the skull will gently stretch the soft tissue in this area causing it to release. You will feel the skull sink lower; the uppermost portion of the spine shift position; and, often observe the head moving from side to side with the release of the occipital base.

Freeing this area will help to resolve tension headaches, enhance nerve communication between brain and body, increase fluid drainage from the skull; and, correct misalignments of the upper spine. Releasing the occipital base also unlocks related emotional and psychological factors, so the guide may assist the traveler in resolving these as well.

Releasing areas of cross-restriction is just one of many techniques a guide can use to work with the traveler's physical body. I have described the process in some detail to illustrate the far-reaching effects of a simple "hands-on" procedure that addresses physical symptoms and prepares the guide and traveler for the deeper emotional and psychological components of the somatosynthesis work.

Other somatic therapists have used similar techniques. Wilhelm Reich, for example, had a method of working with the "muscular armoring" of the body, which he viewed as the physical expression of underlying emotional barriers to experiencing joy and excitement in life. For Reich, there were seven rings of cross-restriction: 1) pelvis; 2) central abdomen; 3) respiratory diaphragm; 4) chest; 5) neck; 6) mouth and jaw; 7) eye region. Upledger, by contrast, proposes four important cross-restrictions: 1) pelvic; 2) respiratory diaphragm; 3) thoracic outlet; and, 4) occipital base.

Of course, as I guide, I may have decided not to release cross-restrictions and instead have chosen some other method of physical intervention. Joint mobilization may have been more appropriate for the physical conditions of a given traveler, and I might have used any of several procedures to accomplish this task.

Unwinding is one such procedure where the guide facilitates the movement of a joint in whatever direction the body desires. Ankles, knees, hips, shoulders and neck are common areas where unwinding is a useful technique, although the entire body can undergo unwinding.

If I were unwinding a neck, for example, I would gently hold the traveler's head in my hands and follow whatever movement the head and neck make. The traveler's head may twist and turn, move forward or arch backward. The head may move continually for periods of time, then pause for a while. I would passively encourage the body to follow this pattern of movement until all movement ceased, or until the desired range of motion in the joint was achieved.

It's like dancing with a partner: the traveler's body leads as you follow. Nothing is forced although movement is sometimes probed. I might gently nudge the traveler's head to the right and see if movement picks up from there. If it doesn't I would nudge it in another direction and wait for the traveler's body to engage in further motion. Once the traveler begins to move, the unwinding occurs with a choreographed logic of its own. The movement can be simple or complex; rapid or slow; jerky or smooth.

I feel that by just holding a body part I telegraph an unspoken message that "It's OK" for that part to do what it needs in order to heal. Travelers will often report feeling out of control of their bodies—like their body is moving itself. They will also challenge the technique, claiming that the movement is being induced by me. In this case, I simply remove my hands for several moments and allow the traveler to observe their body moving without my presence.

Through this technique the body appears to reverse the trauma a joint was subjected to: hence, the name *unwinding*. Figure 4.8 illustrates the kind of unwinding motion that will often take place around a joint.

During an unwinding, it is not uncommon for a traveler to relive a traumatic event and feel the emotions surrounding that experience. Thus, the physical and psychological aspects of trauma stored in the body can be resolved.

As a guide, I might determine that the traveler simply needs *steady pressure* in one, or more, areas of the body. In this case, I would not specifically be waiting for a release to take place, although one may occur. Like any form of manual therapy, sustained pressure affects the body in a number of ways: by aligning and repositioning body structures; through pressure massage of the body; and by reflex stimulation. The need for steady pressure may arise when the traveler's body moves away from confronting physical or psychological issues.

For instance, I have witnessed travelers who continually move their pelvis and lower back to avoid confronting the physical and psychological pain in this area. Steady pressure, which offers firm but passive resistance to movement, will "pin down" the traveler in this area, preventing further motion of avoidance. Thus, the traveler's body will be directed to deal with the physical and psychological concerns at hand.

At other times, steady pressure can be used to support a traveler having difficulty connecting the physical and psychological components of a problem. A gentle, steady hand in the middle of the chest (near the heart), for example, can help make this link and allow the healing journey to proceed.

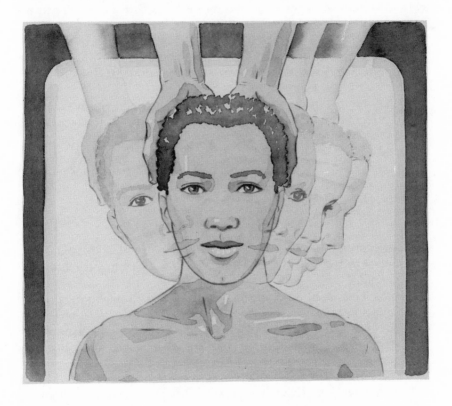

Fig. 4.8: Illustration of an unwinding where the head and neck undergo many different motions as tension, pain, and the emotional memory of trauma are released.

❖

The human *energy field* is also responsive to therapeutic touch. In the following somatosynthesis session, I used the traveler's energy field to work with the physical and psychological issues surrounding an injury to the shoulder. The traveler was a forty-two year old, female athlete named Chris, who, until two years earlier, competed in national swimming contests. She severely injured her right shoulder after diving clumsily and hitting the side of the pool. Surgery was required to repair a torn ligament and shoulder separation. I first saw Chris after three operations to repair the shoulder. She had a large surgical scar from her shoulder to just above her right biceps, and her right arm hung painfully rigid at her side. She was understandably frustrated by her unsuccessful surgeries and her inability to swim for the past two years.

I began our first treatment session by palpating her energy field. Starting at her feet, I scanned her field with my hands held several inches above the surface of her body. It felt as though she had an invisible garment wrapped around her, but at the shoulder there was a void. After talking her through a relaxation, I enlisted her help in working with the shoulder.

"Bring your awareness to your right shoulder," I suggested, "and just experience that area of your body."

After several minutes in silence, Chris offered that she saw colors in the shoulder.

"There's an area of gray, right over the main injury site," she said, "it's surrounded by red, with a small patch of yellow trying to push through from one side."

Colors have been traditionally associated with monitoring and modulating the human energy field. Based on Chris's visualization of the colors in her shoulder, it seemed appropriate to continue working with her energy field. I asked her what color she felt belonged in her injured shoulder.

"Green," she answered; "that's a color I associate with life and healing."

I cupped her shoulder with my hands—one on top, one on bottom—and visualized a flow of green between them. Chris assisted by also visualizing green in this area, and describing what she felt take place within her shoulder.

"I see wave after wave of different hues of green," she recounted. "The gray area seems to be disappearing and I feel strength moving back into my shoulder."

After ten minutes of visualizing green in her shoulder, I asked Chris to bring her attention to her uninjured left shoulder.

"What's it like to be aware of that shoulder," I queried.

"That's funny," she said, "for so long I've just focussed on my injured shoulder that I almost forgot I have another shoulder. My left shoulder feels strong, and it feels like it really wants to help my right shoulder heal. In fact," she added, "I can see my left shoulder sending the color green over to the right shoulder."

Chris came to realize that both shoulders had very different messages for her. The right shoulder represented the rigid, inflexible, traumatized person she had been in the past. The left shoulder was the strong, vital, but yielding person she could be in the present and future. One shoulder represented what she had been, the other represented what she could become.

This drama between her past and her potential was being enacted in other areas of her life as well. Chris was just beginning to "get her feet under her" after a divorce which, coincidentally, was finalized within hours of her accident. She had recently graduated from school, landed a new job and was feeling her emergence as a strong, independent woman. This contrast between opposing parts of herself represented by each shoulder did not escape her. I concluded this first session by asking her to consider how she could incorporate this insight into her life now.

"I've never looked at these two sides of myself," she noted. "The injury seems to have trapped me in my past self. Whenever I think about my body, I think about my right shoulder, never my left, and I think about the person I used to be. I'm not that person, and I don't want to be that person again. I want to let go of that past self and grow into the strong person my left shoulder represents. I guess, I'm trying to heal my life in exactly the same way I need to heal my shoulder. From now on, when I think about my shoulder, I'm going to be aware of the left shoulder first and use that shoulder to help my injured shoulder. I can send the color green from my left shoulder to my right, and help my right shoulder heal."

Fortunately, we were able to decode the messages contained in Chris's body. She left feeling much less shoulder pain, and much more confident about what she needed to do to heal herself.

Cross-restriction release, unwinding, sustained pressure, and *modulation of the body's energy field* demonstrate different approaches to the therapeutic use of human touch. Each of them represent a slightly different way a guide can work with the traveler. Often, I will incorporate them all within a single somatosynthesis session, as they seem appropriate to the traveler's needs.

Of course, these are not the only methods of therapeutic touch that can be used, but they share an important trait that allows them to be easily incorporated into the somatosynthesis work. *Minimally invasive*, they encourage the traveler's healing process to unfold from the inside out. Compared to the deep goading of a tight muscle or a forceful thrust to correct spinal alignment, the techniques mentioned so far coax the body rather than coerce it; they imply possibilities rather than impose certainty; they ask the guide to be a humble servant rather than an all-knowing dictator; and they place great reliance on the traveler's "inner compass," which always seems to point in the right direction for the healing journey.

Within the human body light force often accomplishes more than heavy force, and there is actually a biological law to support such a paradoxical belief! Called the *Arndt-Schultz Law*, after the two German doctors who first described it in 1899, the law states that:

> Light stimuli enhance the function of biological systems; moderate stimuli inhibit the function of biological systems; and heavy stimuli arrest the function of biological systems.

In the somatosynthesis work, the guide seeks to enhance the healing response of the traveler through minimally invasive physical intervention.

Sometimes it is necessary for a guide to be directive—to force a bone from one location to another; to insist that a joint move past a restrictive barrier; to wrestle with a tight muscle until it gives up. When this happens I feel like a guide who has not really heard what the traveler's body needs, so that now the healing journey must proceed by my decree. I also feel that when I force physical change within the traveler, I do not always allow for the deeper psychological and emotional issues to surface and change simultaneously.

We can change physical posture more swiftly than psychological posture—the body heals more rapidly than the mind. Our goal in somatosynthesis is to touch the mind through the body, to guide both body and mind on the journey towards healing and wholeness.

5

Touching Mind and Emotion Through the Body

"The body is the temple of the soul," says an Eastern proverb. And, when the temple is well-cared for, the human soul flourishes. So it is for somatosynthesis as well: Through the body we seek the soul—through Soma we find Psyche. Caring for the temple is just the first step in the somatosynthesis work; allowing the human soul to flourish completes the process. Working with the traveler's physical body merely paves the way for reaching the traveler's deeper psychological ground. Once this deeper ground is found, the traveler is able to glimpse at his or her innate wholeness, discover the obstacles towards realizing this wholeness, and develop the inner resources to overcome these restraints. This is the true healing journey of somatosynthesis, a journey which turns upon the use of human touch. Through touch, the guide and traveler not only attend to the needs of the physical body but also gain access to the innermost sanctum of the psyche.

Gaining access to the psyche through the body is an astonishing process. It ranges from simply placing a traveler in touch with the mental images behind physical symptoms to a profound exploration of the intricate nature of a human being. Here too I have adopted a straightforward approach to reaching the psyche through the body—one which emphasizes the inherent ease and naturalness of the process. I have tried to avoid burying the actual techniques under heavy psychological theory, for the somatosynthesis guide, while working with the human psyche, is not trying to mimic a psychotherapist. There is a substantial difference between approaching the psyche through touch and approaching the psyche through talk. Much of what may take several sessions of therapeutic dialogue to achieve often can be done in a few moments using touch.

I am reminded of a session with a career woman in her forties who since adolescence had developed a very tough, aloof, intellectual exterior to cover a deep-felt sense of vulnerability and isolation. Her parents had died when she was eight years old, and she had been shuttled from household to household throughout her life. Her exceptional intelligence made her quite good at sparring intellectually, but it also kept her true feelings camouflaged. On the verge of being in touch with her emotions, she put forth a barrage of intellectual arguments and managed to avoid dealing directly with what she felt. Not surprisingly, traditional psychotherapy was difficult for this woman—she admitted "going through" several therapists in the past few years. She came to see me because she was having pain in her middle back that made it difficult to breathe.

Without saying a word, I applied a firm but steady pressure over her chest, which I refused to release even when she insisted I was hurting her. Instead, I asked her to use her mind to focus on the area of her body under my hand and, as the pain increased, to focus even harder. She did, and moments later she began to cry, heaving her chest and arching her back off the table with each sob. Through her tears she admitted to how tired she was of maintaining this intellectual armor, and how all she really wanted was to connect with people in her life. The muscles in her middle back released through her crying, and when she was through she had no pain.

Moreover she had been placed in touch with her emotions in a way she had not allowed herself for many the years. The session ended, but the real healing journey had just begun; this woman had finally taken her first step on that journey. I doubt that so much could have been achieved so quickly through talking alone. Used insightfully and incisively, touch penetrates where talk does not.

Road Map for a Healing Journey

Figure 5.1 is an outline of a somatosynthesis session—a road map of the journey taken by traveler and guide. The three important points on

this map are numbered in the order encountered during a somatosynthesis journey. Obviously, the body (soma) is the point of departure. We
start with the body because somatosynthesis travelers usually begin
therapy out of concern for physical problems, and through touching the
body the guide addresses these physical concerns.

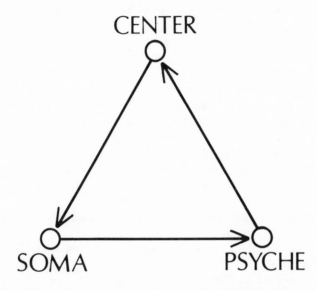

Fig. 5.1: The somatosynthesis road map illustrating the healing journey from Soma to
Psyche to Center.

In the previous chapter, we looked at various ways in which a guide
uses touch to work with the traveler, and thereby begin the somatosynthesis journey. Once begun, the guide assumes the responsibility of
directing the journey through each point on the map. The first portion of
the somatosynthesis journey is from soma to psyche—the subject of this
present chapter. To complete this first segment the guide must assist the
traveler in reaching the psychological issues—thoughts, emotions and
feelings—related to the areas of the traveler's body the guide is working
with.

Arriving at this second point (psyche), the guide continues to work
with the traveler's body while helping the traveler understand and gain
insight into the psychological elements of the healing journey. But

somatosynthesis strives for more than just providing the traveler with deeper access to the psyche.

In the second phase of the journey, the guide facilitates the traveler's movement from psyche to center. *Center* is a place within the traveler that is distinct from body, thoughts, and feelings. We will say more about the center later, when we consider this second portion of the somatosynthesis journey. Now I will briefly discuss it through the experience of a traveler I guided.

❖

Arlan was man in his late forties who came to see me because of pain in his left shoulder. After a period of relaxation and inner reflection on both his shoulders, Arlan came to realize that his left shoulder pain represented his resistance to exploring deeply held feelings about being physically abused by his father as a young child. When he shifted his attention to his right shoulder, however, he was aware of a "gung-ho" energy that wanted to deal directly with the situation and finally get over it. I intervened physically to help Arlan's left shoulder, and I asked him to give a voice to each shoulder, listening to what they had to say.

"It's like a mad house in there," he observed, "one says 'Go!' then the other says 'Stop!'

"'Go! Stop! Go! Stop!'" he said in frustration, "they just keep going back and forth."

Arlan went on in a state of confusion between these voices for about 10 minutes. Then, seemingly out of nowhere, he shouted in an uncharacteristically loud voice,

"Enough already, I'm in charge!"

That voice was Arlan's center. With it, he was eventually able to bring these two warring, inner voices under control and gain mastery over the forces contributing to his shoulder pain.

The function of the center is to bring about a synthesis of soma and psyche. In Arlan's case both soma and psyche were divided within, and the center's task was to step in to bring order—like a mediator negotiating between two parties or a parent settling a conflict between two rival siblings. Thus helping the traveler find his or her center is the second step of the somatosynthesis journey. Having the traveler use this center to synthesize soma and psyche is the final step of the process.

Here we have an account of the somatosynthesis map—an overview of the journey from soma to psyche to center and back. We should read this map, bearing in mind Korzybski's wise saying that, "the map is not the territory." For the territory covered in each healing journey is one of varying terrain, special to each traveler and uniquely navigated by each guide.

On the path, there are only a few assumptions we need to make about the relationship between guide and traveler. First, and foremost, is a belief in the inner process of the traveler: that in each traveler lies an "inner wisdom," an "innate intelligence," a "higher self" that continually seeks wholeness and fulfillment. Nature shows us this fundamental aspect of life. We believe that a seed will sprout roots and grow into a bush; that a bush will sprout buds that open to become flowers; and that flowers will turn their petals to always seek the light.

In nature we need merely nourish and support the growing plant—its inner wisdom will dictate the manner and moment of flowering. In working with human nature, a similar truth holds: We need merely support and encourage the process of growth while an inner wisdom dictates the manner and moment of unfoldment. As a guide, we can no more force a person through any phase of the somatosynthesis journey than we can force a rose to open. There is a level of respect, belief and faith in the inner process of both plant and person that allows us to participate in their unfolding, but not to control it.

In a similar way, the inner process of the guide is also valued. For the guide's inner wisdom leads the traveler to discover his own. It is the guide's sensitivity to the traveler's needs that propels the journey forward. The traveler is like a growing plant, the guide like a master gardener. And like a true gardener, the guide is conscious of the plant's need for soil, water and light, and careful to give only the right amount of each to support the plant's growth.

One important way a guide becomes attuned to the traveler's needs is by maintaining an *open focus* throughout the somatosynthesis journey. By this, I mean that as the journey proceeds, the guide continually ponders the question, "What is emerging here, and what is my role in helping the traveler take the next step?" Answers to this question allow the guide to direct the journey's course.

Open focus sounds like a contradiction in terms because we normally associate *focussing* with narrowing our field of vision, and closing down our perspective. However, adopting an open focus widens the guide's vision and enlarges the guide's perspective of the route the traveler may take on the healing journey.

Driving a car is a good example of open focus in action. When you drive, you always focus sufficiently far ahead to maintain a sense of what is next to come. Focussing only on the road immediately ahead will limit your vision, not allowing you to prepare for a bend in the road or an upcoming detour. On the other hand, focussing too far ahead will cause you to miss the more immediate conditions that you encounter as you drive.

An open focus places your vision at just the proper distance ahead— maintaining keen awareness of what is likely to emerge, yet being able to see all that transpires from moment to moment. A guide must also maintain a focus which gives clear vision of the journey ahead, while always remaining aware of the moment to moment progress of the traveler. This allows the guide to continually interact with the traveler— through soma and psyche—and direct the further progress of the healing journey.

These are the three key elements of this journey beyond the body: the somatosynthesis road map, the inner wisdom of traveler and guide; and the guide's open focus. With these kept in mind, the guide can adapt many specific techniques for this passage from soma to psyche to center and back. The techniques a somatosynthesis guide might use seem to fall naturally into a particular phase of this healing journey, and we can explore them in that way.

From Soma to Psyche

The journey beyond the body commences as traveler and guide move from soma to psyche. It is the beginning of the traveler's glimpse into a reality deeper than the body's physical condition. Access to the psyche's realm requires a relaxed, inner focus that enables the traveler to pay attention to subtlety of feeling and thought. The guide is already in touch with the traveler through palpation and the therapeutic administration of touch. This continued touch helps the traveler relax, while the guide's carefully chosen words deepen the relaxation and turn the traveler's awareness within.

My preference is to use the traveler's breath as a means of relaxation and refocussing. Ordinarily, I talk the traveler through three stages of the this process: body, mind, and inner focus. First, the traveler is invited to close his or her eyes, focus on the breath, and allow it to deepen naturally. Then I encourage the traveler to feel that each inhalation and exhalation takes the body a little further into relaxation. I usually have my hands on the traveler now, making it easy to monitor the relaxation response. This response almost always includes a noticeable decrease in the rate of breathing, audible sighs of relief and some muscular twitching.

Beyond the body is the mind. And relaxing the mind is a more subtle task, given the incessant flow of thoughts in and out of our consciousness. Here too the breath is a valuable tool. I ask the traveler to observe the rhythmic pattern of the breath without exerting any control over it. Then I offer the traveler a mental image which allows the thoughts to exist without disrupting the mind's tranquility: imagining the thoughts to be clouds floating by on a calm summer day or feeling the mind is a leaf floating in a quiet pond while the thoughts gently ripple the pond's surface.

Such images are particularly helpful for travelers who overly identify with their intellect. For example, any time I sense a traveler struggling with the separation between thoughts and feelings, I will suggest a return to this image; with the mind relaxed, the difference between the two becomes clearer.

Relaxing the mind is also preparation for turning the traveler's focus within. To accomplish this inward turning, I invite the traveler to locate the "center point of being," a metaphorical place easily found with eyes closed and a simple question held in mind: "Where is my center point?" The answers, while unique to each, are shared by many: "the space between my eyes," "the center of my chest," "my solar plexus," or "the middle of my abdomen." Once found, the traveler is encouraged to become more aware of this "center point." As a somatosynthesis session proceeds, this becomes a point to which the traveler can return again and again, to integrate and synthesize the emerging issues of the healing journey.

Traveler and guide will often observe a profound shift in the atmosphere of the journey once the center point is found. Relaxing the body and mind becomes more than just letting go of muscles and thoughts. Developing an inner focus leads to more than just thinking about one area of the body. Like moving from an air-conditioned office outside into a humid summer day, traveler and guide move into a tangibly different state of awareness.

Frequently the guide is first to register this shift. The reciprocity of the process is obvious: As the guide touches and talks the traveler through successive levels of relaxation and inner focussing, the guide too relaxes and focusses within. An inexplicable bonding with the traveler is felt: Through touch the physical boundary between the two seems to disappear, and a bonding beyond the body occurs.

Helping the traveler find his center point, leads the guide to discover his own. There is a feeling that both are linked via these points of inner awareness, and the real exchange can begin. Like a telephone connection, the inner wisdom of both traveler and guide seem to freely communicate, beyond words but with perfect clarity and understanding—an experience often characterized by a mild euphoria. This deep communion is a well-spring of knowledge for both voyagers: The guide can tap into it to direct the healing journey; for the traveler, it provides access to the deeper issues and insights the journey requires.

This turning point is not always reached as early as I have described, but it is a critical part of the somatosynthesis journey. Whether it is achieved in the early or late stages of the process, it denotes a point of engagement between traveler and guide with maximum therapeutic potential. I believe that at this transition point both voyagers experience a shift in awareness commonly referred to as an *alternative* or *altered state of consciousness* (ASC).

What is unique in somatosynthesis, is the use of human touch to bring about this ASC, something I have termed a *touch-induced altered state of consciousness* (TASC). From the verbal reports of experimental subjects to the objective findings of scientific instruments, there is a lot we know about altered states of consciousness. This knowledge makes it easier to grasp the significance of TASCs in somatosynthesis.

The perception of critical shifts in awareness (ASCs) during therapy is not unique to somatosynthesis. Psychologist Eugene Gendlin called this subjective shift in awareness a "felt shift" and developed an entire psychotherapeutic approach around its induction. Research later showed that objective correlations to this phenomenon do exist.

The brain wave activity of therapists and clients were independently recorded throughout a psychotherapy session while the session was simultaneously videotaped. After the session, the videotape was viewed separately by both therapist and client who were asked to note the point at which they felt the therapy was most effective. The brain wave recordings examined at those points showed an unexpected degree of synchronous activity between both therapist and client.

A more remarkable finding was obtained by Shealy and Green, while monitoring well-known spiritual healer Olga Worrall treating a subject at a distance. Worrall was stationed in one room while the subject was seated in a separate room about thirty feet away, separated by a wall. Both Worrall and the experimental subject were connected to sophisticated recording devices which monitored brain wave activity, heart rate, and respiration. At the precise moment Worrall said she "visualized" placing her hands on the subject's body, the recording instruments showed a dramatic, synchronous shift of the functions being monitored—brain wave, heart rate and respiration changed at the same time and in the same direction for both individuals. Even ordinary experience gives rise to familiar instances of ASCs. The difference between our ordinary state of wakefulness and the "half-sleep/half-wake" state that precedes sleep is similar to the shift perceived as guide and traveler enter a TASC. An "aha" experience, which resolves a tough problem in a flash of insight, is another example of this shift in awareness. Athletes frequently report such shifts in awareness: a "runner's high," a basketball player's "hot hand," a bowler being "in the groove," or a baseball hitter's rhythm.

Perhaps the most common example of this shift in awareness comes in conversation between two people. Everyone has had the experience of "talking past" someone else—a situation where words fly back and forth yet little communication takes place. Then at a certain point a shift takes place. There is the feeling of "I've got it!" and a sense of real understanding that transcends the need for further talk.

All of these examples are indications of body and mind coordinating to provide access to a different state of awareness: a realm giving rise to thoughts, feelings and actions beyond those ordinarily deemed possible. During a somatosynthesis journey access to this realm while not guaranteed to traveler or guide, is frequently granted to both through human touch.

Human touch can rapidly induce an altered state of consciousness—a phenomenon which escapes most somatic and psychological therapists. I have frequently observed myself and a traveler slipping into a TASC after a mere 25 to 30 seconds of touch. TASCs, like other altered states, come about through the coordination of body and mind. Touch relaxes the body and goes beyond the boundaries normally imposed by the mind. When I touch I am no longer a small self bounded by my skin. When I touch, the traveler becomes an extension of me, and I in turn become an extension of the traveler.

Barely perceptible within the energy field, or deeply felt within the body, human touch implies that we are more than separate, fragmented selves. Travelers will often say they are unable to feel where their skin ends and mine begins. And frequently we will both feel "lost in touch," as our experience of time and space are endowed with eerie new traits.

Time may appear to dilate or contract: "time passed so slowly" or "I can't believe we've been here this long, it just feels like a few minutes have passed"—are phrases commonly heard from travelers, and also experienced by guides. Body space is altered: "I felt incredibly light, as if I were flying and had left my body behind"; "I felt like I was floating, hovering in the air above my body"; "I felt my body expanding, growing larger and larger throughout the session"—are sensations also shared by travelers and guides. These are the qualities of touching—so different from ordinary experience—that propel the healing journey into an altered state.

The goal of somatosynthesis, however, is not merely to marvel at touch inducing altered awareness, but to use this shift in consciousness to penetrate the deeper realms of the psyche. Here we are not alone, for there is a long tradition of using altered states of awareness in the healing process. Most notably this occurs in *shamanism*, a practice certainly older than recorded history. Shamans emerged as personal and social healers harnessing the forces of nature, and working with human nature to bring about the healing of individuals and groups.

Traditionally shamans were the doctors and the priests, the visionaries and mystics, the wise men and wise women, the first guides of the healing journey. An ailing person, or an ailing society would turn to the shaman— whether to heal a physical or psychological malady or to determine the clan's next move to more fertile, bountiful lands. Shamans used drugs, drumming, dancing, chanting, fasting, exertion, sensory deprivation, prayer, and human touch. With these tools they brought about various states of ecstacy, reverie, trance, and illumination—in themselves in individuals and in groups. From these altered states came the visions, the images, and the methods by which the shaman healed.

We have lost the way of the shaman in modern medicine, but glimpses of this tradition still remain. From the gentle smile of a caring physician, to the reassuring touch of a concerned therapist these small, ordinary, unnoticed gestures are still capable of producing subtle alterations in our state of consciousness. Simply feeling that "I am not alone," that "someone cares," helps us connect with a realm of being beyond our ordinary experience of separation and isolation. This is a healing experience. Other forms of therapy do even more. I have no doubt that induced alterations in consciousness occur in all therapy based on human touch. Many somatic therapists are aware of this but simply attribute such occurrences to the profound relaxation produced by touch.

Fig. 5.2: Southern African rock painting of a shaman in the middle of a circle of dancing figures. The shaman is touching a figure lying down before him.

When I first began to practice as a chiropractor, my patients regularly reported sensations like floating, being out of body, and loss of skin boundary. I just reassured them that such feelings were a normal consequence of touch and left it at that. I even tried just touching someone with the intent to help or heal—without any specific therapy in mind—and found that similar shifts in awareness happened.

Ultimately I began to realize that these shifts in consciousness were not secondary effects of touching; they were real doorways to the healing process. To walk through these gateways is to reconnect with the way of the shaman. In this sense somatosynthesis reclaims the shamanic vision. As the journey moves from soma to psyche, the guide assumes the role of the shaman. Let us now look at some of the specific techniques to carry the healing journey from soma to psyche.

Somatic Imaging

The traveler's ability to image somatically is the basis for many of the techniques in this early phase of the healing journey. We spoke about somatic imaging earlier, and I would like to show how it is actually used in therapy. The process begins with the guide's decision of where to intervene. Through palpation the guide determines where and how touch will be applied therapeutically—from deep within the traveler's body to the outer limits of the traveler's energy field.

Touching not only initiates physical changes but also brings the traveler's awareness to a given area. The guide can then verbally direct the traveler to continue focussing on this area while the traveler allows any related images to emerge. As these somatic images take shape in the traveler's mind, they can be shared openly with the guide.

Our language for describing physical sensation lends itself to somatic imaging. We are accustomed to using metaphors to describe our physical condition, particularly in the case of pain or discomfort. A "stabbing" pain, a "wrenched" neck, a "churned up" stomach, a "burning" sensation, a "shooting" pain, a "pins and needle" sensation, a "tight" muscle, these are examples of the images embedded within commonly used phrases. Somatic images range from the mundane to the bizarre. However, when they arise from a relaxed and inwardly focussed traveler, these images, however strange, are almost always related to the deeper issues underlying physical conditions.

❖

A typical example of using somatic imagery is the case of a young man in his thirties named Daniel who sought my help for his severe lower back pain. With his lower back and pelvis sandwiched lightly between my hands, I verbally guided him through a relaxation and inner focussing. Then I asked him to bring his awareness to his painful lower back and simply let any images of that area come into his mind.

"It's very tight on both sides of my spine," he noted. "Like the strings of a guitar that have been tightened too much."

Another example of somatic imagery comes from a middle-aged woman named Jeannette, whom I first saw because of recurring headaches, neck and shoulder pain. As she lay on her back, I held her neck and asked her to be aware of any images that emerged related to her pain.

"I feel as though someone has a knife in my neck," she reported. "I can almost see the blade with a hand holding it into my flesh."

The image was so vivid for her that her body recoiled as she shared her vision with me. I asked her to stay with that image and describe the hand holding the knife into her.

"It's a man's hand," she said, "but I can't see past his wrist."

Rather than have her try too hard, I asked her to relax while she still focussed on the hand. After four or five minutes, the image seemed to change spontaneously for her.

"It's like watching a camera, slowly moving up this man's arm," she exclaimed. "I can even tell that he's wearing a black leather jacket. His shoulder and neck are coming into view now."

"Oh my God," she cried out, "it's David, it's David!"David and Jeannette were involved in a relationship ten years ago. Jeannette left that relationship because David physically abused her. Since married, she had also been through several years of psychotherapy surrounding her relationship with David. She felt that David was a part of her past that she had moved beyond. Consequently, she was very surprised to encounter him in this way.

Somatically derived images are not confined to inanimate objects like strings and knives. They will often appear as *people with given attributes*: a painful area becomes an angry individual; a tight area feels like an overburdened person; while an area of numbness is experienced as a scared or fearful person.

The possibilities are endless and vary from traveler to traveler depending on the specific body area the image emerges from and the deeper issues which the image represents. Such images may represent imaginary people, someone actually in the traveler's life or different aspects of the traveler's personality. Qualities or feelings may also arise without being tied to the image of a person. When the traveler focusses on the lower back, anger may be experienced; awareness of the chest and middle back might bring sadness; and tightness in the shoulders could give rise to fear.

Some travelers may experience physical sensations: One body area may feel "light" and have a "floating" quality about it, while another area may feel "dense" and "grounded." Here too the feelings and qualities which surface will depend on the inner forces being expressed through a given area of the traveler's body.

Occasionally, a body area will be experienced as an *animal*, with traits related to a traveler's underlying issues. Ben was a man in his early 30's with no specific complaint other than chronic fatigue. To my palpation, the energy field surrounding his liver was excessively active. I rested my hand gently beneath the right side of his rib cage and asked him to bring his awareness to this area. After several minutes, Ben shared the imagery that began to unfold:

"I see a lone, silver wolf standing on a small hill," he recounted. "It's slowly walking in my direction."

As the wolf came closer to Ben, his whole body began to tense.

"The wolf is snapping at me," he screamed; "I can't move, and it's eating my liver."

This was a very Promethean image. Eventually the wolf did kill Ben although he was conscious throughout his symbolic death and remained conscious afterwards. Once the wolf had eaten Ben, it turned around and began to offer him messages about the inner conflicts in his life. (I'll say more about interpreting and working with somatic images later). Afterwards Ben informed me of his Native American heritage and told me that the wolf was his totem sign.

Another interesting variation of somatically derived images occurs when a traveler identifies a body area with a *place*. An area of pain may feel like a cave and the traveler may feel trapped within. Or a painful area could be experienced as an arid desert, with the traveler lost under the hot sun. Travelers will report a variety of terrain associated with body areas: rocky, treed, hilly, meadow-like, mountainous, flowing like a river or ocean, swampy. Sometimes the place will be a well-defined structure, like a house with the traveler wandering around inside.

Not all somatically derived images are visual. Some travelers image better acoustically. For one traveler various areas of discomfort along either side of his spine had distinct musical tones associated with them. At other times I have asked a traveler to "give a voice" to an area of the body and then listen to the message that area speaks. Many travelers will simply perceive areas of color rather than distinct images. Areas in pain will appear red, for example, while areas of abnormal function will seem grey or black. Simple patterns of darkness or light may predominate the images of other travelers.

Certainly I have merely sampled the unlimited possibilities of images that a traveler may experience. For the catalog of somatically derived images would be as vast as the human psyche itself. Regardless of their actual form, it is the symbolic value of these images which makes them so important. Symbols are the language of the psyche. Traditional psychotherapy has long relied on symbolic expression: free association, hypnosis, dream analysis, and ink-blot tests are familiar examples.

Every dreamer knows that the human psyche uses symbols to weave incredibly complex tales out of everyday images. In psychotherapy it is common to speak of the human unconscious expressing itself through symbols. Symbols are windows on this unconscious realm. They make different portions of the unconscious available to our conscious mind. I often use the term *not-yet-conscious* to describe that portion of the psyche lying just outside our field of awareness, waiting for a chance to emerge symbolically. *Somatic imaging* is a powerful way of using our bodies to access this not-yet-conscious domain.

Somatosynthesis attempts to widen this not-yet-conscious sphere and make more of our unconscious self available to us. Somatic imaging is a principal tool for accomplishing this. Imaging is so fundamental to the way the human brain and nervous system work that I have met few people who could not make good use of this tool.

It is really up to the guide to encourage the process of somatic imagery within the traveler, to trust the traveler's inner wisdom, and ultimately to accept whatever imagery results. Time and time again, regardless of how outlandish a traveler's imagery initially seemed, I have experienced that trusting the traveler's inner process led the somatosynthesis journey in the right direction. Once the traveler acknowledges a connection with somatically derived images, access to the psyche is established, and the somatosynthesis journey is underway.

There are many ways for guide and traveler to interpret and work with somatically derived images, and thus many potential directions for each somatosynthesis journey to take. Here I would like to examine some of the common ways that the somatosynthesis process continues, once access to the psyche is established.

Tactile Intervention

Touch is the "second therapist," the "silent guide" of a somatosynthesis journey. Upon establishing a connection with the traveler's psyche, touching alone is often the only requirement for moving the healing journey forward. In the last chapter I mentioned the 3 D's (depth, direction and duration) of somatic therapy. I also gave an account of some actual ways of using these aspects of touch for working with the traveler's physical body: releasing areas of cross-restriction, unwinding a portion of the body, or working with the traveler's energy field.

But these three qualities of touch also have very specific effects beyond the traveler's body. In fact, they form the basis of a *language of touch* through which the guide can communicate deeply with the traveler. All of us have used this language of touch at some point in our lives. Take a moment and ask yourself how you would touch someone else if you wanted to:

- communicate love
- demonstrate support
- display anger
- show caring
- ask them to come closer
- tell them to keep their distance
- express fear
- communicate joy
- restrain them
- release them

Even from this brief list I think you will see that there is a quality of touch, a degree of depth, direction and duration appropriate for each quality listed. For example, a light, sustained touch might communicate love; a moderate, sustained touch might express support; while a heavy sustained touch might indicate restraint. Light stroking often communicates caring, while heavy shaking could transmit anger, anxiety or fear.

Above and beyond its therapeutic benefits, human touch is a language through which the guide can steer the healing journey. Through touch the guide can facilitate the emergence of a range of emotions and qualities from the traveler. Many travelers who have difficulty communicating verbally, readily receive and respond to messages encoded through touch.

I remember a middle-aged male traveler named Roger, a salesman who was constantly on the road. He was divorced, overweight, overworked, and caught in a stressful lifestyle. Roger was also a person who kept his feelings bottled up. One particular somatosynthesis journey with Roger consisted of nothing more than my lightly holding his head. I was not entirely sure of why this seemed appropriate, but I sensed that Roger needed to feel support coming from someplace in his life.

As I gently supported his head a few inches off the surface of my treatment table his whole body began to shake violently. He started perspiring profusely and was obviously out of control of his body. For nearly 15 minutes this ordeal continued before gradually subsiding. There was an unmistakable air of sadness in the room as Roger spoke in a shaky voice.

"I can't let myself cry," he said; "I want to but I can't. So I let my body cry for me."

Roger's uncontrollable muscular contractions were his body's way of crying to release pent up stress. Not only had his body received my non-verbal message through touch, but it had responded in kind by crying without ever uttering a sound. Touch is a powerful means of helping a traveler enter the realm of the psyche and stay with the feeling content of their healing journey—particularly when those feelings are inaccessible verbally. Communicating through touch does not depend on a person's ability to be articulate. It bypasses the limitations of language and thereby circumvents the problem of fitting one's experience to the words available in a given human language.

Verbal Intervention

Just as it is important for the somatosynthesis guide to understand and use tactile intervention (touch), it is equally important for the guide to use psychological intervention (talk) as well. Basically a guide can make three kinds of verbal interventions to advance the traveler's journey through the psyche: (1) content-oriented interventions; (2) process-oriented interventions; and (3) purpose-oriented interventions.

For example, a guide might ask a traveler: "How many areas of knifing pain do you feel?" or, "Can you describe what objects are in the foreground of that image and what objects are in the background?"

These two questions are examples of *content-oriented* verbal intervention, asking the traveler for psychological *content*—the facts and figures of consciousness. Content-oriented interventions are useful in sharpening the traveler's psychological focus. For a new traveler, content-oriented interventions are a way of capturing, and holding onto, the symbolic content of the psyche—"Can you describe that image in more detail?"

For a traveler whose mind begins to wander, content-oriented interventions are a way of getting back on track—"Bring your attention back to the house you first saw: can you see what color the outside is painted?" The guide may choose to amplify some aspect of the traveler's experience, and content-oriented interventions serve that purpose—"Of all the different colors you are aware of, select the one that seems most related to the pain you are presently experiencing."

In contrast to content-oriented interventions, *process-oriented* interventions ask the traveler to be in touch with feelings and emotion—"What was it like for you to experience that image?" Process-oriented interventions are generally wide-open. They presuppose little and allow the traveler to respond from an inner experience in-process. In other words, if a traveler was experiencing sadness, a process-oriented intervention would seek to elicit that feeling. A content-oriented intervention, however, would have the traveler describe what gave rise to the feeling of being sad. Process-oriented interventions help the traveler stay in touch with the feelings and emotions that are part of psychological issues. This effectively deepens the traveler's experience and moves the somatosynthesis journey forward. Thus most of the guide's psychological interventions will be process-oriented.

Purpose-oriented interventions invite the traveler to seek insight and meaning in the healing journey—"How might you use the messages contained in that image, in your life right now?" They provide powerful motivation to initiate a healing journey—"How important is it for you to work through your anger?" And they are equally powerful means of motivating the traveler to incorporate the effects of the healing journey in daily life—"Are you now willing to acknowledge your anger when it arises?"

These psychological interventions, combined with the therapeutic use of touch, provide the somatosynthesis guide with dynamic tools for the healing journey. Like any craftsperson, the guide should have knowledge of the basic techniques for using these tools. Then the guide's creativity and sensitivity can build on this foundation, adapting the use of these tools to the specific requirements of the traveler and the healing journey.

Body Maps

Creating a *body map* is a somatosynthesis technique which uses all of the tools we've discussed so far. Body maps help guide the healing journey by identifying the emotional, psychological and spiritual issues related to specific areas of the body. To create a body map, the somatosynthesis guide uses a combination of tactile and verbal intervention with the traveler, recording the results on an outline of the body. A sample body

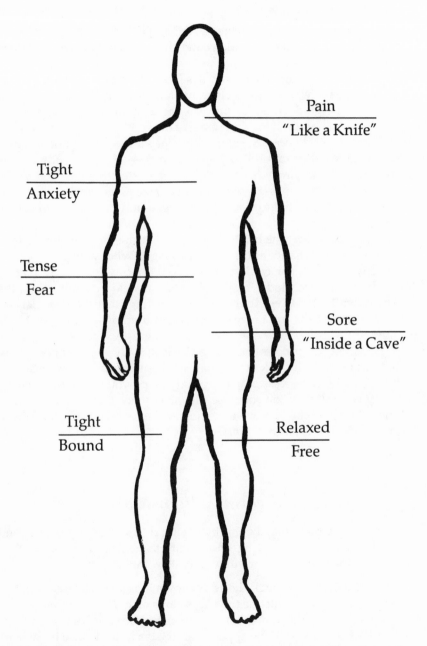

Fig. 5.3: Example of a body map showing the physical and psychological attributes of various areas of the body.

map is shown in figure 5.3, where a simple stick figure has been labelled with both the physical sensations and the emotions related to various body areas.

Body maps are derived in two ways. The physical condition of various areas of the traveler's body is often the starting point for a body map. In this case the guide seeks to uncover the emotional, psychological or spiritual issues underlying these areas of the body. At times, however, the traveler's inner concerns are more apparent—unresolved emotions, psychological conflict, unfulfilled spiritual longing. Here the body map is created by identifying what body areas are related to these deeper concerns. So a body map is created by mapping the psyche to the body or by mapping the body to the psyche. In either case, it is a useful tool to initiate the healing journey.

Body maps chart the healing journey. They are dynamic portraits of the traveler that change as the traveler changes. When pain is relieved or underlying psychological issues resolved, the traveler's body map is similarly altered. Body mapping is a model-in-miniature of the somatosynthesis process. In actually constructing a map both traveler and guide draw on the full range of techniques used on a somatosynthesis journey.

Describing the process of creating a body map gives us the opportunity to take an in-depth look at a somatosynthesis session. As we examine more closely the process of making body maps, you may wish to create one of yourself or of someone else. However, if you create a body map of yourself alone, you will have to modify the following instructions to account for the absence of a guide.

Creating a Body Map

Creating a body map begins by having the traveler in a relaxed and comfortable position: lying on a comfortable surface or seated in a comfortable chair. Then the guide can follow these steps:

1. **Draw a simple stick figure as shown in figure 5.3**. Use a separate piece of paper and write the traveler's name on it. As an alternative you might like to use the figure that appears in the *Modified Body Accessibility Questionnaire* (found in the appendix of the book) to create a body map. This would allow you to relate the accessibility of various body areas to

their physical condition and also to the related emotional and psychological issues.

2. **Explain the process to the traveler**. Tell the traveler you will be touching selected body areas, and asking for her/his awareness to be brought there. There are many ways that people speak about their awareness of an area:

(a) Visual images ("I can see ....")

(b) Somatic images ("This area feels as though ....")

(c) Auditory images ("It's as though I could hear this part of my body saying ....")

(d) Simple impressions ("I'm aware of ... related to this area.")

Reassure the traveler that there are no right or wrong responses. The process works best when the traveler is as honest as possible with whatever emerges in a given area.

3. **Guide the traveler through relaxation and inner focussing**. Consult chapter four for a sample relaxation and inner focussing script. You can use that one or create a similar one of your own.

4. **Lightly touch the next area of the body you wish to map**. The figure used in the accessibility questionnaire shows ten areas of the body you can work with. The first several times you do this exercise take one area at a time and proceed through the entire exercise. Later you may selectively choose one of these areas to work with, or apply the exercise to any other area of the body. Almost always, different issues are related to the different sides of the body. Therefore treat both right and left sides of the legs and arms separately. As you touch the traveler's body be aware of the onset of a TASC (touch-induced altered state of consciousness).

5. **Ask the traveler to bring her/his awareness to this area**. You can use the following intervention, or one similar to it:

"Bring your awareness to the area of your body I'm now touching. Without trying to control or analyze this area, just allow yourself to experience it."

6. **Ask the traveler to physically map this area**. Use the following interventions or ones similar to them:

(a) "What's your body like in this area?"

(b) "How does you body move in this area?"

(c) "Does this area of your body feel the way you would like it to?"

(d) "Are you comfortable with this area of your body?"

7. **Ask the traveler to psychologically map this area.** Use the following interventions or ones similar to them:

(a) "What's the experience of this area like for you?"

(b) "How do you experience this area now?"

(c) "What emerges for you as you experience this area of your body?"

(d) "What quality does this area express for you?"

(e) "What story does this area of your body have to tell?"

(f) "What message does this area of your body have for you?"

8. **Wait patiently and allow whatever emerges for the traveler to come through.** Do not rush the traveler to identify the issues underlying a given body area. Trust the traveler's inner wisdom by accepting whatever emerges as what needs to emerge. If the traveler is having difficulty mapping this area try another intervention. If that does not work skip this area temporarily, go on to another area, and return to this area later.

9. **Locate the process-oriented material in the traveler's response.** Actively listen to the traveler's response, searching for process-oriented material (feelings, images, issues, qualities, etc.). Confirm your sense of the process-oriented material, by repeating it back to the traveler:

(a) "So there's some sadness associated with this area?"

(b) "This area is like a river moving through rapids."

(c) "It sounds like this area has something to do with your relationship with your husband."

10. **Label the traveler's body map with the psychological material discovered in the previous step.** Write in a few key words that summarize the psychological issues underlying this body area.

11. **If you are finished with all body areas, then go to step 12;** otherwise, repeat the process beginning with step 4.

12. **Guide the traveler out of the TASC.** You can use the following intervention, or one similar to it:

> "Bring your awareness back to your breathing and as you do carry back with you whatever it is you now know. Take a few minutes to feel how you might use this knowledge in your life now."

> [Pause for a few minutes.]

> "Bring your awareness back to your breathing again. When you're ready take several deep breaths, stretch if you need to, and then open your eyes."

The Unfolding Journey

Starting with a somatically derived image, a simple process-oriented intervention can sometimes serve to unfold an entire somatosynthesis journey. For example, the guide would invite the traveler to "stay in touch with that image and allow it to evolve." Some travelers can take such a minimal request and, with little or no further input from the guide, complete a somatosynthesis journey. The initial image will blossom into a rich symbolic odyssey. These travelers will readily connect with the psychological content behind their physical conditions, and even direct the guide to areas of their body where touch would benefit this unfolding process.

Such an experience can be quite a surprise to the guide. I imagine it to be similar to a mountain-climber who hires a guide to assist with an ascent up a mountain the climber has never tackled before. Just as the guide prepares to lead the climber through the ascent, the climber takes off as though they have traveled this route many times before.

❖

Cynthia was a 26-year-old woman who had lost her mother at age five. She had never really grieved this tremendous loss and subsequently developed a well-maintained, intellectual defense against her feelings about her mother's death. When I first saw her, she complained of middle back and chest pain and severe headaches. Although she was guarded against acknowledging her feelings from our first session, it was apparent that Cynthia had exceptionally good access to her not-yet-conscious. Once she was relaxed, her focus directed within, she was quite adept at allowing rich, symbolic imagery to emerge and unfold.

In the beginning of our work together her effortless access to the psyche made guiding her sessions relatively easy and straightforward. Over time she became more comfortable with her feelings—at first simply acknowledging their existence, then actively working through the emotions surrounding the death of her mother. As we went on I began to notice that in each session I was making fewer and fewer psychological interventions. At the beginning of one session Cynthia informed me that she had a splitting headache and that her entire body, from upper chest to head, felt tense and uncomfortable.

"I'm never really sure what to expect in these sessions," she admitted, "and I am not sure how well I can participate today."

"That's fine," I reassured her, "just relax and let your awareness drift to the upper portion of your body."

After talking her through a relaxation and inner focussing, I asked her to become more aware of this upper area of her body. We had worked together enough that I didn't feel the need to suggest anything more specific than simple awareness of this area. As it turned out, this was enough for Cynthia.

"The first image I have is of a heavy gray mass," she said, "it's shiny, and polished on the outside."

There was a calm, intense quality in her voice that let me know she was truly engaged in this image. I moved my hands to the base of her skull and gently applied a little traction. I had already made the decision to allow whatever emerged for Cynthia to take shape without my intervention. I'd simply be there to make sure she didn't get off course. At the start I had no idea of the direction we were headed. Several minutes later the following saga unfolded for Cynthia. I listened closely and said little.

"It's not really just a mass," she observed; "it's more like a mountain, and I'm climbing it. It's hard to get a toehold as I move up. Every so often I see a trickle of water that breaks through the outer surface, and that makes it easier for me to wedge my boot into the side of the mountain."

For the next five minutes, Cynthia stopped talking, while I continued to apply gentle traction at various locations on her skull. Spontaneously she picked up the tale again.

"I can see the top of the mountain now," she said; "I know how important it is to reach the top, but the climbing is very difficult right now. I'm fighting for every inch I climb. I'm temporarily stuck at this present location, unable to get a good toehold. As I look around for one I can see inside the mountain; there's red clay there; it's damp and moist inside the mountain. I've got to break through the surface."

After spending several minutes in silence she admitted to feeling a burning pain at the base of her skull. I took that as an indication to return my hands to that area, and re-apply gentle traction. As I did the burning subsided and Cynthia again went into a relatively long few minutes of silence. She came out of this period with a burst of energy.

"I feel a force on top of the mountain, pulling me upward," she exclaimed. "It's like a Will much greater than mine that makes my journey to the top inevitable. I know I'll make it now."

"It's funny," she said parenthetically; "this greater Will seems part of me, but at the same time it's much larger than me as well."

As Cynthia related this phase of her journey her head, neck and chest melted under my hands. Finally she made it to the top of the mountain.

"There's nothing up here except blue skies and the mountain top," she proclaimed triumphantly. "I feel like I can put my arms around the mountain. It's actually much smaller than it seemed while I was making the climb. I feel a sense of expansiveness and broadness up here, more than a sense of being up high. The top of my body feels warm and comfortable, while the bottom part feels very connected and rooted to the mountain underneath it."

I let Cynthia stay at the top of her mountain for awhile longer; then I concluded the session with a simple, purpose-oriented intervention.

"Slowly bring your awareness back to your breathing, and as you do be open to the meaning of this journey in your life now."

With little hesitation Cynthia derived the meaning from her journey.

"Slowly I'm letting my feelings trickle through like the water coming from within the mountain. As I let this happen I'm better able to ascend the mountain, which I can now see is the hard intellect I have constructed around my soft core. I'm always frightened that if I really connect with my feelings I'll lose my mind. But on top of the mountain I had both, and that felt great. Feeling the power of a Will simultaneously part of me but larger than me makes me realize how little I have to struggle to climb this mountain. I simply need to drop my resistance to that Will."

When Cynthia finally sat up, she suddenly remembered what had prompted her to see me today.

"I almost forgot," she added; "my headache's no longer with me; my head feels like its floating above my body."

For an experienced traveler such a self-directed journey is possible. Cynthia's journey, the exception rather than the rule, shows the remarkable human capacity to continually seek healing, wholeness and meaning in our lives. A journey like this also presents a different set of challenges for the guide. With little intervention to move the journey forward, the guide assumes the role of monitoring the traveler's progress and ensuring the journey stays on course. Usually the guide has a more active part to play.

Counter-Imaging

To move the somatosynthesis journey forward the guide can help the traveler develop a *counter-image* to the initial somatic image. As the name suggests, a counter-image is one that stands in opposition to the original image. This image/counter-image technique is particularly effective when applied to a well-defined source of pain or discomfort. If the original image is a "knifing pain" in the lower back, the counter-image may be "pulling out the knife"; if the image is "churned up" intestines, the counter-image may be "a calm sea"; if the image is of muscles "tied in knots," the counter-image may be "a hand untying the knots"; and so the process goes.

Working with an image/counter-image pair allows a traveler to experience two different and opposing conditions—one representing a present state, the other representing a possible future. The dynamic tension thus created can be a potent therapeutic force. Many image/counter-image pairs represent unresolved inner conflicts within the traveler. Having such an inner conflict displayed by the body gives the traveler a unique opportunity to gain insight into the conflict and ultimately to come to terms with it.

When asked to develop a counter-image to a tight, tense right shoulder, one traveler simply chose his left shoulder which felt relaxed and at ease. As the journey proceeded this traveler discovered that the right shoulder was a stressful, ever-striving side of his personality, while the left shoulder was a nurturing, caring side of his personality. The "striver" was dominant, while the "nurturer" had little to say in this man's life. At the conclusion of the journey the traveler came to the realization that the only way to solve and prevent the recurrence of his shoulder pain was to give the "nurturer" more opportunity for expression in his life.

Another traveler imagined her tight neck muscles as river rapids. The counter-image was a calm, tranquil portion of the same river. During her journey she realized that the river rapids represented her nervous anxiety about being in control of every aspect of her life. Calm water, on the other hand, represented a deep-felt need to be peaceful and to "go with the flow" in her life.

Image/counter-image pairs can reveal different aspects of the traveler's personality—often a source of the issues lying beneath overt physical conditions. Later I will describe additional techniques for working with those elements of the traveler's personality that emerge during a somatosynthesis journey.

Image/counter-image pairs also give travelers the opportunity to discover the process through which an image is transformed into its counter-image; this can be useful to the guide as well. For example one traveler imagined that his painful back muscles in spasm were actually over-tightened guitar strings. The counter-image was obvious: Loosen the strings. As the guide I enlisted this traveler's help in locating the beginning and end of six guitar strings—three on either side of his spine. Then I proceeded to simulate unwinding the pegs for each string by gently twisting the traveler's skin in a counter-clockwise direction. The traveler assisted the process by informing me when each string was loose enough.

In another instance, a traveler complaining of burning pain in his left leg saw frayed nerve ends in that area. The traveler happened to be an electronics engineer whose image and counter-image obviously came from this area of expertise.

"There's a circuit overload," he said confidently, "because there aren't enough intact fibers to carry the electrical signals on that nerve."

Like a lineman who just discovered a break in a power main he added, "the nerve ends need to be spliced together with more fibers before it burns out completely."

His image was the frayed nerve, his counter-image was to splice the frayed ends. Thus the entire session consisted of the traveler meticulously helping me locate several dozen nerve ends on either side of the frayed area and simulating the process of soldering them back together. During this operation the traveler monitored the burning sensation and when it stopped he let me know that we could stop finding and soldering nerve endings in his leg.

Image/counter-image is such an easy method of working with the psychological issues beneath physical conditions, that I encourage travelers to use the technique on their own. I present it to them in five steps which you might like to try yourself:

Image/Counter-Image Exercise

1. Relax and allow an inner focus to develop.

2. Bring your awareness to a particular area of your body and let an image of that area emerge.

3. Now let a counter-image emerge and develop as well.

4. Ask yourself the question, "How will this image become its counter-image?"

5. Let yourself imagine the shift from image to counter-image taking place as indicated by the answer to the question asked in step 4.

Subpersonalities and the Healing Journey

Most travelers encounter some aspect of their personality on a somatosynthesis journey. A voice given to a somatic image; conflict between image and counter-image; or just experiencing the feelings surrounding a physical condition, call forth various facets of the traveler's personality.

Unresolved personality issues are often at the core of our physical symptoms. Typically psychotherapists seek to handle these issues through the mind. But somatosynthesis includes the body in this process, adding another dimension for reconciling conflicting elements of the traveler's personality.

The structure and function of our personality is reflected in the anatomy and physiology of our body. Our personality, like our body, is composed of many diverse elements that must function together as a whole. Each organ, each muscle, each cell has a unique set of actions it must perform for the sake of the whole. Yet the performance of our organs, muscles and cells must be controlled and coordinated so the right actions happen at the right time.

Likewise the various components of our personality have unique actions to perform on our behalf. These personality components operate so independently at times that they might well be called *subpersonalities*. Giving a name to these subpersonalities (organs of our personality) helps us readily identify their function.

For example, within each of us we could easily find one or more of the following subpersonalities: the "judge," the "critic," the "nurturer," the "victim," the "rescuer," the "emotional wreck," the "know-it-all," the "child," the "parent," the "introvert," the "extrovert," the "aggressor," the "lazy bum," the "overburdened," the "striver," the "peace-maker," the "mystic," and the "saint." Although they differ greatly, each subpersonality has a role to play in our overall, healthy personality. Like each organ, the function of our subpersonalities must be coordinated and controlled.

An over-functioning or under-functioning organ or muscle distorts the body, while an over-functioning or under-functioning subpersonality distorts the psyche. Muscle tightness on the right side of the neck can cause pain, and distort the posture by pulling the head to one side. By the same token, if the psychological issues beneath that muscle tension have to do with unchecked aggression, for example, then the traveler's "aggressor" subpersonality is distorting the psyche, causing it to be pulled in one direction.

Within the body resolution may involve decreasing muscle tone on the tight side, while increasing muscle tone on the other side. Psychologically resolution may involve decreasing the influence of the "aggressor" and increasing the influence of the "nurturer" subpersonality. In many instances the traveler will have already identified the non-tense side of the body as the "nurturer" subpersonality.

Thus, the guide's use of touch to correct the muscle imbalance can symbolically correct the psychological imbalance as well. What is wrong with the body is reflected in the mind. What is done to the body is incorporated by the mind. In both cases, physically and psychologically, a balance between two different forces is achieved. Ultimately the healing journey should arrive at a point where control and coordination of body and mind rest with the traveler. The constant presence of the guide is no longer required.

Somatosynthesis will frequently unearth the traveler's subpersonalities. The techniques for furthering the healing journey from soma to psyche have the potential to do this. Helping the traveler identify and better understand the personality forces at work in the body are major goals of this first phase of the somatosynthesis journey. During a single journey, many different subpersonalities may surface for the traveler. The guide's task is to facilitate their emergence and help the traveler synthesize the roles these subpersonalities play.

❖

For a traveler named Paul, multiple subpersonalities arose on one somatosynthesis journey. I saw Paul for complaints of pain in his left shoulder blade and his lower back. He was a thirty-three year-old recently married lawyer who left a successful Los Angeles law practice to move to a suburb of Washington, D.C., where his new wife had received a prestigious university fellowship.

Our session began as usual. I assessed his body to determine where I would intervene physically and guided him through relaxation and inner focussing. I placed one hand under his left shoulder blade while the other rested lightly on his chest. When invited to just experience this area, Paul quickly became a lawyer again. He proceeded to describe in minute detail how his shoulder blade felt crunched; how his muscles were tight; and how the pain radiated down to his lower back—content-oriented answers to a process-oriented intervention.

To circumvent this situation, which happens frequently with travelers possessing well-developed intellects, I challenged Paul to respond to my interventions in a different way. Instead of speaking what was on his mind, Paul had to arrive at a single word that captured the essence of his myriad thoughts. During this process the following subpersonalities emerged:

The Worrier. Moving to the East Coast was Paul's undoing according to the Worrier. He was living on savings, uncertain about opening his own law practice and unsure of the wisdom of leaving a lucrative, well-established professional life in Los Angeles. The Worrier was represented in Paul's body by the crunched, tight, painful feelings in the shoulder blade area.

The Free Man. Paul found a counter-image to the Worrier in a subpersonality called the Free Man. There was no need to worry about living on savings or opening a private practice, said the Free Man. After all, Paul and his wife would eventually be going back to Los Angeles when her fellowship ended. What mattered was that Paul lived a life "free" from all these worries. This freedom was represented in Paul's back and shoulder blade before his current pain and tension.

The Peace-Maker. There was some truth for Paul in both the Worrier and Free Man subpersonalities. It was up to the Peace-Maker subpersonality to work out a solution between the Worrier and the Free Man that would help Paul take the next steps in his life. The Peace-Maker seemed interested in coming to a decision that would include the most useful aspects of both the Worrier and the Free Man.

The Resister. This was an interesting subpersonality that emerged for Paul once he began to let the Peace-Maker work out a solution. The Resister actually enjoyed the way things were right now and wanted to block the Peace-Maker's attempts to settle the conflict between the Worrier and the Free Man. In a sense, the Resister was a counter-image to the Peace-Maker. As the journey evolved, Paul wound up mediating between these four subpersonalities. Each of them was given time to speak, while Paul listened to their message and observed their effect on his body. My gentle physical intervention helped his back and shoulder blade to release, and as this occurred the Peace-Maker's task seemed easier. Throughout the journey the Resister constantly challenged Paul to bring forth his will and determination to arrive at a solution.

Ultimately the Peace-Maker reached a workable compromise: Paul could open a small-scale, low-key, private practice. This would allow him to work at what he enjoyed without the stress of recreating the practice he left in Los Angeles. With a solution in hand, Paul's physical discomfort disappeared. Finding the balance between several opposing subpersonalities was the key for this traveler—combined physical and psychological intervention enhanced our progress towards this end.

Working with the traveler's subpersonalities is an important method of addressing the psychological components beneath physical conditions. Pain and discomfort is often associated with one or more dominant subpersonalities. Pain is a loud message that something is out-of-balance, physically and psychologically. Asking the traveler to listen to the voices behind the pain—the various subpersonalities—is a step towards re-establishing balance within body and mind. Not all subpersonalities are trouble-makers. In the case cited above, for example, the traveler discovered that some of his less dominant subpersonalities were actually waiting to help. The guide is also there to assist the traveler in finding a center point of coordination and balance amidst the competing energies of various subpersonalities.

There are many variations on the techniques that apply to this first phase of the somatosynthesis journey—the movement from soma to psyche—but these are the major themes: a belief in the traveler's inner process; the use of various forms of somatic imagery to connect bodily events with psychological issues; helping the traveler come to terms with these psychological issues, particularly those related to the personality; and the use of touch to support and guide the entire process.

There is no perfect therapeutic technique, one that will work under any set of conditions. On the somatosynthesis journey, therapeutic technique is a combination of many factors, none more important than the guide's creative ability to adapt any technique to the unique needs of a given traveler. This is especially true as the healing journey passes into its second phase—the movement from psyche to center. Reaching the center is like ascending a mountain: There are many paths to the summit.

6

The Journey Beyond Body and Mind

In his poem, "Burnt Norton," T.S. Eliot describes a place he calls, "the still point,"

> At the still point of the turning world. Neither flesh nor
>   fleshless;
> Neither from nor towards; at the still point, there the
>   dance is.
> But neither arrest nor movement. And do not call it fixity,
> Where past and future are gathered. Neither movement
>   from nor towards,
> Neither ascent nor decline. Except for the point, the still
>   point,
> There would be no dance. And there is only the dance.

Center is the traveler's still point: neither body nor mind but a dance encompassing both. Were the somatosynthesis journey to stop with the psyche, it would be only partially complete. Helping the traveler discover the psychological factors underlying physical conditions is an important step. Adding therapeutic touch to this process enhances the effect.

True healing comes as the traveler is able to synthesize these changes of body and mind into a new vision of self. Unless the traveler learns to balance the competing demands of the psyche, the imbalance will continually recreate physical pain and discomfort. Moreover, unless the traveler learns to retain the bodily changes brought about through touch, continued physical pain and discomfort will prolong the existence of unresolved psychological issues. This point of synthesis is the *center* of the healing journey. By definition, the somatosynthesis process is always moving towards this center. This is what it means to believe in the traveler's inner wisdom—that innate intelligence forever seeking wholeness. It also means that often the guide needs to do very little to help the traveler find this center. For the traveler's inner compass frequently points in the right direction. However, the guide must be able to read the signs that the traveler is approaching the center and then encourage this process along.

Another way of viewing the "center" is that part of us which acts as a "witness" or "observer." The following exercise will allow you to experience this aspect of your center. You may wish to have someone else guide you through this exercise. If that is not possible, modify the following instructions to account for the absence of a guide.

Discovering Your Center

1. Begin by finding a relaxed and comfortable position: lying on a comfortable surface or seated in a comfortable chair. Take a moment to focus on your breathing, and relax your entire body. Close your eyes and draw your awareness within, as though you could look within your body.

2. Scan your body from your head to your feet, searching for an area that seems to draw your attention to it. This could be an area of pain or tension, an area that was previously injured, or simply an area of special significance to you.

3. Let a single image of that area form in your mind. Don't try too hard to create the image, just let it arise of its own accord. Accept whatever image comes to you, regardless of how unlikely it may seem.

4. With your eyes still closed imagine that you could see that image projected about two feet in front of you. Look at it. What's it like to see that image from your body there in front of you?

5. Now, in your mind, push that image away from you. Push it away as far as you like, and note how your experience of that image changes.

6. Bring the image back to its original position. What's that like now?

7. Next bring the image even closer to you, as close as you are able to? How is that experience different?

8. Finally return the image to its original position, and note what it's like to have it there again.

9. Before ending this exercise take a moment to reflect on what you now know about the area of your body you chose to work with. How can you use this knowledge in your life?

10. Slowly bring your awareness back to your breathing, and when you're ready, stretch your body, take some deep breaths and open your eyes.

To do this exercise you first needed to find your center, even though no specific instructions were given to that effect. It was your center which allowed you to view this somatic image in front of you, and at various locations away from you. In this way your center was an observer of the relationship between you and this image.

Was it easy to see the image of this body area in front of you? If it was then you experienced another important function of your center: helping you disengage from this area of your body. Disengagement or *disidentification*, as it is often called, is also an important part of the somatosynthesis process. Disidentification is not dissociation. The exercise does not ask you to do away with your feelings and thoughts about this area of your body. You are not asked to repress or ignore them. On the contrary, the exercise asks you to observe your thoughts and feelings, and observation is a function of your center. Through disidentification you can observe what occurs in your body or mind without becoming totally enmeshed. It's a way of stepping back and discovering what is going on.

When we are in pain, we so quickly identify with the physical attributes of our discomfort—tension, aching, burning, throbbing—that we easily miss the underlying messages. Roberto Assagioli was fond of saying, "We are dominated by everything with which our self becomes identified. We can dominate and control everything from which we disidentify ourselves."

How easy was it for you to move the image away from your body? And what feelings were present when you did this? Answers to these questions tell you how well you are able to disidentify with that portion of your body and the related feelings. Disidentification may allow a traveler grappling with physical pain, for example, to step back from that pain and experience anger beneath the pain. An event associated with that anger may have been long forgotten. Through disidentification the traveler may rediscover it and thereby see the current pain and anger as reactions of the body and mind to that initial occurrence. Resolving the traveler's reaction to that initial circumstance may be an important step in relieving the physical pain and the anger.

When we are too caught up in the activities of our body or mind, we are unable to see beyond them—we are too identified. But from our center we can observe what lies beyond this identification. I often explain to a traveler that body and mind are like a puppet show. If we were in the audience watching such a show, we would see various puppets come on stage: some might have happy faces, while some might have sad faces; some might be angry and screaming, while others might be loving and quiet; some might move slowly as though in pain, while others might jump up and down with glee. These puppets are like the different aspects of our body and mind.

In a good show, the puppets seem endowed with a life of their own, and the audience can easily identify with the different characters that appear on stage. Of course the puppets are actually controlled by a puppeteer who pulls the strings and gives them life. We're trying to find that puppeteer within ourselves, I tell the traveler. We are trying to find that center.

One traveler I worked with had so much anxiety about being touched that initially our healing journeys were mostly verbal. Patricia was a bank teller in her mid-forties with headaches and chronic neck pain. When touched around her neck and head, she had sensations of spinning and began to faint, even though she was lying down. During my first session with Patricia, I merely talked about disidentification and guided her through a simple exercise. I also asked her to practice this exercise at home each day. At our second meeting I asked what it was like for her to do the disidentification exercise daily.

"I had the image of a core," she said, "around which were wrapped many outer layers—my body, feelings, desires, and thoughts."

I then talked with her about subpersonalities and their relationship to events within the body and mind. I asked her to imagine herself sitting on a bench outside a house. She was to let her various subpersonalities emerge from the house. She narrated the scene as follows:

> The "You Should Patricia" is coming out first, shaking her finger, as if to tell me what I should and shouldn't do. The "Dilettante" is coming out next saying, "Should I do this, should I do that, flitting from one side to the other." Next the "Indecisive" emerges shaking her head with indecision, "Yes, no, maybe, yes, no, maybe...." Here comes the "Paragon of Virtue!" She's really the queen of them all—no faults, no failings—but she's like ice, she's really cold! I see Patricia peeking out from the door [an assumed reference to the traveler's center]. She knows perfection doesn't exist. She wants me to come inside and talk.

Now Patricia moved inside, and continued her account:

> There's someone in the closet, she's coming out now and saying, "I'm scared to death." [Traveler starts to cry.] She's slowly moving towards the door. I feel sorry for her. I want her to change, she has the willingness to change. I want to help her change.

I asked the traveler if everyone in the house had been accounted for. She wasn't sure, at first, until she realized there was an upstairs.

> No, upstairs there's a little girl. [Traveler starts to cry again]. I never forgave her, I blamed her all these years. She needs to be told, "I'm sorry." He shouldn't have done that to her. She feels ashamed and guilty.

Patricia continued looking around the upstairs and became aware of someone in a closet:

> Someone's hiding in another closet. I don't know who it is. Oh, she's the Angry One. I can't let her out, she might hurt everybody. I know she's hurting me now [traveler starts to cry]. She's sitting on a volcano, and I don't know how long she can stay there. She's trying very hard. Maybe I can give her a message for now: "Relax and stay there a little longer." I'll see what I can work out for her freedom with a volcano erupting. She's not very happy but I guess she's all right for now. I'll

open the closet door part of the way and keep the chain
on it. Next time, I'll remove the chain and open the door
fully.

After looking around inside this house for several more minutes
Patricia realized that she had discovered all the important subpersonalities. She decided to walk back out of the house and sit on the bench
again.

"It was a glass house," she concluded, "and the whole experience was
kind of fun!"

I asked Patricia to spend the time between now and our next meeting
getting to know these subpersonalities a little better. When I next saw her
she decided to have all the subpersonalities in her house meet in the living
room—all except the one sitting on top of a volcano. With her subpersonalities assembled in front of her, Patricia asked the little girl she had
found upstairs to leave her seat and come closer. As the child came closer
to her, Patricia began to cry, and that child's story began to unfold.

Patricia's father was a prominent official in the State Department, and
as a result of his position he and Patricia's mother spent most of their time
travelling overseas. Instead of being with their parents, Patricia and her
two brothers, were sent to a boarding school near their home in New
Haven, Connecticut. The school was a place filled with haunting, disturb-
ing memories for Patricia. Her face tensed with pain and her voice barely
audible, she spoke with great difficulty about her years there.

As she labored with this account, it began to dawn on me what was
taking place: Patricia must have been abused sexually while in boarding
school. Working with other travelers who were sexually abused as children, one gets to know the characteristic aura that envelopes someone
who reconnects with that ordeal. It's a very difficult fact to admit, especially for a mother of six, in her late-forties, who feels the experience
should long have been over with.

Finally Patricia brought herself to openly share her inner child's dark
secret. She whispered, tearfully: "I'm embarrassed to say this, but you
should know that for the seven years I was at this boarding school, I was
repeatedly abused sexually by one of my teachers."

With that first admission, the entire, tragic affair came out. From age
seven to fourteen, Patricia's violin teacher, an older man in his late sixties,
engaged her in sexually abusive acts. Through her sobs she shared her
shame, guilt, anger, and confusion over this time in her life. In her young
mind Patricia began to fuse her sexual abuse with her pain over being left
behind by her parents and so blamed herself for both circumstances:

I wanted to be a perfect student. I thought if I were good enough in school then maybe my parents would come and take me back with them. But I knew because of what had happened I could never be perfect, never good enough. I felt that I deserved not to be with my parents because of what I had done with him [her music teacher].

This was not the first time Patricia had dealt with her feelings surrounding these issues. She had been under therapy, on and off, since she was twenty. In fact, at 23 she suddenly awoke from sleep, feeling her personality completely dissociated from her physical body—her body felt as though it were on one side of the room and her mind on the other. This dissociated state continued for several days until she was finally hospitalized. Although never as bad as it had originally been, she periodically re-experienced episodes of dissociation throughout her adult life.

Patricia lived in terror of these times which rendered her incapable of functioning. A task as simple as going to the grocery store became more than she could handle. Ordinarily she was heavily sedated when these states arose, and they would pass in several days. These states of dissociation were always accompanied by severe neck pain and headaches—the physical symptoms which led Patricia to see me.

However, when I first touched her neck and head, the feelings of dissociation intensified, her entire body became tense and rigid, and she became extremely anxious. Now this conglomeration of physical and psychological events was beginning to come together for both Patricia and me.

She realized that dissociation was what she experienced while being abused sexually. In order for that sexual abuse to continue repeatedly, she really did separate her body from her mind. It was the only defense she was able to muster back then: giving up her body but keeping her mind. Her headaches and neck pain were physical manifestations of this defensive reaction. So my touch recalled those early sexual incidents and consequently brought on the dissociation Patricia used to deal with them.

In previous therapy over the years, Patricia had addressed her feelings of anger towards her music teacher, even feeling that she had grown through this anger to a point of forgiveness.

"But I never forgave that poor little child," she said in muted tones. "After all these years, I still blame her."

Over the next several sessions, Patricia got to know her "inner child"— to learn her hopes, her fears, and her unfulfilled needs. Then, at the beginning of a subsequent journey, Patricia smiled and said with a voice of unusual clarity,

> The blame is starting to loosen. I feel that I've been able to start forgiving that little girl. There's another voice that has popped up in these past few weeks. I've started to call it "Slugger" because she's someone who doesn't give up [a reference to Patricia's real desire to work through her psychological and physical issues.]

I asked Patricia to be in touch with her body at this point, and she responded, "I feel like one of those 'roly-poly' dolls that you can knock over but it rolls with the punch and rights itself again." Patricia now went back into the house where she originally met her various subpersonalities.

"Why don't you re-introduce yourself to them all," I suggested.

"I'm in charge," she said emphatically to them, "and we're all filled with power."

I was actually a little startled by the strength of Patricia's statement. I reached for a pen to jot down the word "Center?" in my notes. There's a real feeling of excitement when a traveler approaches her center, like watching a marathon runner in the last 100 yards before the finish line—and Patricia was there. She continued to speak from this newly found part of herself.

"The volcano watcher can come out of the closet now," she said, "she needn't worry, the volcano can erupt slowly. We'll just take all these feelings in manageable amounts."

"Oh, someone's opened all the windows," Patricia exclaimed. "The house is starting to perk up. Things are looking brighter."

Patricia concluded this journey by simply saying, "All of you [referring to her subpersonalities] have something to bring to this house."

Patricia had found her puppeteer. Through discovering her center, Patricia began the process of reconciling her physical body and psychological processes. Eventually this breakthrough allowed us to include touch on our healing journeys.

❖

While Patricia clearly illustrates a traveler moving from subpersonalities through disidentification to the center, the process is often more subtle. Bruce, a traveler in his early-sixties, had initially come to see me for complaints of lower back and neck pain. Although he no longer had lower back pain, the somatosynthesis work was valuable to him, and he continued his sessions on a regular basis. Bruce had also undergone several years of psychotherapy and was well-aware of his emotional and psychological issues. During one session I found myself using gentle pressure in his neck and upper back. I asked him to focus on this area and let his experience of it unfold. He rendered the following account of his journey:

> I'm on a small island of land between two rivers. The river on the right symbolizes "what I have been" in my life until now [a time in the traveler's life when he began psychotherapy and made some significant, more healthy life changes.] The river on my left represents "what I may become" in my life beginning now. I can see the two rivers converging about 100 yards down stream, and I'm walking in that direction. This river is much larger now than either of the two rivers that feed into it.

I began applying very light traction at the base of Bruce's skull and slowly following the movement of head from side to side as the neck muscles relaxed and tension was released. I invited Bruce to become the river now and experience its journey from this confluence until it joined the ocean. As he did, he resumed his narrative:

> As I move along, I'm aware of the scenery along the banks of the river. Cattle and horses are grazing on either side. There's a bend in the river, and now we're passing through a small village. How interesting, on the river's banks are various scenes from my life—people, places and events that marked turning points for me. There are my parents waving to me as I pass by; they're both dead now; my former wife and our children are also there. Good friends are along the river's bank, and I can even see the house where I was raised.

> At the end of the village the river begins to move over rocks, picking up speed and creating a series of whirlpools and rapids. Nothing but rocks line the banks of the river now, and the water has deepened as it cuts a path through this gorge. Up ahead I can see the ocean— it's vast and unending. It's rough going at first; there's more turbulence where the fresh river water meets the sea.

[The traveler pauses for about a minute.]

Finally, there's calm and I'm floating in a deep ocean of tranquility.

Bruce's journey, though not as explicit as Patricia's, was nonetheless as powerful. Where Patricia's was rich in detail, Bruce's was rich in symbolic imagery. The two rivers at the beginning of his journey were two poles of Bruce's psyche: a composite representation of the forces of transformation (what I may become) and permanence (what I have been). This is an archetypal conflict, reflecting tension between two opposing forces that underlie many of the conflicts within the human psyche. But the conflict was resolved through coincidence of these opposing forces, and the resulting journey on a single river was Bruce's synthesis of these two streams of being. In this single river he had found his center.

After passing through Bruce's personal realm of being (all the scenes with his family and friends) the river deepened as it approached the sea. And when the river finally reached the sea Bruce reached his still point. Conflict, turbulence and rapid movement then yielded to the quiet tranquility of a vast ocean. A somatosynthesis journey like this exerts a powerful influence through symbolically synthesizing and integrating important elements of the traveler's life.

Bruce's journey also illustrates a second key aspect of our center: It provides access to a transpersonal realm. For Bruce this realm was symbolized as a vast ocean.

Body and mind are the two major components of our personal self. And I first described the center as a witness, or an observer found beyond our body or mind; helping to synthesize and integrate these two aspects of our being. *Transpersonal* is another way to say "beyond the personal"; "beyond the body and mind" ("trans" is the Latin prefix meaning beyond). But transpersonal goes far beyond "witnessing" or "observing."

Transpersonal also means *spiritual*, where "spiritual" indicates far more than what religious denomination you are. This transpersonal or spiritual domain is often difficult to describe, because words do not convey the breadth and depth of transpersonal experience. As a reality beyond body and mind, it is also a reality beyond words. Mystical experience, self-realization, self-actualization, enlightenment, unity, wholeness, and oneness are frequently used words, but even these cannot contain the reality.

Of course, this is not such an unfamiliar problem. Many people have had a transpersonal experience which defies verbal description. If you have ever witnessed a breath-taking sunset over the ocean, for example, then tried to describe it to someone else, you know the problem. Your words may capture the colors that were present or the feelings evoked in you but the *gestalt*, the whole of it, would still lie beyond your words. Chances are that you would end up saying, "You need to have experienced it to really appreciate what I'm trying to describe." And that is precisely the nature of the transpersonal, it is a direct experience.

It also turns out that transpersonal experience is really not so far removed from our everyday lives. Stopping to admire a flower, being present at the birth of a child, gazing into the eyes of a lover, creating something as simple as a sand castle or as complex as a symphonic score, enjoying beauty in any form, these activities draw us outside of ourselves—even if only for an instant. And the *transpersonal* literally lies "outside of the person."

We often speak of a "transpersonal self" as though it represents a separate part of us. This is confusing because we do not possess a transpersonal "part" in the same way we might have a "part" of ourselves that is angry, sad or in pain. The transpersonal is an experience, not an entity. It is an experience investigated by human beings for many thousands of years. There are many ways to interpret, understand and partake of the transpersonal experience.While I'd prefer to speak about the "transpersonal realm of being," that's a cumbersome term so I'll frequently use "transpersonal self" in its place.

Transpersonal experience is often called mystical simply because the true nature of the experience lies hidden from us. What is it about the flower that causes us to linger so long? Why does the miracle of birth inspire such awe? How does love touch us so deeply? From where does creativity spring? Why does beauty captivate? There are no comprehensive answers to these questions, and in this sense the experiences that give rise to these questions are mysterious. In fact, in the search for wholeness and meaning in our lives, it is the very mystical or mysterious quality of these experiences that draws us to them, time and time again.

This drive towards the mystical, the transpersonal, the spiritual, was described by Albert Einstein as the "most beautiful emotion we can experience." And this is the essence of the somatosynthesis journey—the rediscovery of wholeness through connecting with the transpersonal or spiritual dimension of our self. Said in another way, the transpersonal realm is that part of us that is never separated from the whole. Einstein felt that this part lay hidden from us and that our challenge was to rediscover this transpersonal realm, removing the barriers separating us from the whole:

> A human being is a part of the whole, called by us "Universe"; a part limited in time and space. He experiences himself, his thoughts and feelings as something separated from the rest—a kind of optical illusion of his consciousness. This delusion is a kind of prison for us, restricting us to our personal desires and to affection for a few persons nearest us. Our task must be to free ourselves from this prison.

An age-old technique for freeing oneself from this prison is to answer the question—What is the transpersonal self?—in negative terms. This is the approach taken for thousands of years by Eastern mystics who enumerated all the qualities not possessed by the spiritual self. Not good. Not bad. Not pleasure. Not pain. Not success. Not failure. Not body. Not mind. The first dictum of Chinese Taoist philosophy holds that the Tao expressed in writing is not the real Tao—and such is the truth of the transpersonal "self." Even in Christianity we find the phrase, "He who knows Me, knows Me not." The transpersonal or spiritual self is beyond the grasp of our finite mind.

To better understand what transpersonal experience *is*, I would invite you to try the following exercise:

Rediscovering Your Transpersonal Self

1. Find a comfortable position to sit in or lie down on your back. Begin by focussing your awareness on your breathing. With each exhalation allow your body to relax just a little more. With inhalation feel that you are breathing in a wave of relaxation that starts at your head and flows all the way down your body to your feet.

Now let your mind follow your body into relaxation. With each inhalation and exhalation feel that your mind is better able to relax and find a comfortable, calm, quiet place to be.

2. Ask yourself the question, "Who Am I?," and let the answers to that question emerge. Most likely they will come in several common forms: I am this body; I am my mind; I am this thought of myself; I am a doctor; I am a teacher; I am a good person; I am a bad person; I am a husband; I am a wife; I am male; I am female; I am black; I am white. There are many possibilities. Spend several minutes letting various answers to this question surface.

3. Next systematically repeat the following high-lighted phrases several times each to yourself, and read the associated text at least once.

I have a body, but I am not my body. My body may find itself in different conditions of health or sickness; it may be rested or tired; it may bring me pleasure or pain, but that has nothing to do with who I really am. My body is a precious instrument of experience, which allows me to function in the world, but it is only an instrument. I treat it well; I seek to keep it in good health, but it is not myself. **I have a body, but I am not my body.**

I have feelings, but I am not my feelings. These feelings are countless, contradictory, changing, and yet I know that I always remain I, my self, in times of hope or of despair, in joy or in pain, in a state of irritation or of calm. Since I can observe, understand and judge my feelings, and then increasingly learn to control, direct and use them, it is evident that they are not me. **I have feelings, but I am not my feelings.**

I have desires, but I am not my desires. My desires are aroused by drives both physical and emotional and by outer influences. They too are changeable and contradictory, and alternate between my attractions and repulsions. Sometimes my desires are met, and at other times they remain frustrated, yet I can never confuse my desires with who I really am. **I have desires, but I am not my desires.**

I have thoughts, but I am not my thoughts. My mind gives rise to my thoughts which help me comprehend the world around me and my world within; but still my thoughts are not me. **I have thoughts, but I am not my thoughts.**

I am what remains, a Center of Consciousness and Spirit.

4. After repeating these phrases, just relax and let yourself be in touch with the response you have to them, in body and mind.

5. When you are ready, take a couple of deep breaths, stretch, and then open your eyes.

This exercise affords you the opportunity to experience the difference between your personal self and transpersonal self, as both answer the fundamental question, "Who Am I?" After initially relaxing, step 2 captures the response of your personal self to this question. As you can see, your personal self is defined by the cluster of things with which you identify—body, mind, thoughts, feelings, social roles. Not only is your personal self defined by these identifications, it is also limited by them.

These are the limitations that occur for a traveler who identifies with the anger of a "striver" subpersonality, for example, and develops a set of tight, painful neck muscles as well. In this traveler's mind, a voice is saying "I am angry," and this traveler's body is expressing this underlying anger through tension and pain.

As long as the traveler holds onto this anger, it will drown out other voices within and restrict the free, natural movement of the traveler's body; thus, the traveler is dominated, and therefore limited, physically and psychologically, through the personal self's identification with this anger. The goal of the somatosynthesis work is to free the traveler from these limitations of body and mind.

The transpersonal self is beyond limitation. And step 3 of this exercise presents a systematic way of disengaging from the limiting identifications of the personal self, to discover this transpersonal self. Here we also see the center functioning to disidentify us from each limiting identification, thereby providing access to our transpersonal self.

So the movement of the somatosynthesis journey from psyche to center is a movement away from the limitations of body and mind and a movement towards the transpersonal. It is the exceptional traveler who manages to make the journey from soma to psyche to center in one somatosynthesis session. Commonly, the traveler will spend a number of sessions on the first phase of the somatosynthesis journey. The journey's first phase—the movement from soma to psyche—gives the traveler an opportunity to explore the personal self (body and mind) and begin the process of disidentification.

The very fact that the traveler continues to work on disidentifying from the limitations of body and mind will often propel the journey into the second phase with little prompting from the guide. At other times, the guide may choose to steer the healing journey towards the traveler's center in a more direct manner.

In a similar way access to the transpersonal realm of the traveler can be spontaneous or planned. Often the resolution of personal issues—subpersonality conflicts, psychological issues beneath physical symptoms, image/counter-pairs—creates a vacuum into which transpersonal energy rushes. The journey taken by Bruce illustrates this. Personal conflict (the two streams) was resolved by the center (the one river) which lead to the transpersonal (the ocean).

Oceans, mountains, vast horizons, brilliant light and awe-inspiring visions represent the kind of transpersonal imagery that spontaneously emerges for many travelers. These are images that convey the wholeness, oneness, vastness and grandness of transpersonal experience.

This theme of moving from the personal through the center to the transpersonal is presented in the journey of a traveler named Michelle. Like Bruce, Michelle had no specific physical complaints; she had also been through traditional psychotherapy for years; and she was aware of many of her emotional and psychological issues. With Michelle lying on a table, I was drawn to the area of her upper back and chest. Supporting that area with one hand underneath and the other hand on top, I guided her through relaxation and asked her to focus her awareness there. I asked her what kind of "place" she experienced from this area of her body. With very little additional intervention, the following journey unfolded:

> I'm on a the side of a hill, overlooking a hilly terrain with mountains far in the distance. I see a path in the distance that leads down the hill. I feel drawn toward the path.

> [The traveler pauses for a few moments.]

> I'm on the path now, walking down the hill into a forest of pines. I want to stop here for awhile and enjoy the cool, quiet comfort this forest affords me.

> [The traveler is silent for about five minutes.]

Oh my, there's a light dancing in front of me, beckoning me to follow it. It's leading me through the forest, and suddenly it disappears into a small cave. I'm not sure if I should follow the light inside.

[Michelle hesitates for a moment, trying to decide whether to go into the cave.]

I'm going inside too. It's surprising how comfortable it feels in here, even though I don't see any windows or a light source. Now I see a fire going and some utensils spread around the floor—obviously someone lives here.

[The traveler starts to laugh.]

It's me, I'm the one who lives here! I can even see a window now; it's round and in the middle of one side of the cave's wall. As I look out, I realize that I'm no longer in the forest but high on top of a mountain. I can look down and see everything. I can see the other side of the world.

Michelle enjoyed this view of her world for the next several minutes until we concluded the session. I asked her to spend some time in silence and allow the meaning of this journey to develop for her. In our discussion afterwards, Michelle informed me that the hilly terrain she was in initially represented the conflicts or "bumps in her life." The path down the hill into the forest was an opportunity for her to descend into the deeper levels of her psyche from where these conflicts emerged.

Michelle was surprised at how comfortable it was for her to be in this forest. The dancing light symbolized that part of her that "always wants to lead me home" (her center). When she finally found "home," symbolized by the cave, Michelle could look down on the hills, the forest and the path. She saw what she had come through to get there, contained in one whole, all-encompassing (transpersonal) view. "This is a view from my 'higher self,'" she said.

❖

The transpersonal realm is not always the end point of the somatosynthesis process. Sometimes a guide may use transpersonal resources to facilitate a traveler in other phases of the healing journey. Using transpersonal resources is particularly effective when travelers are "stuck," as the following traveler was.

Georgia was a sculptor in her early thirties, who initially saw me for complaints of headache and neck pain. Like many of the travelers I have worked with, she had been in traditional psychotherapy for years, and also felt she had a good grip on her emotional and psychological issues. But throughout the course of treatment, little attention had been paid to her body. While she had resolved many of her psychological problems intellectually, they were very much with her physically. In one particularly evocative session, I was supporting her underneath, and on top of her chest. When I asked her to be aware of this area, she responded, "It's like a brick wall, a long, high brick wall."

"What's it like to feel that wall?" I interjected.

"Lots of different feelings," she said, "sadness, anger, fear, hurt, and frustration. I thought I got rid of most of these feelings long ago," she added, "I don't understand why they are still with me."

"What's on the other side of the wall?" I queried.

"I don't know," she said, "it's too high for me to see over."

"Can you climb up?"

"No," she responded quickly.

Georgia stayed in this predicament for several minutes feeling trapped by this brick wall of her emotions. I waited to see if she could find a direction to take. When it was obvious she couldn't, I suggested that she try a new perspective.

"Imagine that your body could float and that you could rise higher and higher, high enough so you can look down on the wall and see both sides simultaneously."

After several minutes of silence, Georgia reported that she was indeed hovering over the wall.

"I have a floating sensation throughout my body," she noted. "It feels very peaceful and serene. I wish I could just stay here."

"What's it like to look down on the wall now?" I asked.

"On the other side of the wall is the sea," she observed. "That brick wall is holding back the sea."

I allowed her to stay in that lofty place for several more minutes and then gently suggested that she come back down to the side of the wall she was trapped behind. When she did, she had a new sense of possibility, the wall no longer seemed insurmountable, for she now understood its significance.

"Each brick in the wall represents one of the emotions I've been holding onto in my body," Georgia informed me. "If we can dislodge the bricks, then we can let the sea in and wash the emotions out."

In an interesting combination of physical and psychological intervention, Georgia identified the emotion associated with each brick and also the area of her chest wall where the brick was located. I then simulated the removal of the brick by pulling it from that area of her body. When one brick was removed, we moved to the next and then the next. As each brick was removed more of the sea leaked through. Finally after removing one brick the sea came crashing through, toppled the wall and flooded the entire area. Georgia was left floating on the surface of the water.

"I haven't drowned in these feelings," she exclaimed joyfully, "I'm floating again, and it feels good."

Georgia had journeyed from soma to psyche where she got "stuck." I had her tap into a transpersonal resource (floating above her body) in order to move through the block she encountered. This access not only allowed her to work with the emotional issues, but also showed me what type of touch to use to support her healing process.

Working With The Inner Healer

The "inner healer," "inner sage," "inner wise person," "inner doctor," or "inner physician" is a unique way of mobilizing the traveler's transpersonal healing tools. This imaginal figure embodies the forces within the traveler seeking wholeness and life. Throughout the ages and across the cultures of the world the inner healer, as the "life force," has been called by many names: from the *vis medicatrix Naturae* (the healing power of nature) of Hippocrates to the "will to live" of western medicine. Figure 6.1, exhibits some of these names for the inner healer as the life force.

Names for the Life Force

NAME	CULTURE/NATION/PERSON
Mana	Polynesia
Huna	Polynesia
Vis medicatrix Naturae	Greek (from Hippocrates)
Pneuma	Greek (from Galen)
Mumia	Greek (from Paracelsus)
Dynamis	Greek
Baraka	Moroccan and Persian
Mungo	Central Africa
Elima	Congo
Ch'i (or Ki)	China (Japan)
Prana	Hindu
Eckankar	Pali
Manna	Israel
El	Israel
Reiki	Japan
Numen	Roman
Ka	Ancient Egypt
Hike	Ancient Egypt
Kerei	Indonesia
Tondi	Sumatra
Tinh	Vietnam
Orenda	Native American (Iroquois)
Manitou	Native American (Algonquin)
Wakan	Native American (Sioux)
Wakonda	Native American (Omaha)
Maxpe	Native American (Crow)
Digin	Native American (Navaho)
Dige	Native American (Apache)
Hullo	Native American (Chickasaw)
Vital fluid	Medieval alchemists
Elan vital	Early Europe
Animal magnetism	Anton Mesmer
Magnetic fluid	Anton Mesmer
Will to live	Western medicine
Orgone energy	Wilhelm Reich (USA)
Universal Intelligence	Chiropractic (USA)
Vivaxis	Frances Nixon (USA)
Eloptic energy	T. Galen Hieronymous (USA)
L-fields (life fields)	Harold Saxon Burr (USA)
M-fields (morphogenetic fields)	Rupert Sheldrake (England)
Paraelectricity	Ambrose Worrall (USA)
Bioplasma	Russian
Kirlian energy	Czechslovakian

Figure 6.1

Working with an inner healer makes the healing life force come alive for the traveler. As an imaginal figure, the inner healer may appear to the traveler as a living or non-living entity—people, animals, plants, rocks, lights, and sounds are some common images. Some travelers are simply aware of a voice or just a presence. The inner healer may be familiar, a family member or friend, endowed with special significance for the traveler—a spiritual personage or treasured keepsake—or a totally novel image. The traveler may listen to, speak with, or otherwise observe and interact with an inner healer. In the following case study, an inner healer helped a traveler and me understand the basis of recurrent lower back pain.

❖

Jill was a woman in her mid-thirties with incapacitating lower back pain for three months before her first visit with me. She had difficulty walking, sitting or standing, and had been out of work since her back pain began. At the beginning of this session I obtained permission from Jill to work with her inner healer, after explaining that it was a personification of the inner forces working to help her heal.

With one hand underneath her back and the other on top of her lower abdomen, I guided this traveler through relaxation and inner focussing. From previous discussion with the Jill, I was aware that she had easy access to internal images. So I presented her with the following request: "Silently ask to be placed in contact with your inner healer, and wait until you feel that inner healer is with you." Five or six minutes passed while Jill was absorbed in a quiet, inner focus. When she emerged, she was indeed in touch with an inner healer.

"I see a female image coming toward me," she reported. "She's tall and has long, flowing black hair. This woman is standing in front of me now."

"Ask her if she has a name," I interjected.

"She says her name is Amma," Jill answered, "and that she is here to help me."

While Jill was getting to know her inner healer, I was aware of a strange sensation at the skin surface and in the energy field over her right ovary. It felt like an energy vortex, a whirlpool of energy, rushing into a tightly congealed mass deep within her body.

"Ask Amma if she can help me understand this impression," I requested.

Jill paused in silence for two or three minutes and then repeated what Amma had shared with her.

"Amma said the mass you feel is related to the medical operations that have been performed on my body," Jill let me know.

"The mass is composed of the fear, anger, and pain associated with my hysterectomy [the traveler had undergone a complete hysterectomy while in her early 20's, after being injured in an automobile accident] and my resulting inability to have children," she went on.

"Amma says that mass of emotions needs to be released from that area and placed in a basket of light which can then be removed from my body," Jill concluded.

Jill's inner healer had given us a clear indication of what the next steps were. Like handling fragile eggs, the traveler picked up each emotion—anger, fear, and pain—and carefully placed them in this basket of light. Then, I gently pushed the skin of her abdomen in several directions, asking her and her inner healer which direction felt right for the basket to be removed. We finally agreed that it should come straight out and up through her abdominal wall. As she relaxed, I began to pull this symbolic mass from her.

Suddenly she began to push and cry and breathe very rapidly. Her cries turned to screams, and she began to sweat profusely. It was obvious that we were in the middle of a birthing process, which lasted for 10 to 15 minutes. Then, with one final tug and push, it was over—the basket of feeling had been born! We both breathed a deep sigh of relief.

"It was a C-section," I said.

"I know," she whispered.

Afterwards I asked Jill to thank her inner healer and make an agreement that she could meet her again whenever she needed. Jill had been in traditional psychotherapy for several years as a result of the accident, her operation, and her inability to bear children. She thought that she had worked through her feelings, but she had not released these intense emotions from her body. This somatosynthesis journey proved to be the turning point in Jill's condition; her health steadily improved from then on.

There are many ways a traveler can make contact with an inner healer. For example, the traveler can be seated in a serene place, while the inner healer walks in from a distance; the traveler can walk up to the inner healer; a picture of the inner healer can be drawn in the mind of the traveler; or the traveler can watch a blank movie screen and the inner healer's image projected upon it.

❖

Helping the traveler discover and work within the transpersonal sphere is what distinguishes somatosynthesis from many other forms of therapy. So often we are content to make the body feel better by relieving the pain and discomfort of a physical condition. We also settle for merely identifying and analyzing the psychological and emotional issues that we face. Somatosynthesis asks more of the healing process: it assumes that all human beings possess potentialities that surpass the ordinary limits of body and mind, and it attempts to marshal these resources for the healing journey.

Coming Home:
Grounding the Somatosynthesis Journey

Descending from a climb is as important as reaching the summit; grounding the somatosynthesis journey, as important as the journey itself. In concluding a somatosynthesis journey, I hope to see the creation of an environment within the traveler that allows for continuance of the healing process after the journey's end. Additionally, both the traveler and guide need to emerge from a mutually shared TASC. Of course, determining when to bring the journey to closure is a matter of discussion as well. Sometimes the healing journey proceeds through a well-defined set of stages—a beginning, middle and end stage. It is then obvious when the end is reached. The traveler's physical body often gives evidence of the journey's end. Muscular relaxation, the release of movement restrictions, or the reduction of pain, may reach a maximum and, despite continued intervention by the guide, no further change is observed. Psychological cues mark the journey's end as well.

The traveler's symbolic journey may reach conclusion: a high mountain may be scaled; the traveler may flow down the river and reach the ocean; opposing voices within the traveler may be brought together; and afterwards there is really nothing further to be done. A guide may also elect to conclude the healing journey for other reasons, like the length of time the journey has taken, or the traveler's physical exhaustion. Most often, the beginning, middle and end of a somatosynthesis journey is not so well demarcated, and a combination of factors coupled with the guide's subjective impression determines the conclusion of the healing journey.

Helping the traveler make a transition between the altered state of awareness, characteristic of the healing journey and an ordinary state of awareness is important. Frequently, a TASC is so enjoyable that the traveler does not want it to end. A guide can encourage a graceful transition from a TASC by successively focusing the traveler on more superficial levels of awareness. For example, I might begin by asking a traveler to focus her awareness on the mind, then on the breath, then on stretching the body, and finally, when she is ready, to open her eyes and sit up. Roughly speaking, this is just the reverse of what took place at the outset of the somatosynthesis journey, when the traveler was invited to develop a relaxed, inner focus.

Breaking the bond of touch between traveler and guide is done with care. Several travelers have asked me to leave my hands on them for several minutes after the conclusion of the journey and then gradually remove them. In the extreme, I will even ask the traveler to inform me when it feels all right for me to stop touching. I have also borrowed a page from the clinical notebook of Milton Erickson, the famous psychotherapist, who often left his patients with the reassurance that "my voice goes with you." My reassurance to travelers is that "my hands go with you."

Actually, it is not uncommon for a traveler to report feeling the presence of the guide's hands hours, sometimes days after a somatosynthesis journey. I believe there are two factors at work here. One is the lingering, after-image sensation common to all of our senses. Look at any object long enough, for example, then close your eyes, and you will see the object's after-image against the black background of your closed eyelids. Take your thumb and press it hard into the palm of the opposite hand. If you remove it quickly, you will feel the after-image sensation of it's pressure on your palm.

Positive events are recorded and recalled through the body in precisely the same way that problem events are. One traveler made it clear to me how this worked.

"I felt the stress of that situation about to over take me, and my neck muscles about to tighten up as usual," she said. "But simultaneously I also felt the presence of your hand holding my head and neck the way you often do. Neither the stress of the situation nor the tightness ever developed."

Ultimately travelers can learn to heal and help themselves without necessarily relying on the actual or imagined presence of the guide. But the guide should always respect the powerful bond of human touch, especially when that bond is about to be broken.

In grounding the healing journey, the guide has the opportunity to recapitulate the journey's course and to challenge the traveler to carry back the journey's meaning. This can be as simple as summarizing where the traveler has been and asking the traveler to allow the meaning of that journey to emerge. The traveler can be taken back to a particular physical condition or psychological issue and asked to discover what is new as a result of the healing journey.

Sometimes it is necessary to "tidy up" the loose ends of a somatosynthesis journey. One traveler I guided, had been in touch with herself as a four year-old girl throughout most of the healing journey. As it turned out, the adult traveler was a person this little girl finally felt that she could trust. At the conclusion of the journey, however, the little girl was reluctant to let the adult traveler go. The adult traveler needed to hold the little girl, give her a big hug, tell her she loved her, and promise that she would be back whenever the little girl was in need. Once this was done the adult traveler could leave and the healing journey be brought to conclusion.

In other instances travelers have needed to climb down a mountain, thank their "inner healers," or say good-bye to various subpersonalities before completing their healing journeys. All of these methods assist the traveler in departing the healing journey while retaining its essence. This final phase of somatosynthesis beckons the traveler to connect with the powerful transformative force contained in the meaning and purpose of the healing journey.

With the ending of the journey, the real healing begins. When asked how a somatosynthesis journey could be incorporated and integrated into his life, one traveler observed, "It doesn't end here, does it? Now I have the choice to allow this journey to express itself through my life."

7
Healing Journeys With Exceptional Travelers

Guiding a somatosynthesis journey is a special privilege. With every traveler unique and all journeys different, I am constantly filled with excitement and awe as each epic of healing unfolds. In this way I have learned the most about somatosynthesis from just being with travelers on their journeys. From the many accounts of somatosynthesis journeys which I have recorded, I have selected several for inclusion here. Some of the following journeys illustrate particular aspects of somatosynthesis that I have discussed earlier. Other journeys were included because they touched me in a special way. All give a feeling for the many directions the healing journey may take. My comments at the end of each selection highlight important aspects of the journey for both traveler and guide.

Past Presents

Lily had an air of fretful calm about her. She sat on the examination table staring blankly at me, with two jet black braids falling symmetrically past each shoulder. I wheeled my exam stool around the table, past her clothes which were folded neatly in the corner—a simple smock with vivid reds, yellows and greens, quite a contrast to the doleful person in front of me.

"She's different!" I thought to myself, as I began to take her history. In fact, she was a woman in her early thirties with a bizarre history of auto-immune disease. Her immune system attacked the proteins produced by her body as though they were unwanted, foreign intruders. This resulted in a wide array of symptoms: severe joint pain, muscle weakness, lethargy, and increased susceptibility to disease. All of this because her immune system confused "self" with "other," and treated portions of Lily's body as though they were not her own. She told me of going from specialist to specialist and having test after test with no conclusive results.

"You're rejecting your body," I blurted out in the middle of my history-taking, "why?" I realized I may have spoken out of turn; after all, I hardly knew this woman.

"I think you're right," she offered, "but I don't know why."

I told Lily that on several occasions I had observed that people with massive allergies or systemic immune problems were often psychologically rejecting their physical body or some other part of themselves. I also informed her that "hands-on" therapy, combined with attention to emotional/psychological issues often proved effective at uncovering and resolving the basis for such wide-spread, perplexing physical problems. I was not at all surprised when she informed me that she had been in psychotherapy on and off for nearly ten years. She also related her experiences with hypnosis, biofeedback and nutritional therapy. None of these methods had proven effective.

This brief discussion paved the way for Lily to share a few important aspects of her life, which had bearing on her present condition. She pulled her hair back to expose a large, disfiguring scar on her right neck and shoulder where she had been severely cut by the blades of a fan. At three years old, while reaching out to her mother, who was adjusting the position of a fan, her mother's arm knocked the fan off a table and onto Lily. Lily also tentatively put forth that she had been the object of childhood sexual abuse, but offered no further details. This did not seem the time to pursue this matter further, so I thanked her for providing me with these details and continued my physical examination. However I could not help forming some hunches of what had transpired for Lily to bring her body and mind to their present condition.

"Within the two incidents she related were the seeds of her rejecting her body," I thought. "Perhaps we can work through these incidents with her body to help bring about some resolution and acceptance."

This all seemed very logical and gave me added confidence in telling her that I felt we could work together for her benefit. The most difficult part of our first few sessions was establishing a rapport. I often felt like a climber, groping for a finger hold along a wall of sheer rock. Somatic therapy seemed to work fine with Lily, and I did a variety of soft tissue releases, joint mobilization, gentle spinal correction, and energy field techniques. But the journey from soma to psyche was more arduous. Somatic imaging, image/counter-image, subpersonalities, guided imagery, all the interventions that usually worked well with travelers did not seem to take hold. We did achieve a superficial depth in some areas. While I was holding Lily's injured right shoulder, she became aware of her fear and sense of being punished because she reached out for love.

"I know my mother wasn't punishing me," she said, "but somehow I got that the fan falling on me was a punishment for wanting my mother to hold me at that moment."

A similar theme emerged around the incidence of sexual abuse. Again Lily felt her body was being punished when she reached out for love. In this case, her grandfather was the perpetrator. Of course, this was similar to my original hypothesis about why Lily was rejecting her body. She felt it had been punished, and she had dissociated herself from her body as a result. For three or four sessions, this was about as far as we journeyed together.

In fact, this was territory she had covered several times in psychotherapy and hypnotherapy. What was different now was the integration of her body into the process. Still there was little change in the doleful air about her. I actually began to question whether we were moving in the right direction, until I walked into her treatment room nearly 45 minutes late one day. Even after I explained to her that I had an emergency right before seeing her, Lily was still upset with my lateness.

"I have a real problem with waiting," she said. "I feel like I'm on death row, waiting to die."

A lot of people have expressed anger at me for being late, but no one had ever told me they felt as though they were waiting to die. After asking Lily to lie down and relax I suggested that she focus on that image of waiting to die. "I'm alone," she said softly, "in a hut, waiting to die."

As she began, I knew by her voice that we had the "live issue."

"I'm afraid, I'm alone, and I feel betrayed by him," she whispered. "I loved him, but that love was betrayed."

"Who, Lily, who betrayed you?" I asked.

"The chief," she cried in a soft monotone, "when they found us out, I was sentenced to die."

Lily was speaking as though she were commenting on a scene taking place outside my window. There was little hesitation in her voice, although I was still unsure about exactly what tale was being told. Bits and pieces of a story line were coming together, but the events were somewhat jumbled. She kept rambling on about a poor young girl who received a death sentence because of her love for a chief. Finally I intervened and asked Lily the name of this young girl.

"Her name is Morning Lily," she responded, "she's a young Native American girl of fifteen."

"Tell me about Morning Lily," I requested, before Lily could continue rambling. Now began an incredible tale.

> She was the only child in her family. Her parents raised her as a very creative, intelligent girl. Even at an early age, her singing, dancing and story-telling captivated the members of the tribe. As word of Morning Lily's exceptional talent spread among her people, she was requested to come and perform for the tribal chief. He too was taken with her grace, poise, intelligence, and charm. After speaking with her parents, the chief arranged for her to stay with him, so that she would be able to perform at his pleasure. Of course, her parents were quite excited about this because it meant that they too would have an elevated status in the Native American community.

> Morning Lily was trained to sing, dance and tell stories, but no one had trained this young girl to handle the feelings that emerged for this chief. The chief already had several wives, and it was against the community's customs for him to take on another wife as young as Morning Lily. His feelings for her also grew, and not long after she was with him they became lovers. Of course their affair was conducted in secret. Although Morning Lily fell deeply in love with the chief, she was never able to openly acknowledge this amongst her Native American community.

> Eventually their relationship was exposed, and to save the chief's honored position Morning Lily was blamed for the seduction. She was immediately isolated in a hut

by herself to await the deliberations of a tribal council. A decision was reached that she should sacrifice herself at the next full moon, committing her own death with a special ceremonial knife. The full moon was two weeks away, and Morning Lily waited alone, still unsure why her love for the chief had led to her death sentence.

Lily now breathed a sigh of relief, which immediately seemed to lift her out of the story she had just narrated.

"I've known about this," she said to me, "at least bits and pieces of it, but I did not know the whole story."

Lily then told me how once during hypnotherapy, this story about Morning Lily started to come out. But her hypnotist was uncomfortable working with what he perceived to be "past life regression." The same story began to emerge during Lily's current psychotherapy sessions. But her therapist told her that she artificially created the reality of Morning Lily, to enable her to handle the sexual and psychological abuse she experienced in this lifetime. I assured Lily that it didn't really matter to me if the hypnotist or psychotherapist was right. I professed a neutrality of belief in regard to past lives and reincarnation. What I did know was that, contained within Morning Lily's saga, was the central issue surrounding the physical conditions that Lily manifested. Regardless of whether this was a true past life experience or Lily's fabrication to handle early childhood trauma, it was an apt metaphor. Lily recognized this relationship as well.

"Lily is attempting to get rid of Morning Lily," she observed," isn't she? That's where my massive auto-immune problems are coming from. One part of me is literally trying to rid itself of another part of me."

I agreed that what was taking place in her body and what was evolving in her psyche were symbolically equivalent. She continued to draw the analogy further.

"I'm beginning to understand why I am so anxious when I have to wait," Lily remarked. "It recreates Morning Lily's waiting for her death. She's scared, but she has to die."

"What a strange coincidence," Lily mused. "For the last five years I've worked as a hospice nurse, helping other people face death, while really I needed to help a part of me die."

It was clear that Morning Lily would have to die for Lily to continue living. But it seemed too soon for that to take place. Lily, after all, had really just discovered her existence. I felt that Morning Lily had some important teachings to impart to Lily. Over the next several weeks Lily got to know Morning Lily. A different area of Lily's body became the focal point of each journey. These areas also had a special significance for Morning Lily. One area was related to her femininity, another to her sensuality, a third to her intelligence, a forth to her deep, emotional expression, and so on. For Lily these were attributes missing from her life. After a few moments of holding these areas on Lily body, she would contact Morning Lily and allow Morning Lily's voice to speak to her. In this way Lily came to know this young, Native american girl whose wisdom was so needed. Morning Lily's full moon finally came. And, at the beginning of one journey, both Lily and I knew, without saying a word, that it was time for Morning Lily to die. While supporting Lily in her chest and upper back, I asked for her help.

"You of all people know what Morning Lily needs to hear as she approaches her death," I avowed, referring to Lily's expertise in hospice work.

After a long silence Lily spoke softly to this young girl, "I love you, don't be afraid to let go, I'm here with you. When you're ready to go, I'll take your hand and walk along beside."

By custom Morning Lily was to take her life in public. When she was ready to leave her hut, Lily ushered her to the location where this drama was to be played out.

"She's waiting," Lily said nervously, "she's not ready to go just yet. I'm not sure why, but she's waiting."

At this point I was waiting too, holding Lily's head and merely allowing the events to unfold as they would. In a short time, the reason for Morning Lily's hesitation became known.

"She's waiting for him to be there," Lily stated. "She wants to die looking into his eyes."

The chief was not supposed to be present at such an event, but Lily was sure he would come anyway. After another long silence, Lily said, "I see him now, way in the back of the crowd gathered around Morning Lily. No one else is aware of his presence, but he's here and now we're ready."

I placed one hand over the area where Morning Lily was about to plunge a knife into her body.

"She's done it," grimaced Lily, as her body relaxed down into the table she was lying on.

Again dense silence pervaded the journey, broken in time by Lily's voice.

"Morning Lily's spirit is hovering high above this scene," she reported. "She's peaceful and very happy. And my spirit has risen to meet her there. We're joined together in spirit now."

There was little else to be said. Within a week Lily lost her job as a hospice nurse. The next time I saw Lily she looked different—she had on make-up, lipstick, and a colorful outfit. The air around her was different too. She first told me how angry she had been in the last two weeks, and I nearly broke out laughing.

In the several months we had worked together, she had never expressed this depth of emotion. An aliveness and vivaciousness was about her, even as she told me about her woes—her bank accidentally closing her checking account and all of her checks bouncing; her building being sold and her need to find another apartment to rent. Somehow the issues were not as important as her response: She began to feel in touch with the movement of her life. While gently holding the back of her head, I pointed out this new found emotional reaction to her, and she lamented, "But I'm not used to being this close to my emotions, it's a bit overwhelming."

Helping Morning Lily die was helping Lily to live. All of her problems were not solved—physically or psychologically. In fact, Morning Lily's death was just the beginning for Lily.

"This isn't easy," she noted at the end of one journey. "Although I no longer need Morning Lily as a frame of reference for my life, now I have the job of replacing her with something else. That's a real challenge."

My journeys with Lily stand out among the travelers I have guided. The sheer dramatic content is one reason. But there are also important lessons I learned as her guide. To this day I harbor an ambivalence towards past life experience. Perhaps it is because the idea of the human soul dropping one body to pick up another seems too inelegant, too mechanistic, given the little I intuit about the beauty and splendor of Nature. Yet I am fully convinced of the authenticity of Lily's story, not so much in historical accuracy as in its deep meaning for her healing. Obviously, one could draw a relationship between the Native chief and Lily's sexually abusive grandfather. Morning Lily's death by knife, and Lily's accidental disfigurement with a fan strike a similar equation. It is possible that in young Lily's mind, this fantasy world was constructed to help her deal with the troublesome reality of her actual life.

But the coping mechanism began to spill over into her body in the form of systemic dysfunction. It also appeared to drive the choices Lily made in her life—working as a hospice nurse seems more than mere coincidence. The common thread in all this—her body, her job, the dramatic story of Morning Lily—is simply that Lily's not-yet-conscious was attempting to express itself in her life. She was continually attempting to heal herself.

When she was unable to express her not-yet-conscious through story, she expressed it in her work; when that failed, she expressed it in her body. One of the basic premises of somatosynthesis is a belief in the power of the traveler's not-yet-conscious—the traveler's inner wisdom. Regardless of the form, helping the traveler manifest this inner wisdom enhances the healing process.

If there is another lesson to be learned from these journeys with Lily, it is that healing is not necessarily curing. When Lily finally allowed Morning Lily to die, all of her physical and psychological problems did not simply vanish. In fact, certain issues were even more graphic in Lily's life since she no longer had Morning Lily to diffuse them. Reaching one's center is the epitome of the somatosynthesis process, and Lily reached her center through the death of Morning Lily. Once reached, the center is able to integrate and synthesize the physical and psychological issues of the traveler. The symbolic and poetic joining of Lily and Morning Lily in spirit represents this synthesis. However, it was not the culmination of Lily's healing process—just the beginning.

Crystal Visions

Barbara was a 36-year-old traveler who had experienced several months of severe lower back pain and headaches before I first saw her. Previous somatosynthesis sessions were successful in relieving much of her pain and allowing her to resume a normal life. Since some lower back pain was still with her I began this session by supporting Barbara in the lower back and pelvic area. As she began to relax I guided her attention within and asked her to be in touch with whatever was emerging in her life now.

"I'm inside a crystal," she said. "It's a beautiful crystal full of light, and I am touching the facets. In the center there is a ball of radiant, white light."

For the next five minutes, Barbara described how wondrous it was being inside a crystal. But after a few moments in silence her vantage changed.

When asked to be aware of the direction in which she was headed, Barbara replied, "I'm travelling upwards, higher and higher."

At a certain point, Barbara felt that further movement upward was blocked.

"I can't go higher than this," she reported. "It feels as though I am moving into a dense area of congestion. There's a dark, black, heavy area over my right arm."

I suggested that she envision herself moving through that area of congestion, no matter how long it took. Her body shook as she experienced the pain in that area.

"There's a lot of pain," she cried out, "a lot pain."

Within a few moments the pain began to dissipate and the restriction to her upward movement lessened.

"The congestion is clearing," she observed, "and I can move higher, I can fly again."

Again at a certain point her further upward motion was halted. She reached another point of congestion and intense pain—this time over her left breast. I guided her into this area of darkness and congestion, where a vivid, visual experience began to unfold.

"There's a knife and a hand," she said nervously. "I feel as though I am being stabbed and also backed up against a wall."

"Oh, my God," she exclaimed. "It's my father. He's stabbing me right here [pointing to her left breast] and I'm lying in a pool of blood. He's looking at me, and saying, 'I'm sorry, I'm sorry.' Now he's turning around and walking away."

Barbara related how symbolically this felt like what her father had done to her as a young child, when he abandoned her and her mother. Like many travelers, Barbara had been through years of psychotherapy around her father's abandonment. She was aware of the effect his leaving had on her emotionally, but unaware of the impact of those psychological effects on her physical body. Barbara stayed with this poignant scene for a long while, choosing not to say anything else. She emerged from this inward focus and remarked how the crystal had grown larger around her. "The congestion has gone," she reported, "but there's still some pain here [pointing to an area over her left breast]. The pain feels trapped in here."

I felt this was an appropriate moment for me to physically intervene with Barbara's pain. With her help, we determined where on her chest wall this pain could exit. I gently separated the skin over this area with my fingertips, as if to make a portal for the pain to pass through. As I did this, Barbara's pain grew worse, and spread to other areas of her body.

"The pain is really intense," Barbara let out. "I can feel it in my lower back, and calves, and even in my head."

I continued to separate this area with my fingertips, and gently pressed the tissue in the direction of the exit point. Her body moved from side to side, and Barbara continued to experience much pain for the next few minutes. Finally, the pain subsided, and Barbara found herself back in familiar surroundings.

"I'm back in the crystal now," she smiled, "and the light is even brighter. It's different in here now, I can see a door in the crystal. It's a door through which I can exit and return."

Barbara's journey was brought to conclusion, as she focussed on it's meaning in her life now.

"Within the crystal I have access to past experiences which still influence my body and my mind," she noted. "But the crystal is a source of light, and through that light I have access to my higher self, my spirit. That leads me beyond what I am now and shows me what I may be."

Barbara illustrates a traveler working from her center throughout the somatosynthesis journey. The typical transition from soma to psyche to center collapsed into a single movement from soma to center. That crystal, with a light in the center, was Barbara's symbolic representation of her center. This center integrated both higher and lower realities for her. As she moved upwards—into the higher reality of her spirit—she encountered a variety of physical and psychological impediments. Physical intervention provided doorways for Barbara to move through these impediments. Literally and symbolically, simulating a passageway on Barbara's skin was an example of this. It allowed her to move through the physical pain, and psychological trauma, of her father's abandonment. Once accomplished, she was again back at her center, aware that she could move through such impediments whenever she needed to, as the newly found door in the crystal demonstrated.

High Points of the Healing Journey

Mountains are evocative and powerful symbols of the traveler's integrating center. Here are two short accounts of travelers journeying to a mountain.

Douglas was a lively septuagenarian who came to see me because of severe neck pain from an arthritic condition throughout his spine. I guided him through a deep relaxation, and asked him to focus on the painful area in his neck, allowing whatever related images to emerge. Douglas immediately seized upon the image of his neck being crowded, an accurate representation of spinal arthritis. But the image went further, carrying him back to a time 30 years earlier when he had been stationed with the State Department in Tokyo.

"It's an amusing image," he observed. "It reminds me of the crowded streets of downtown Tokyo during the daytime."

As I gently mobilized his head and neck, he stayed with that image for some time, remembering what it was like to be in the middle of this busy metropolis. He also remembered that while in Tokyo a sight that gave him peace and restfulness was the view of Mount Fujiama. So the counter-image Douglas chose to work with was being at Mount Fujiama. It was a very special experience for him.

In real life he felt close to the Japanese spiritual traditions surrounding the mountain. Thinking about how the Japanese related to the mountain brought him peace, comfort and physical relaxation. Envisioning himself on the mountain led him to feel the same sense of "connection with life" present when he actually walked on Fujiama. That connection, he noted, was very important to him. When I asked him what inner quality would help most in his life now, he paused for a moment, then said, "My own spirituality, I need to connect with that peace within. The peace I found on Fujiama."

With mobility restored to his neck and the severity of his pain diminished, we concluded this healing journey.

Laureen had no specific physical symptoms during this somatosynthesis session, although I had been seeing her for several months because of an injury to her neck and shoulder. Assessing her physical body I was drawn to her left upper chest and upper back area. With my hands supporting this area above and below, I guided Laureen through a relaxation and asked her to focus on this area. I invited her to imagine standing in that area of her body and to be aware of what images surrounded her there. Laureen felt as though she were lost in a desert with no apparent direction to take. At my request she imagined her body hovering over the desert as she scoured the terrain for a path to take.

"I see a path now," she reported. "It leads from where I am, to an oasis, and from there to the mountains."

After descending back to the desert floor, I encouraged Laureen to walk that path and simply be aware of whatever unfolded for her on this journey. Meanwhile I continued to physically intervene in her upper chest and back after which I also moved my hands to gently apply traction to her neck. Laureen was so deeply engrossed in her journey that verbally interacting with me was virtually impossible. When I asked her to share her experience with me she took several minutes to exit from her silence, and then spoke in a barely audible whisper. I decided not to continue guiding her journey verbally. I simply monitored her body, looking for visible signs of change. Her breathing, level of muscular relaxation, discernible alterations in her energy field, audible sighs and sounds were some of the cues to the progress of her healing journey. This journey in silence went on for nearly one-half hour. When her bodily changes indicated the end of the journey was near, I slowly guided her out of the deep TASC she was in. I asked if she would share what the journey was like.

> It was very easy and comfortable for me to stay in the oasis. I didn't want to leave, but something kept drawing me on. I was afraid the journey to the mountains would be difficult, but as it turned out, it wasn't. When I finally reached the mountains, I climbed the highest peak. I had a profound awareness of everything around me. I felt the sky, the air, and the sun. I was aware of everything, and I felt at one with everything. And I feel extremely calm and peaceful now.

Often very little urging is needed for the traveler's journey to unfold. Simply pointing a traveler in the right direction, as I did by having Laureen rise up and see the path, is enough. It is a delicate decision the guide makes about the amount of verbal intervention necessary for the traveler. For some travelers journeying in silence is a powerful experience. Laureen, for example, clearly reached her center on the mountain. Even though she was not able to narrate the journey while it happened or fully describe its effect on her afterwards, the results of having been to the mountain were clear to me in other ways: physical changes, the content of her journey, and the feeling I had upon listening to her speak of where she had been.

A Golden Thread of Synthesis

Carla was a vivacious, energetic woman in her mid-thirties who came to see me with complaints of lower back and shoulder pain. Before we began our session Carla informed me that her husband had just received a transfer to California. This posed a dilemma for her because she was in the final stages of opening her own small boutique. I talked her through relaxation and inner focusing, then asked her to bring her awareness to the pain in her lower back. It was obvious to both of us that this pain was related to the conflict she had around her husband's transfer. Supporting this lower back area with my hands, I asked her to give the area a voice and be in touch with what her lower back told her about her current situation.

"There are two voices there," she said after a moment's pause. "One is a voice of bitterness and grief over not being able to manifest my dream of opening my own shop. But the other is a voice of freedom; I grew up in the area where he was transferred to, and I would be very excited about moving back there."

We treated these two voices as two subpersonalities being expressed by Carla. The tension between them was being manifested in her spine. I asked Carla to discover what the needs of each of the subpersonalities was."That's pretty easy," she remarked. "One voice would like to let go of the bitterness and grief, while the voice of freedom would like to retain that freedom."

When asked what she felt we could do with these different voices she responded quite vociferously,

"Let's kill that voice of bitterness and grief!"

But she immediately backed off and said, "No, no, I don't really want to kill it, they [the two subpersonalities] should be synthesized [her word, not mine!]."

Carla was an experienced traveler, so I simply asked her to allow that process of synthesis to happen. She first described a beautiful golden rope to me.

"It feels like love," she said. "and the rope is tying both of these subpersonalities together."

As the joining of the two continued Carla reported that arms were extending from this synthesized entity. These arms were reaching out to "encompass the world."

"These symbols are deeper than I can understand," Carla mused. "I can only feel what they mean."

As the joining of the two continued Carla reported that arms were extending from this synthesized entity. These arms were reaching out to "encompass the world."

"These symbols are deeper than I can understand," Carla mused. "I can only feel what they mean."

Ultimately the two subpersonalities fused into one, with a single face, and arms transformed into wings.

"I don't understand what this means," Carla stammered, "but it feels right."

The whole journey lasted about 45 minutes, and near its conclusion I asked Carla to be aware of what inner resources this experience had made available to her now. She was silent for several minutes, and chose not to say anything in response. Afterwards I also asked Carla to be aware of where this experience fit into her life now. Again she was silent for several minutes and chose not to say anything. Concluding the journey I asked her if there was anything she did want to share.

"The image of my higher self, the single face with two wings, was overwhelming," she related. "I really didn't understand all the imagery that emerged for me, and therefore I couldn't say anything when you asked me. But I'm very relaxed now, and I don't have any back or shoulder pain."

The healing movement from soma to psyche to center was clearly displayed in this traveler's journey. Underlying Carla's lower back pain (soma) were two conflicting subpersonalities (psyche). The winged entity rising from the synthesis of these two subpersonalities was her center or "higher self" in Carla's words. Carla's inability to verbalize all of her experience was really insignificant when compared to the physical and emotional impact of the journey. Carla's journey is a classic example of the synthesis of two conflicting subpersonalities that were causing physical distress.

The Inner Healer in a Bikini

Charles was a tall, well-built, 26-year-old football player who came to see me after injuring his shoulder on the playing field. He had been treated by a variety of specialists for this shoulder pain but to no avail. For our first several sessions I manipulated the shoulder and applied traction, which brought only temporary relief. Something else needed to be done, but my initial assessment of Charles was that he would not be a good candidate for a somatosynthesis session. I felt that his orientation was towards resolution of this problem on a strictly physical basis.

However, at our next meeting, against my better judgment, I asked him if he would really like to get to the bottom of this shoulder problem. "Sure Doc," he replied.

I gently cupped his shoulder with both hands and asked him to focus on his breathing and relax. I told him that it was often possible to visualize a person in a problem area of the body. "You have an 'inner healer,'" I said, "someone who might tell us why this shoulder problem remains."

As Charles continued to relax, he drifted into a TASC. Within moments of focussing on this inner healer, he began to exclaim, "This is incredible! This is incredible! What a sight! What a beautiful sight!"

At first I was really excited that he had contacted the image of an inner healer so quickly.

"What's your inner healer like?" I said. "What are you seeing?"

"You won't believe this," he began, "but I'm watching this absolutely beautiful woman in a very skimpy bikini."

Charles went on to describe the aesthetic form of this woman whom he was watching from behind. His comments made me gasp—and really wonder if I had done the right thing. An inner healer in a bikini, I thought, how can this work?

"Trust the process," I kept telling myself, "you'll never go wrong if you trust the process."

"OK, Charles," I said, "can you talk with her?"

"No," he replied, "she won't turn around."

So Charles followed this inner vision down the beach, marvelling at her beauty. Every so often he would tap her on the shoulder in an attempt to get her to turn around. When she finally did, he began to describe what he saw in even more glowing terms.

"Her eyes are lovely," he proclaimed. "Her face is soft and beautiful. And the rest of her body is exquisite."

Meanwhile I was still a little nervous, trying to figure out how I could rescue what appeared to be a doomed therapy session.

"Ask her what her name is," I interjected.

He paused for several seconds while he mentally asked to be introduced to this image.

"Joanna," came the reply, "her name is Joanna."

Suddenly Charles exploded with amazement again, "I don't believe this," he let forth, "she's actually telling me why I have this shoulder problem."

Joanna explained to Charles that his shoulder pain was the result of his trying too hard to please other people and feeling inadequate when he failed to live up to their supposed expectations. It was a behavioral pattern he had adopted early in life, she said. It had developed from the feelings of inadequacy arising when he compared himself to his father. This problem affected him in football, work situations and his marriage.

All the while Charles just nodded as if he were in total agreement with this inner healer. "Damned if she isn't right," he said, "she's right, she's absolutely right."

It was obvious that Charles was deeply involved in this healing process now, much to my amazement and delight.

"Ask Joanna where I can place my hands to help this shoulder," I suggested.

Charles contemplated the request for several seconds and then reported where Joanna recommended that I place my hands on his shoulder. I happily complied with these instructions and left my hands there until informed by Charles, through his inner healer, to remove them.

"Son of a gun," he exclaimed, "it feels better, it really does."

At the conclusion of this session, I asked Charles to thank Joanna for being with us and to make an agreement with her that the two should meet again whenever it was needed.

Charles went out of town, and I did not see him again for several weeks. When I next had a chance to ask him how his shoulder had fared during this time, he shared how he had met with Joanna again.

"It only bothered me once," he recalled, "one morning while I was shaving."

"But I called Joanna back and had her put her hands on my shoulder the way she had you touch me," he beamed, "and the pain went away in a few minutes."

Over the next several sessions Charles met a number of beautiful women who served as "inner guides" for him. Eventually that process shifted and Charles was placed in touch with other images that existed at much deeper levels in his psyche. But the initial process was a pointed and amusing reminder to me of the uniqueness of each traveler's inner experience. Any image that's valid for the traveler can be used in the healing process.

Charles's saga actually had another humorous twist. After each session he went home and told his wife all about the strange but effective healing process he was involved in. At first she was excited and pleased by what she heard. However, Charles reported, she soon demanded to know who these beautiful women were that her husband was discovering with such regularity. With my own confidence bolstered by Charles's experience I told him to reassure his wife that if she wanted to come in for treatment we could no doubt find some gorgeous men for her to meet as well.

While this session with Charles may have been the most humorous healing journey I've taken, it also contains some important lessons. One lesson concerns the guide's trust of the traveler's "inner wisdom," even when the "inner healer" seems more like an "inner jester." I honestly felt like calling this journey to a halt several times. In the end, both Charles and I learned more about the healing process by persevering with what unfolded before us.

A second lesson is how valuable the traveler's inner wisdom can be for the guide. I received useful information about how to intervene physically from this traveler's inner wisdom. On a somatosynthesis journey there are always more therapeutic entities than just the physical presence of the guide. There is the guide's inner wisdom and the guide's touch, but most of all there are the different forces in the traveler seeking wholeness and healing. The guide's job is to find the course of the swiftest wind and steer the healing journey in that direction. And this is best done by tapping into, and using, all the forces within the traveler.

Lastly I feel it necessary to acknowledge the role that humor does play in healing. Humor, when used appropriately, is a wonderful way to ground a particularly intense journey or diffuse a highly charged emotional issue for the traveler—it can bring out the sheer joy of being human, even in the face of difficulty and despair. As one quip put it, "the best way to combat gravity is with levity."

At the Helm of Healing

Somatosynthesis sessions can evoke powerful images, filled with meaning and purpose for the traveler. The following traveler is Andrew, a thirty year-old male who came to see me ostensibly for lower back pain. For many years he has worked alone as a carpet layer and carpenter. Now his physical condition threatened his livelihood. One particularly evocative session prompted him to write down his experience which follows:

The image is clear, invoked by the constant, nagging pain in my lower back. I see myself through the eyes of an oarsman, struggling to pull his oars through the water. Although the boat moves forward while I am rowing I can only clearly see where I have been, not where I am going. The soreness is resolute, and I am growing more and more fatigued by the work of trying to get somewhere that I cannot see. Why is this image so important to me now?

Throughout most of my adult life I have sought the luxury of solitary work. Somewhere along the line I lost the ability to trust others, believing myself to be the only one that could do things right. Thus the image of the solitary oarsman in his vehicle of choice makes perfect sense.

I believe in choice, and I believe that we choose our own ways of suffering. The boundaries between physical and emotional pain are amorphous at times—physical distress is so often a manifestation of some underlying agenda. I turn to my inner physician, asking why I have lower back pain and how it is related to this powerful scene of solitary struggle. "I need help," I admit to myself.

Pow! Suddenly the wind fills sails that have appeared on the boat, the sky turns a brilliant blue, and I can see where I am going. I am no longer traveling in a rowboat powered by my stubbornness, but a beautiful sailboat through which I have harnessed the wind to drive me toward a distant but clear destination. I understand that the wind may slacken at any time but I am willing to take that risk in exchange for the opportunity to see where I am headed. I am at the helm of my sailboat. And I am a physician healing himself.

The traveler lay on his back during this session, while my hands remained relatively stationery—one hand underneath and one hand over top his pelvis and lower back area with a very light pressure applied in a downward direction. Afterwards the traveler reported a substantial reduction in lower back pain. Several days later he was offered a partnership in a small construction firm, which now requires him to manage the efforts of others rather than work alone.

A somatosynthesis journey is an opportunity for travelers to create and experience their own personal mythology. No one can tell the traveler's story as well as the traveler. A guide can help the traveler flesh out body areas, feelings, issues, symbols, and images, but ultimately it is the traveler alone who stitches together a quilt of meaning out of these various and sundry patches. Andrew's account of his journey shows how marvelous the traveler's end-product can be. Andrew's account also makes me note that I encourage travelers to write down their journeys.

Like a dream, a somatosynthesis journey is often vivid and intense in the moment. One feels that it will never be forgotten. Then once the journey is through, the feelings and the meaning of the journey seem to linger, but the details become hazy and are slowly lost. These details, the images and movement of the journey, are useful to the traveler. Re-reading a previous journey can recall important truths that have diminished over time; help a traveler remember valuable inner strengths that were discovered; and re-inspire the traveler to continue moving along the healing journey.

The Center of the Maze

Cheryl was a middle-aged traveler who experiences a lot of pain in the neck and between her shoulders. During this session she was lying on her back, and my hands were resting lightly, one underneath and the other on top of her upper chest and shoulders.

"Bring your awareness to this area," I suggested, "and just allow yourself to experience it."

Initially she had a lot of resistance to experiencing this area of her body. After several minutes she off-handedly described the area as feeling like an abstract painting.

"What's in the painting?" I asked.

"Forms," she replied, "just a lot of forms."

"Can you visualize this painting in three-dimensions instead of two?" I queried.

"Yes," she responded, "the painting has become a maze of geometrical forms. I'm walking in this maze and I'm lost."

Cheryl found it difficult to discover a way out of the maze. I suggested that in her mind's eye she allow her body to float above the maze and discover the way out. She tried this and reported a very peaceful sensation of being in contact with her higher self as she floated above the maze. I took this to mean that she was in touch with some aspect of her transpersonal self and suggested that she use this contact to help her get out.

"My higher self," she said, "informs me that to find the way out I must first find the center of the maze."

From her vantage point above the maze Cheryl discovered a path to the center. She then returned to the person still lost in the maze and carefully traversed the path she had discovered leading to the center. When she finally arrived at the center of the maze she was excited, happy and free of pain. The connections between the events taking place in her life and her healing journey were obvious. She recounted how her life reminded her of being lost in a maze and how she literally shouldered the pain and stress of trying to find a way out. At my next session with Cheryl she told me that whenever she felt mounting stress building up in her body, she now paused for a moment and quickly found the center of her maze.

Cheryl's journey is yet another instance of the importance of the center to the traveler's healing process. I particularly liked this journey because of the metaphor of the maze and the simple practicality the traveler attached to finding its (her) center. She could immediately apply the journey's experience in her life.

The Plastic Healer

John was a 35-year-old rock-climber who came to see me several months after a climbing injury. He had fallen off a thirty-foot high cliff onto his back, fracturing several vertebrae and shattering his left foot and wrist. An operation was necessary to remove a portion of one lumbar vertebra pressing against the spinal cord, and a pin was implanted into his ankle. He was told it was very unlikely that he would walk normally again, but John was very determined and refused to accept such a dismal prognosis.

While still lying in his hospital bed, he continued to run the small electronics firm that he had recently started. John also had several hobbies, including working with plastics. It was something he enjoyed doing with his young son. Together they worked with a variety of different types of plastics—heating them, molding them into desired shapes and allowing them to set.

"I'm not sure why," he said, "but for the past several weeks I've been telling my wife that these plastics have something to do with my recovery."

In particular, John had searched out and found a hard-to-locate company that offered hobbyists special low-melting point plastic kits. Called, "Friendly Plastic," this material enabled him to work with plastics at temperatures near the boiling point of water.

As we began this somatosynthesis session it appeared as though John would really benefit from mild traction in the area of the lumbar vertebral fracture. Both he and I had the impression of a lot of scar tissue in this area from the injury and the resulting surgery. With John lying on his back I applied very gentle traction while I asked him to relax and become more aware of what this area felt like. Spontaneously both of John's hands rose above him and worked the air as though they were kneading dough.

"It's the plastic," he exclaimed, "that area feels like plastic that's been molded in the wrong shape."

Using a process that he knew intimately, John did the "inner work" to change that area. He heated the plastic and used his hands to rework it into a shape that felt right, then he let it set. Afterwards we talked about his imagery and how uncanny it was that he was drawn to the plastics several weeks before. Even more surprising to him was the anatomical accuracy of his analogy. As I explained to John, an analogy is often made between *plastic* and human connective tissue (muscles, ligaments, tendons, and membranes). We think of such tissue having two phases of existence. In one phase, called the *elastic phase*, soft tissue is very resistant to change. When a force attempts to change the tissue in this phase that force is absorbed and the tissue restores itself to its original state. This first phase would be equivalent to hardened plastic. The second phase is called the *plastic or viscous phase*. Here the tissue responds to force by altering its shape and conformation, equivalent to the molding of heated plastic.

John immediately understood this equivalence. We then began to devise ways of using the plastic to help him "feel" what needed to take place in his spine and ankle. He made plastic sculptures of the injured body parts, meticulously studying and manipulating them. We also used these models to guide the therapy applied to these areas. In this "Friendly Plastic" John literally had a tangible somatic image that he could use in his healing process.

Anything can be a vehicle of healing, as this journey with John shows. John's experience with the plastic also shows the power of the traveler's healing force, even when it is expressed unconsciously in the traveler's life.

The Knife Edge of Healing

Janice came to my office initially for treatment of her right shoulder pain. After several sessions of manipulating her painful shoulder, it was clear that I was only providing her with temporary relief. She would feel better for an hour or two, sometimes even a day afterward, but ultimately the shoulder pain would return. Janice was understandably frustrated. Having already been treated by several specialists for this condition, she asked if there was anything else we could do. I suggested we try to discover if there were any underlying psychological or emotional issues related to this pain.

"I've been in psychotherapy for years," she assured me, "how will that help?"

I explained to her that many times neither psychotherapy nor body therapy alone is completely effective, but when placed together they create a powerful healing tool. She agreed to try this novel approach. With one hand under, and the other hand on top of her right shoulder I asked her to relax and focus her attention on this area. As she did, an incredible story began to unfold.

"What does the area feel like?" I queried.

"That's strange," she answered, "it feels as though there's something stuck in my shoulder, a knife—not a big knife, more like a small dagger."

When questioned further Janice managed to describe the knife's intricate details. She saw the carved handle, the embedded jewels and the shining steel blade. She also saw a hand holding it.

"Oh, no, it's Charles!" she exclaimed, "he's holding this knife in me."

Charles, it turned out, was Janice's former husband, divorced many years before. With this recognition Janice realized there were unresolved issues from that marriage that she somehow still held onto in her shoulder.

Upon closer inspection of the knife's blade she was able to make out inscriptions of the feelings which were involved. *Anger, rejection*, and *fear* were inscribed on one side of the blade. On the other side, she found the words: *love, understanding*, and *peace*. It then became apparent that it was not so much her former husband who was metaphorically stabbing her as her unresolved tensions over the relationship causing her pain. I asked Janice what we could do with this knife, and she informed me that she would really like to have it removed.

"But the feelings are real," she said, "and I'm not sure they should be removed. I just don't want them to hurt me anymore."

Next, I asked her to successively imagine that she was both sides of the blade. What would that be like? If the blade could speak to her, what would it say? While she continued this imagery, I continued to work with her shoulder—mobilizing the joint, using light traction and stimulating muscle reflex points. Ultimately we arrived at a point of resolution.

"I know what we can do," she proclaimed, "I'll form a protective sheath of these conflicting emotions. Then we can pull the knife from the sheath, leaving the feelings but removing the pain."

Janice formed a sheath of emotions and visualized the knife in that sheath. The light traction I had been using was already "pulling" at her shoulder. We now viewed this traction as symbolically representing the act of removing the knife. With the final tug we both breathed a sigh of relief. It worked. Her muscles relaxed, her range of movement increased dramatically, and her pain was gone.

Janice had to leave town shortly after this session. When I next saw her, I asked about her shoulder. She smiled and told me there had been hardly any pain at all.

"Once when I was brushing my hair I felt some pain," she recounted. "So, I quickly imagined that sheath of emotions and pulled the knife out myself. That was all I needed to do."

Janice exhibited unusual skill for a first time traveler. She was able to view her shoulder pain as conflicting emotions, yet still reach an emotional synthesis. In part, I suspect that over time, and through her previous psychotherapy she had been able to disidentify with the emotions surrounding her divorce. She recognized and acknowledged them, without feeling controlled by them. It remained for this process of disidentification and synthesis to be grounded in her body. The knife was a strong somatic component which anchored this experience. It was the device which moved the healing journey from soma to psyche—discovering the psychological dimension of Janice's physical complaint. And it was also the implement whose symbolic removal represented the healing of both the physical condition and psychological issues of the traveler.

Epilogue

From soma to psyche to center, the somatosynthesis journey proceeds. It is a healing journey that begins with the body, that touches mind, and ultimately reaches the spirit. It is a journey through which we can find meaning as well as healing in our lives; a journey that can release us from our deepest fears and reveal to us our greatest hopes; a journey of emotional expression and compassionate insight; a journey that reveals what we have been and holds out the promise of what we may yet be.

Somatosynthesis is about this intricate relationship between soma and psyche through touch. At the same time it points to a more fundamental reality beyond soma and psyche. Reich touched upon this deeper issue when he asserted that *in function* body and mind could not be separated. However we are accustomed to thinking of body and mind as separate, independently functioning elements, and only occasionally we consider the interdependence between the two. Yet viewing the body and mind as independent or interdependent is, at best, incomplete.

When a similar problem about the independence or interdependence of matter and energy arose in the history of physics, Einstein, like Reich, proposed a functional unity between the two. $E = mc^2$, Einstein's famous equation of relativity, acknowledged the unity between what were assumed to be two basic, separate and distinct aspects of reality: energy (E) and matter (m). Einstein's insight was healing. It connected what was previously thought to be separate; moreover, it showed that what was thought to be separate was never really separate at all. And it is this non-separability of reality that permeated the whole of physics after him.

In a similar way, somatosynthesis points beyond the connection of body and mind, to the inherent non-separability of the two. This distinction between connection and non-separability, while subtle, is none the less important. For it suggests that body and mind, like matter and energy, are not merely interrelated fragments, but arise from an underlying common ground of wholeness.

When we sense the need for wholeness we often attempt to discover and connect isolated fragments to make that whole. Yet we have another option available to us. We can acknowledge that our discovered connections actually point to a common ground of wholeness to begin with. In recent years, investigations in fields as diverse as physics, brain research, chemistry, biology, medicine, and psychology have converged on a similar set of views about the inherent non-separability and wholeness of life.

Beyond the body and mind, beyond emotions and thoughts, beyond matter and energy lies this domain of wholeness. It is a place of healing, for healing and wholeness are but different words (actually the *same* word, at root) for the same truth. It is also a realm of "spirit," when the meaning of that word is abstracted from its common religious interpretation. *Spirit* originally meant that which gives life, and this domain of wholeness is common ground for the diverse aspects that constitute living and being. We *can* touch this place of wholeness where body and mind, emotions and thoughts, matter and energy are given to us as one. We *can* touch this place where healing waters meet.

Appendix

Modified Body-Accessibility Questionnaire

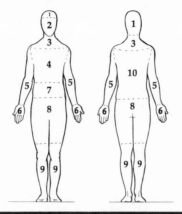

Body Area	Friend of the Same Sex		Friend of Opposite Sex	
	Touched	Been Touched	Touched	Been Touched
1. Head/forehead				
2. Face				
3. Neck/shoulders				
4. Upper Torso/chest				
5. Arms				
6. Hands				
7. Lower Torso/abdomen				
8. Thigh/buttocks				
9. Legs				
10. Back				
11. Sum of all entries in this column				
12. Average Score # on line 11 / 10				

Use the following rating codes:
1 = Never   2 = Seldom   3 = Sometimes   4 = Frequently   5 = Always

References

The following guide to sources and references is intended to assist readers in further investigating the material presented in this book. For each chapter, bibliographic information is given for sources cited in the text: related references are grouped together; additional reading is suggested where appropriate; and comments about the content of the source material are included.

CHAPTER 1. *Where Healing Waters Meet*

References on the convergence of body and mind therapies: *The Healing Mind* by Irving Oyle (Millbrae, California: Celestial Arts, 1979); *Supermind* by Barbara Brown (New York: Harper and Row, 1980); *Beyond Biofeedback* by Elmer and Alyce Green (New York: Delacorte, 1979); *Love, Medicine and Miracles* by Bernie Siegel (New York: Harper and Row, 1986). For sources on psychoneuroimmunology: *Psychoneuroimmunology*, R. Ader (ed.) (New York: Academic Press, 1981); *Foundations of Psychoneuroimmunology*, Locke, et. al (eds.) (Hawthorne, New York: Aldine Publishing Company, 1985); entire issue of *Journal of Neuroscience Research*, vol. 18, no. 1, 1986; "A Brief Tour of Psychoneuroimmunology" by D. Darko in *Annals of Allergy*, vol. 57, no.4, 1986, pp. 233-8. For the study on hypnotically influencing the immune system see, "Hypnosis and the Immune System: A Review with Implications for Cancer and the Psychology of Healing" by H.R. Hall in *Journal of Clinical Hypnosis*, vol. 25, nos. 2-3, 1983, pp. 92-103; the study on depression and immune response, "Stress and Immunomodulation: The Role of Depression and Neuroendocrine Function" by Stein, et. al., appears in the *Journal of Immunology*, vol. 135, no.1, 1985, pp. 827-33.

Candace Pert's comments were reported in *Brain/Mind Bulletin*, vol. 11, no.4, 1986. Paul Bach-y-Rita's experiments with the blind are described in his book Brain Mechanisms in Sensory Substitution (New York: Academic Press, 1972) and "Tactile Vision Substitution: Past and Present" in *International Journal of Neuroscience*, vol. 19, pp. 29-36, 1983. Similar experiments converting human speech to tactile stimulation were conducted by M.A. Clements, et. al. and reported in "Tactile Communication of Speech: Comparison of two computer-based displays" in *Journal of Rehabilitation Research and Development*, vol. 25, no. 4, 1988, pp. 25-44. For more information on the hypnagogic state see previous references to

Barbara Brown and Elmer Green; also *Mind/Body Integration: Essential Readings in Biofeedback*, E. Peper, et. al (eds.) (New York: Plenum, 1979).

Roberto Assagioli wrote very little, his two principal texts being *Psychosynthesis* (New York: Viking, 1965) and *An Act of Will* (New York: Penguin, 1976). However, two good overviews of psychosynthesis are *What We May Be* (Los Angeles: J.P. Tarcher, 1982) by Piero Ferrucci and *A Psychology with a Soul* (London: Routledge and Kegan-Paul, 1987) by Jean Hardy.

CHAPTER 2. *The Primordial Connection*

For Becker's work on regeneration in salamanders: *Electromagnetism and Life* by Robert O. Becker and Andrew A. Marino (Albany: State University of New York, 1982) gives a thorough, but somewhat technical, account of Becker's research; *The Body Electric* (New York: Morrow, 1985) by Robert O. Becker is a less technical treatment of the same material.

Ligeros A. Kleanthes cites evidence of the use of "hand curatives" in many cultures around the world in *How Ancient Healing Governs Modern Therapeutics* (New York: G. P. Putnam's Sons, 1937). For historical background on acupuncture, moxibustion, massage and pulse diagnosis: K. Chimin Wong and Wu Lien-Teh, *History of Chinese Medicine* (Tientsin: Tientsin Press, Ltd., 1932); Ralph H. Major *A History of Medicine* (Springfield, Illinois: Charles C. Thomas, 1954); Effie Poy Yew Chow, "Traditional Chinese Medicine: A Holistic System" in J. Warren Salmon (ed.), *Alternative Medicines* (New York: Tavistock Publications, 1984); *The Chinese Art of Healing* by Stephan Palos (New York: Herder and Herder, 1971). Richard Selzer recounts his experience with Yeshi Dhonden in "The Art of Surgery," *Harper's Magazine*, January 1976, p. 77-8.

On Greco-Roman healing practices: *The Healing Gods of Ancient Civilizations* by Walter Addison Jayne (New Haven: Yale University Press, 1945); *Hippocrates,,* translated by E. T. Withington (New York: G.P. Putnam's Sons, 1927); *Celsus de Medicina*, translated by W.G. Spencer (Cambridge, Mass: Harvard University Press, 1973); *Chiropractic Speaks Out* by Chester A. Wilks (Park Ridge, Illinois: Wilk Publishing, 1973) traces the origins of modern day manipulation to ancient healing practices.

For ancient Egyptian healing practices: *The Healing Hand: Man and Wound in the Ancient World* by Guido Majno (Cambridge, Mass: Harvard University Press, 1975) and Paul Ghalioungui's *Magic and Medical Science in Ancient Egypt* (Amsterdam: B.M. Israel, 1973).

Ibn Sina's (Avicenna) *Cannon of Medicine* was translated into English by O. Cameron Gruner (New York: Augustus M. Kelly, 1970). A description of *sparsha diksha* is found in *Kundalini: The Secret of Life* by Swami Muktananda (South Fallsburg, New York: SYDA Foundation, 1980). Gopi Krishna writes of his spiritual awakening in *Kundalini: The Evolutionary Energy in Man* (Boston: Shambhala, 1970).

Marc Bloch in *The Royal Touch: Sacred Monarchy and Scrofula in England and France*, translated by J.E. Anderson (London: Routledge and Kegan Paul, 1973), gives the most comprehensive account of this subject. The book was originally written in French and provides slightly more information about the use of the Royal Touch by French monarchs. C.J.S. Thompson devotes a chapter to the Royal Touch in *Magic and Healing* (New York: Rider and Co., 1973) where greater emphasis is placed on its use in England.

On seventh-sons: Bloch briefly traces the origin of the cult of the "seventh-son" through various European and some non-European cultures. In particular he sites evidence for a common origin of this practice even in Middle Eastern cultures. Most current writing on shamanism focusses exclusively on Third World cultures in Africa, Asia, Polynesia and the Americas. Little attention has been paid to the European origins of shamanism.For the etymology of the words *heal* and *disease*: Webster's Third International Dictionary (Springfield, Mass: G. C. Merriam, 1971).

Research on spiritual healer Olga Worrall has found its way into mainstream medicine as a 1979-80 display at Harvard Medical School demonstrated. Books about Worrall are *The Gift of Healing: A Personal Story of Spiritual Therapy* by Ambrose A. and Olga N. Worrall (Columbus Ohio: Ariel Press, 1985), *Explore Your Psychic World* by Ambrose A. and Olga N. Worrall (New York: Harper and Row, 1970) and *Mystic with the Healing Hands* by Edwina Cerutti (New York: Harper and Row, 1977). Reports of scientific investigation on Worrall's ability are found in two studies by Douglas Dean: "The Effects of 'Healers' on Biologically Significant Molecules," *New Horizons*, vol. 1, 1975, pp. 215-19 and "The Effects of Olga and Other Healers Upon the Infra-Red and Ultra-Violet Spectrophotometers," Ph.D. Thesis (Princeton: Princeton University, 1983); Robert N. Miller and P. B. Reinhart, "Measuring Psychic Energy," in *Psychic*, May-June, 1975; M. Justa Smith "Paranormal Effect of Enzyme Activity through Laying-on of Hands," in *Human Dimensions*, Summer, 1972; a study by the author entitled "Healer Speeds Up Self-organizing Properties" reported in *Brain/Mind Bulletin*, vol. 7, no. 3, 1982.

"High Tech/High Touch" is described in *Megatrends* by John Naisbitt (New York: Warner, 1982).

The Magic of Touch by Sherry Suib Cohen (New York: Harper and Row, 1987) contains an overview of some of the different forms of touch-based therapies in use today. For a good history of the chiropractic profession see Wilks, cited above, a history of the osteopathic profession is found in *The D.O.'s: Osteopathic Medicine in America* by Norman Gevitz (Baltimore: Johns Hopkins University Press, 1982).

A historical overview of the role of the body in psychotherapy is found in a book by Jungian analyst Deldon Anne McNeely, *Touching: Body Therapy and Depth Psychology* (Toronto: Inner City Books, 1987). See also: *The Book of the It* by Georg W. Groddeck (London: Vision Press, 1979), *Individual Psychology* by Alfred Adler (Totowa, New Jersey: Rowman and Allenheld, 1973) and *Selected Writings: An Introduction to Orgonomy* by Wilhelm Reich (New York: Farrar, Straus and Giroux, 1973).

Palmer's writing on universal and innate intelligence can be found in *Selective Writings of Daniel David Palmer* by Joseph E. Maynard (Marietta, Georgia: Maynard Institute, 1982).

CHAPTER 3. *The Bonds and Bounds of Touch*

Sidney Jourard's original article on body accessibility and his use of the Body-Accessibility Questionnaire is entitled, "An Exploratory Study of Body-Accessibility," *British Journal of Social and Clinical Psychology*, vol. 5, 1966, pp. 221-2. Related works by Jourard: "Self-Disclosure and Touching: A Study of Two Modes of Interpersonal Encounter and Their Interaction," *Journal of Humanistic Psychology*, vol. 8, 1968, pp. 39-48; *The Transparent Self: Self-Disclosure and Well-Being* (Princeton: Van Nostrand, 1964). Rosenfeld's 1976 repeat of Jourard's study is reported in "Body Accessibility Revisited." *Journal of Communication*, vol. 26, no. 3, 1976, pp. 27-30. For a related report on body accessibility see Nguyen, et. al. "The Meaning of Touch: Sex Differences," in *Journal of Communication*, vol. 25, no.3, 1975, pp. 92-103. The body accessibility questionnaire found in the appendix of this book is a modification of the one used in the Nguyen study.

The story of the physician's "white coat" was recounted by Dr. Joseph Flesia of Renaissance International, 1235 Lake Plaza Drive, Suite 130, Colorado Springs, Colorado 80906.

Studies showing that touch enhanced counseling sessions: M. Hubble, et. al., "The Effect of Counselor Touch in an Initial Counseling Session," *Journal of Counseling Psychology*, vol. 28, no. 6, 1981, pp. 533-5, and J. Pattison, "Effects of Touch on Self-exploration and the Therapeutic Relationship," *Journal of Consulting and Clinical Psychology*, vol. 40, 1973, pp. 170-5.

Montagu's classic work *Touching: The Human Significance of the Skin* (New York: Harper and Row) was originally published in 1971 and subsequently revised for publication in 1978 and 1984. The discussion of the importance of touch to the development of the fetus and newborn was essentially gathered from the first four chapters of Montagu's book. Montagu reviews Harlow's monkey experiments on terry-cloth surrogate mothers, and many other research studies on touching. Tiffany Field's study on premature infants was reported by Neala S. Schwartzberg in "That Magic Touch," *Parents Magazine*, February 1989, pp. 87-92. Lowen's comments on sexuality and mother-child bonding appear in *Touching*; also see A. Lowen, *The Betrayal of the Body* (New York: Collier Books, 1969). The latest edition of *Touching* includes an appendix on "Therapeutic Touch" in which Montagu attempts to provide a neurological basis for the effectiveness of laying-on hands healing.

The discussion on boundaries is based on Ken Wilber's *No Boundary* (Boston: Shambhala, 1981) where he describes the creation and implications of boundaries beginning with the boundary of the skin. Wilber demarcates the boundaries we draw, and the battles we then fight, at different levels of our consciousness. He also describes appropriate therapies that can assist in the resolution of self/not-self boundary disputes.

A very readable account of the history of philosophy, including sections on Aristotle and Descartes, is found in T.Z. Lavine's *From Socrates to Sartre: the Philosophic Quest* (New York: Bantam Books, 1984). This book was the basis of a PBS television series of the same name. For related works on philosophy and healing: *The Mechanic and the Gardener* by Lawrence LeShan (New York: Holt, Rinehart and Winston, 1982); Renee Weber's excellent article on the subject, "Philosophical Foundations and Frameworks for Healing," in *Revisions*, vol. 2, no. 1, 1979, pp. 68-87; Larry Dossey's *Space, Time and Medicine* (Boston: Shambhala, 1982). On the general subject of "Fragmentation and Wholeness" see David Bohm's *Wholeness and the Implicate Order* (London: Routledge and Kegan Paul, 1980).

In *The Psychological Birth of the Human Infant* (New York: Basic Books, 1975) author Margaret Mahler describes the stages of boundary-making leading to the "psychological birth of the self." For related information on the problems of faulty boundary creation see: *The Narcissistic and Borderline Disorders* (New York: Brunner/Mazel, 1978) by J. Masterson and

Borderline Conditions and Pathological Narcissism (New York: Jason Aronson, 1975) by O. Kernberg.

CHAPTER 4. *The Language of Touch*

Bekesy's experiments on the skin and his quote about palpation are reported in his book *Sensory Inhibition* (Princeton: Princeton University Press, 1967). Bekesy's work with the skin helped anchor neurophysiologist Karl Pribram's theory of the "Holographic Brain," see *Languages of the Brain: Experimental Paradoxes and Principles in Neuropsychology* by Pribram (Englewood Cliff, New Jersey: Prentice-Hall, 1971).

Toftness has published very little on his work in monitoring human microwave fields, but see "New Device Detects Microwave Emissions in Biological Systems" in *Brain/Mind Bulletin*, vol. 7, no. 3, 1982; "New Technologies Detect Effects of Healing Hands" in *Brain/Mind Bulletin*, vol. 10, no. 16, 1985; and "Spine Thermography at Millimeter Wavelengths" by J. Edrich and I.N. Toftness in *Digest of Chiropractic Economics*, vol. 19, no. 2, 1976.

Research on Therapeutic Touch is reported in Dolores Krieger's books, *The Therapeutic Touch: Using Your Hands to Help or to Heal* (Englewood Cliffs, New Jersey: Prentice-Hall, 1979) and *Living the Therapeutic Touch* (New York: Dodd, Mead, 1987).

On the Einsteinian revolution in physics: Ken Wilber in *The Spectrum of Consciousness* (Wheaton, Illinois: Quest, 1977) reviews the revolution in physics from Newton to Einstein. The quotes from Schroedinger and Eddington were found here; two by Fritjof Capra, *The Tao of Physics* (Boulder: Shambala, 1975; New York: Bantam, 1977) and *The Turning Point* (New York: Simon and Schuster, 1982); *The Dancing Wu Li Masters: An Introduction to the New Physics* (New York: Bantam, 1980) by Gary Zukav; *God and the New Physics* (Simon and Schuster, 1983) by Paul Davies.

Psychology and perception: "Single Units and Sensation: A Neuron Doctrine for Perceptual Psychology?" by Horace B. Barlow in *Perception*, vol. 1, 1972, pp. 371-394 lays the foundation of the orthodox theory of perception along with *The Organization of Behavior* (New York: Wiley & Sons, 1949) by Donald O. Hebb. On Lashley: *The Neuropsychology of Lashley: Selected Papers of K.S. Lashley* edited by Frank A. Beach, Donald O. Hebb, Clifford T. Morgan and Henry W. Nissen (New York: McGraw-Hill, 1960), the introduction by Edwin G. Boring gives a comprehensive view of the significance of Lashley's work to neuroscience; *Neuropsychology After Lashley* (Hillsdale, New Jersey: Lawrence Erlbaum, 1982) edited by Jack Orbach.

On Pribram and the Holographic Hypothesis: "A New Perspective on Reality" in *Brain/Mind Bulletin*, vol. 2, no. 26, 1977 and "Holographic Memory" an interview with Karl Pribram in *Psychology Today*, February 1979 are two non-technical overviews; material in this chapter also comes from a tape of Pribram's presentation at the conference "Coevolution of Science and Spirit" October 13-14, 1979 (New Lebanon, New York: Sufi Order, 1979); *Shufflebrain* by Paul Pietsch (Boston: Houghton Mifflin, 1981) presents a skeptical scientist's view of Pribram's theory and the surprising results of his own experimentation to disprove holographic brain function. Other works by Pribram are *Languages of the Brain: Experimental Paradoxes and Principles in Neuropsychology* (Englewood Cliff, New Jersey: Prentice-Hall, 1971); "How is it that sensing so much we can do so little?" in *The Neurosciences Third Study Program* edited by F.O. Schmitt and F.G. Worden (Cambridge, Mass: MIT Press, 1974); "The Holographic Hypothesis of Memory Structure in Brain Function and Perception" in *Contemporary Developments in Mathematical Psychology* edited by R.C. Atkinson, et. al. (San Francisco: Freeman, 1974); "Localization and Distribution of Function in the Brain" in *Neuropsychology After Lashley*, cited above.

Chung-Ha Suh's remarks were taken from an untitled interview, published by Renaissance International, 1235 Lake Plaza Drive, Suite 130, Colorado Springs, Colorado 80906. H.B. Logan's work on the use of minimal force in spinal manipulation can be found in *Textbook of Logan Basic Methods*, eds. V. F. Logan and F. M. Murray (Chesterfield, Missouri: LBM, Inc., 1981).

For additional material on "cross-restrictions" and "unwinding" see Upledger and Vredevoogd, *Craniosacral Therapy* (Seattle: Eastland Press, 1983). Also see Wilhelm Reich, *The Function of the Orgasm* (New York: Farrar, Straus and Giroux, 1973); M.B. DeJarnette, *Sacro Occipital Technic Manual* (Nebraska City, Nebraska: SORSI, 1984). On learning to diagnose and treat the human energy field, see *Hands of Light* by Barbara Brennan (New York: Bantam Books, 1988) which is a workbook for clinicians.

The Arndt-Schulz Law is defined in any standard medical dictionary, for example *Stedman's Medical Dictionary* (Baltimore: Williams and Wilkins, 1976).

CHAPTER 5. *The Journey Beyond the Body*

Information on psychotherapist Milton Erickson's use of touch, in the form of a handshake, to facilitate trance states is found in *Therapeutic Trances: The Cooperation Principle in Ericksonian Hypnotherapy* by Steven

Gilligan (New York: Brunner/Mazel, 1987). Gendlin wrote *Focusing* (New York: Bantam Books, 1981). Related brain wave experiments were reported in "EEG Patterns Distinctive During Feelings of Insight, 'Mental Block" In *Brain/Mind Bulletin*, vol. 2, no. 13, 1978.

A book about ordinary experience causing altered states of consciousness in athletes is *Sweet Spot in Time* by John Jerome (New York: Avon, 1982). Other sources on altered state of consciousness: three by Stanislav Grof, *Realms of the Human Unconscious* (New York: Viking Press, 1975), *Beyond Death: The Gates of Consciousness* (London: Thames and Hudson, 1980) and *The Adventure of Self-Discovery* (Albany, New York: SUNY Press, 1988); *Altered States of Consciousness*, edited by Charles Tart (New York: Wiley, 1969).

The 1977 experiment demonstrating synchronous electrophysiological changes between therapist and client was conducted by C. Norman Shealy and Elmer Green utilizing spiritual healer Olga Worrall (Springfield, Missouri: Worrall Institute of Spiritual Healing, unpublished paper).

Sources on Shamanism include the classic work by Mircea Eliade, *Shamanism: Archaic Techniques of Ecstasy* (Princeton: Princeton University Press, 1972), *The Way of the Shaman* by Michael Harner (San Francisco: Harper and Row, 1980), Shamanic Voices: A Survey of Visionary Narratives by Joan Halifax (New York: E. P. Dutton, 1979), *Shamanism: An Expanded View of Reality*, compiled by Shirley Nicholson (Wheaton, Illinois: Theosophical Publishing House, 1987), *Up From Eden* by Ken Wilber (Garden City, New York: Anchor Press/Doubleday, 1981).

References on the use of imagery in healing: *Getting Well Again* by Carl O. Simonton, et. al. (Los Angeles: J. P. Tarcher, 1978), *Imagery in Healing: Shamanism and Modern Medicine* by Jeanne Achterberg (Boston: Shambhala, 1985), *Imagery and Disease* by Jeanne Achterberg and G. Frank Lawlis (Champaign, Illinois: Institute for Personality and Ability Testing, 1984), *Minding the Body, Mending the Mind* by Joan Borysenko (Reading, Massachusetts: Addison-Wesley, 1987).

The term *not-yet-conscious* comes from Steven Schatz (Santa Rosa, California: unpublished, undated manuscript). The table of names for the "life force" was found in *The Research Reporter* published by the Holmes Center for Research in Holistic Healing, Los Angeles, vol. 3, no.4, 1979. For further reading on subpersonalities see the works of Assagioli and psychosynthesis cited in chapter 1.

CHAPTER 6. *The Journey Beyond the Body and Mind*

The excerpt from T.S. Eliot's "Burnt Norton" in *T.S. Eliot: The Complete Poems and Plays 1909-1950* (New York: Harcourt, Brace and World, 1971). As a general introduction to transpersonal psychology, Ken Wilber's writings are recommended: *No Boundary* (see reference under chapter 3), *Spectrum of Consciousness* (Wheaton, Illinois: Quest, 1977), *The Atman Project* (New York: Anchor, and *Up From Eden* (New York: Doubleday, 1981). Einstein's quotes on mysticism is from Wilber's book, *Quantum Questions: Mystical Writings of the Great Physicists* (Boston: Shambhala, 1984).

To balance Wilber's account of transpersonal psychology see Michael Washburn's *The Ego and the Dynamic Ground* (Albany, New York: SUNY Press, 1988) which explicitly challenges Wilber's main assertions and presents an alternative view of transpersonal theory.

Also on transpersonal psychology see: *Transpersonal Psychologies* edited by Charles Tart (New York: Harper and Row, 1975); Assagioli's writings referenced in Chapter 1; Carl Jung's writings such as *Symbols of Transformation*, translated by R.F.C. Hull, vol. 5 of *The Collected Works of C.G. Jung* (Princeton: Princeton University Press, 1967); three books by Abraham Maslow, *Toward a Psychology of Being* (New York: D. Van Nostrand, 1968), *Religions, Values and Peak-Experiences* (New York: Viking Press, 1970) and *The Farther Reaches of Human Nature* (New York: Viking Press, 1971).

The exercise "Rediscovering Your Transpersonal Self" was adapted from three sources: Roberto Assagioli's *Psychosynthesis* (see reference above) pp. 116-19, Ken Wilber's *No Boundary* (see reference above) pp. 128-29, and *Beyond Words* by Swami Satchidananda (New York: Holt, Rinehart and Winston, 1977) pp. 85-6.

Bibliography

Achterberg, J. *Imagery in Healing: Shamanism and Modern Medicine*. Boston: Shambhala, 1985.

———and Lawlis, F.G. *Imagery and Disease*. Champaign, Illinois: Institute for Personality and Ability Testing, 1984.

Ader, R. (ed.) *Psychoneuroimmunology*. New York: Academic Press, 1981.

Alder, A. *Individual Psychology*. Totowa, New Jersey: Rowman and Allenheld, 1973.

Assagioli, R. *An Act of Will*. New York: Penguin, 1976.

———. *Psychosynthesis*. New York: Viking, 1965.

Avicenna. *Cannon of Medicine*. O. Cameron Gruner (trans.) New York: Augustus M. Kelly, 1970.

Bach-y-Rita, P. *Brain Mechanisms in Sensory Substitution*. New York: Academic Press, 1972.

———. "Tactile Vision Substitution: Past and Present." *International Journal of Neuroscience*, vol. 19, 1983.

Barlow, H.B. "Single Units and Sensation: A Neuron Doctrine for Perceptual Psychology?" *Perception*, vol. 1, 1972.

Beach, F.A. et. al. (eds.) *The Neuropsychology of Lashley: Selected Papers of K.S. Lashley*. New York: McGraw-Hill, 1960.

Becker, R.O. *The Body Electric*. New York: Morrow, 1985.

———and Marino, A. *Electromagnetism and Life*. Albany: State University of New York, 1982.

Bekesy, G. *Sensory Inhibition*. Princeton: Princeton University Press, 1967.

Bloch, M. *The Royal Touch: Sacred Monarchy and Scrofula in England and France*. J.E. Anderson (trans.) London: Routledge and Kegan-Paul, 1973.

Bohm, D. *Wholeness and the Implicate Order*. London: Routledge and Kegan-Paul, 1980.

———. "The Enfolding-Unfolding Universe: A Conversation with David Bohm." *Revision*, vol. 1, nos. 3 & 4, 1978.

———. "The Physicist and the Mystic—Is a Dialogue between them Possible?" *Revision*, vol. 4, no. 1, 1981.

Borysenko, J. *Minding the Body, Mending the Mind*. Reading, Massachusetts: Addison-Wesley, 1987.

Brennan, B. *Hands of Light*. New York: Bantam Books, 1988.

Brown, B. *Supermind*. New York: Harper and Row, 1980.

Capra, F. *The Tao of Physics*. Boulder: Shambala, 1975.

———. *The Turning Point*. New York: Simon and Schuster, 1982.

Cerutti, E. *Mystic with the Healing Hands*. New York: Harper and Row, 1977.

Clements, M.A., et. al. "Tactile Communication of Speech: Comparison of Two computer-based Displays." *Journal of Rehabilitation Research and Development*,vol. 25, no. 4, 1988.

Cohen, S.S. *The Magic of Touch*. New York: Harper and Row, 1987.

Darko, D. "A Brief Tour of Psychoneuroimmunology." *Annals of Allergy*, vol. 57, no.4, 1986.

Davies, P. *God and the New Physics*. New York: Simon and Schuster, 1983.

Dean, D. "The Effects of 'Healers' on Biologically Significant Molecules." *New Horizons* vol. 1, 1975.

————. "The Effects of Olga and Other Healers Upon the Infra-Red and Ultra-Violet Spectrophotometers," Ph.D. Thesis. Princeton: Princeton University, 1983.

DeJarnette, M.B. *Sacro Occipital Technic Manual*. Nebraska City, Nebraska: SORSI, 1984.

Dossey, L. *Space, Time and Medicine*. Boston: Shambhala, 1981.

Edrich, J. and Toftness, I.N. "Spine Thermography at Millimeter Wavelengths." *Digest of Chiropractic Economics*, vol. 19, no. 2, 1976.

Eliade, M. *Shamanism: Archaic Techniques of Ecstasy*. Princeton: Princeton University Press, 1972.

Ferguson, M. *Aquarian Conspiracy*. Los Angeles: J.P. Tarcher, 1980.

————. (publisher) *Brain/Mind Bulletin*. Los Angeles.

Ferrucci, P. *What We May Be*. Los Angeles: J.P. Tarcher, 1982.

Gendlin, E. *Focusing*. New York: Bantam Books, 1981.

Gevitz, N. *The D.O.'s: Osteopathic Medicine in America*. Baltimore: Johns Hopkins University Press, 1982.

Ghalioungui, P. *Magic and Medical Science in Ancient Egypt*. Amsterdam: B.M. Israel, 1973.

Gilligan, S. *Therapeutic Trances: The Cooperation Principle in Ericksonian Hypnotherapy*. New York: Brunner/Mazel, 1987.

Green, E. and A. *Beyond Biofeedback*. New York: Delacorte, 1979.

Groddeck, G. *The Book of the It*. London: Vision Press, 1979.

Grof, S. *Realms of the Human Unconscious*. New York: Viking Press, 1975.

————. *Beyond Death: The Gates of Consciousness*. London: Thames & Hudson, 1980.

————. *The Adventure of Self-Discovery*. Albany, New York: SUNY Press, 1988.

Halifax, J. *Shamanic Voices: A Survey of Visionary Narratives*. New York: E. P. Dutton, 1979.,

Hall, H.R. "Hypnosis and the Immune System: A Review with Implications for Cancer and the Psychology of Healing." *Journal of Clinical Hypnosis*, vol. 25, nos. 2-3, 1983.

Hardy, J. *A Psychology with a Soul*. London: Routledge & Kegan-Paul, 1987.

Harner, M. *The Way of the Shaman*. San Francisco: Harper and Row, 1980.

Hebb, D.O. *The Organization of Behavior*. New York: Wiley & Sons, 1949.

Hubble, M., et. al. "The Effect of Counselor Touch in an Initial Counseling Session." *Journal of Counseling Psychology*, vol. 28, no. 6, 1981.

Jayne, W.A. *The Healing Gods of Ancient Civilizations*. New Haven: Yale University Press, 1945.

Jerome, J. *Sweet Spot in Time*. New York: Avon, 1982.

Jourard, S. *The Transparent Self: Self-Disclosure and Well-Being*. Princeton: Van Nostrand, 1964.

———. "An Exploratory Study of Body-Accessibility." *British Journal of Social and Clinical Psychology*, vol 5, 1966.

———. "Self-Disclosure and Touching: A Study of Two Modes of Interpersonal Encounter and Their Interaction," *Journal of Humanistic Psychology*, vol. 8, 1968.

Journal of Neuroscience Research, vol. 18, no. 1, 1986.

Jung, C.G. *Symbols of Transformation*. R.F.C. Hull (trans.), vol. 5 of *The Collected Works of C.G. Jung*. Princeton: Princeton University Press, 1967.

Kernberg, O. *Borderline Conditions and Pathological Narcissism*. New York: Jason Aronson, 1976.

Kleanthes, L.A. *How Ancient Healing Governs Modern Therapeutics*. New York: G. P. Putnam's Sons, 1937.

Krieger, D. *The Therapeutic Touch: Using Your Hands to Help or to Heal*. Englewood Cliffs, New Jersey: Prentice-Hall, 1979.

———. *Living the Therapeutic Touch*. New York: Dodd, Mead: 1987.

Krishna, G. *Kundalini: The Evolutionary Energy in Man*. Boston: Shambhala, 1970.

Lavine, T.Z. *From Socrates to Sartre: the Philosophic Quest*. New York: Bantam Books, 1984.

LeShan, L. *The Mechanic and the Gardener*. New York: Holt, Rinehart and Winston, 1982.

Locke, S. et. al. (eds.) *Foundations of Psychoneuroimmunology*. Hawthorne, New York: Aldine Publishing Company, 1985.

Logan, V.F. and Murray, F.M. (eds.) *Textbook of Logan Basic Methods*. Chesterfield, Missouri: LBM, Inc., 1981.

Lowen, A. *The Betrayal of the Body*. New York: Collier Books, 1969.

Mahler, M., Pine,F., and Bergan, A. *The Psychological Birth of the Human Infant*. New York: Basic Books, 1975.

Majno, G. *The Healing Hand: Man and Wound in the Ancient World*. Cambridge, Mass.: Harvard University Press, 1975.

Major, R.H. *A History of Medicine*. Springfield, Illinois: Charles C. Thomas, 1954.

Maslow, A. *Toward a Psychology of Being*. New York: D. Van Nostrand, 1968.

———. *Religions, Values and Peak-Experiences*. New York: Viking Press, 1970.

———. *The Farther Reaches of Human Nature*. New York: Viking Press, 1971.

Masterson, J. *The Narcissistic and Borderline Disorders.* New York: Brunner/Mazel, 1981.

Maynard, J. *Selective Writings of Daniel David Palmer.* Marietta, Georgia: Maynard Institute, 1982.

McNeely, D.A. *Touching: Body Therapy and Depth Psychology.* Toronto: Inner City Books, 1987.

Miller, R.N. and Reinhart, P.B. "Measuring psychic energy." *Psychic,* May-June, 1975.

Montagu, A. *Touching: The Human Significance of the Skin.* New York: Harper and Row, 1984.

Muktananda, S. *Kundalini: The Secret of Life.* South Fallsburg, New York: SYDA Foundation, 1980.

Naisbitt, J. *Megatrends.* New York: Warner, 1982.

Nguyen, T. et. al. "The Meaning of Touch: Sex Differences." *Journal of Communication,* vol. 25, no.3, 1975.

Nicholoson, S. (ed.) *Shamanism: An Expanded View of Reality.* Illinois: Theosophical Publishing House, 1987.

Orbach, J. (ed.) *Neuropsychology After Lashley.* Hillsdale, New Jersey: Lawrence Erlbaum, 1982.

Oyle, I. *The Healing Mind.* Millbrae, California: Celestial Arts, 1979.

Palos, S. *The Chinese Art of Healing.* New York: Herder and Herder, 1971.

Pattison, J. "Effects of Touch on Self-exploration and the Therapeutic Relationship." *Journal of Consulting and Clinical Psychology,* vol. 40, 1973.

Peper, E., et. al. (eds.) *Mind/Body Integration: Essential Readings in Biofeedback.* New York: Plenum, 1979.

Pietsch, P. *Shufflebrain.* Boston: Houghton Mifflin, 1981.

Pribram, K.H. *Languages of the Brain: Experimental Paradoxes and Principles in Neuropsychology.* Englewood Cliff, New Jersey: Prentice-Hall, 1971.

————. "How Is It That Sensing So Much We Can Do So Little?" *The Neurosciences Third Study Program.* Cambridge, Mass: MIT Press, 1974.

————. "A New Perspective on Reality." *Brain/Mind Bulletin,* vol. 2, no. 16, 1977.

————. "Holographic Memory." *Psychology Today,* February 1979.

Reich, W. *Selected Writings: An Introduction to Orgonomy.* New York: Farrar, Straus and Giroux, 1973.

————. *The Function of the Orgasm.* New York: Farrar, Straus and Giroux, 1973.

Rosenfeld, L. "Body Accessibility Revisited." *Journal of Communication,* vol. 26, no. 3, 1976.

Salmon, J.W. (ed.) "Traditional Chinese Medicine: A Holistic System." *Alternative Medicines.* New York: Tavistock Publications, 1984.

Satchidananda, S. *Beyond Words.* New York: Holt, Rinehart and Winston, 1977.

Selzer, R. "The Art of Surgery." *Harper's Magazine.* January 1976.

Siegel, B. *Love, Medicine and Miracles*. New York: Harper and Row, 1986.

Simonton, C.O. and S.M. *Getting Well Again*. Los Angeles: J. P. Tarcher, 1978.

Smith, M.J. "Paranormal Effect of Enzyme Activity through Laying-on of Hands." *Human Dimensions* Summer, 1972.

Spencer, W.G. (trans.) *Celsus de Medicina*. Cambridge, Mass: Harvard University Press, 1973.

Stein, M., et. al. "Stress and Immunomodulation: The Role of Depression and Neuroendocrine Function." *Journal of Immunology*, vol. 135, no.1, 1985.

Tart, C. (ed.) *Transpersonal Psychologies*. New York: Harper and Row, 1975.

———. (ed.) *Altered States of Consciousness*. New York: Wiley, 1969.

Thompson, C.J.S. *Magic and Healing*. New York: Rider and Co., 1973.

Upledger, J.E. and Vredevoogd, J. *Craniosacral Therapy*. Seattle: Eastland Press, 1983.

Washburn, M. *The Ego and the Dynamic Ground*. Albany, New York: SUNY Press, 1988.

Weber, R. "Philosophical Foundations and Frameworks for Healing." *Revisions*, vol. 2, no. 2, 1979.

Withington, E.T. (trans.) *Hippocrates*. New York: G.P. Putnam's Sons, 1927.

Wilber, K. *Spectrum of Consciousness*. Wheaton, Illinois: Quest, 1977.

———. *The Atman Project*. New York: Anchor, 1980.

———. *No Boundary*. Boston: Shambhala, 1981.

———. *Up From Eden*. New York: Doubleday, 1981.

———. *Quantum Questions: Mystical Writings of the Great Physicists*. Boston: Shambhala, 1984.

Wilks, C. *Chiropractic Speaks Out*. Park Ridge, Illinois: Wilk Publishing, 1973.

Wong, K.C. and Lien-Teh, W. *History of Chinese Medicine*. Tientsin: Tientsin Press, Ltd., 1932.

Worrall, A.A. and O.N. *Explore Your Psychic World*. New York: Harper and Row, 1970.

———. *The Gift of Healing: A Personal Story of Spiritual Therapy*. Columbus Ohio: Ariel Press, 1985.

Zukav, G. *The Dancing Wu Li Masters*. New York: Bantam, 1980.

Index

Actherberg, J. 9
acupuncture 35, 36, 39, 52, 53
Adler, A. 54-56
Africa 49, 61, 77, 78, 171
AIDS 9, 70, 75
allergies 178
altered states of consciousness
    (ASC) 128-130, 141, 175
    touch-induced (TASC) 128,
    129, 141, 143, 174, 175, 188,
    191
amoeba 27, 28, 34
Arndt-Schultz Law 120
Assagioli, R. 14, 155
Avicenna (Ibn Sina) 39, 53

Bach-y-Rita, P. 22, 89
back pain 1, 2, 5-7, 93, 108, 110,
    132, 161, 172, 184, 190, 193,
    194, 195
Becker, R.O. 29-32
Beckett, W. 45, 46, 49
Bekesy, G. 90-93, 9
bioenergetics 55
biofeedback 9, 178
birth 11, 12, 18, 22, 25, 32, 52,
    59, 67, 69-72, 74, 163, 173
body accessibility
    questionnaire 62, 140
body maps 138, 140, 143
Bohm, D. 99, 100
brain waves 13, 128, 129

cancer 9, 75
Catholic Church 43-45
character armoring 55
chest pain 144
China 35, 47, 49, 171

chinese medicine 35
chiropractic 8, 11, 52, 53, 56, 57,
    88, 89, 106, 171
Christianity 43, 164
Craniosacral Therapy 114
cross-restrictions 107, 108, 110,
    112, 113, 115, 119, 135
curaceptive reflex 34

dance 11, 86, 89, 115, 130, 153,
    168, 180
DeJarnette, M.B. 114
depression 10, 11, 57, 92
Descartes, R. 45, 76, 78, 79
diaphragms (also see
    cross-restrictions) 108,
    110-113, 115
    occipital base 113-115
    pelvic diaphragm 110
    respiratory diaphragm 110,
    111, 115
    thoracic outlet 112, 113, 115
    urogenital diaphragm 108
disidentification 155, 156, 160,
    166, 199

Eccles, J. 102
Edrich, J. 94, 95
Egypt 40, 47, 49, 64, 171
Egyptian gods
    Horus 40
    Isis 40
    Osiris 40
Egyptian medical papyri 40
    Berlin 40
    Smith 40
Einstein, A. 99, 100, 102, 163,
    164, 201

electromagnetic fields   30, 31,
    53, 93, 95, 96
emotional point   20
emotions   16, 20, 22, 84, 113,
    121, 138, 163, 170, 173, 183
Erickson, M.   175
Europe   42, 45-47, 49, 171

Freud, S.   12, 54-56, 76

Galen   39, 171
Gendlin, E.   128
gestalt   163
Greatrakes, V.   46
Greece   37, 38, 47, 49
Greek Gods
    Aesculapius   37-39
    Apollo   37, 38, 94
    Coronis   37
    Hygeia   37, 38
    Panacea   37, 38
Green, E.   118, 119, 128
Groddeck, G.   54-56

headaches   34, 35, 46, 113, 115,
    132, 144, 146, 156, 159, 169,
    184
hearing   21, 22, 90, 101
Hippocrates   38, 39, 53, 170, 171
holograms   77, 102-104
hospice   181-183
Hubble, M.   66
human brain   18, 21-23, 34, 56,
    66-68, 70, 101-104, 106,
    112-115, 201
hypnagogic state   13
hypnosis   10, 134, 178, 179, 181

imagery (types)
    birthing process   173
    cave   7, 8, 134, 168
    center of the maze   195, 196

core with many layers   156
electrical circuit   147
friendly plastic   197, 198
inner healer in a bikini   190,
    191
knife   19, 25, 133, 146,
    181-183, 185, 198, 199
mountains   26, 144-146, 152,
    167, 168, 174, 176, 187, 188
oarsman in a boat   194
ocean   6, 134, 161-163, 167,
    174
river   84, 134, 143, 147, 161,
    162, 167, 174
straight jacket   24, 25
strings of a guitar   132, 147
wolf   134
immune system   9-11, 22, 23, 75,
    76, 178
auto-immune disease   178,
    181
India   47, 49
innate intelligence   56, 125, 154
inner wisdom of traveler and
    guide   81, 125, 126, 128,
    135, 142, 154, 184, 193
intervention
    by the guide   21, 43, 115, 120,
        135, 137, 138, 141-146, 150,
        151, 167, 170, 174, 179, 186,
        188
    content-oriented   137, 138,
        150
    process-oriented   137, 138,
        142, 143, 150
    purpose-oriented   137, 138,
        145
    tactile   115, 120, 135, 137, 151,
        186
    verbal   137, 138, 151, 170, 188

Jesus 40, 43, 48, 49
Jourard, S. 60, 62, 64

King Olaf 42
King's evil (scrofula) 42, 45
Krieger, D. 96, 98, 105
Krishna, G. 48

Lashley, K. 102, 103
laying-on hands 38, 40, 46-48,
 50-52
 saludors 46, 47
 septennaires 46, 47
 seventh-daughter 46
 seventh-son 46, 47
 St. Marcoul, patron saint of
  47
 the healer of Vovette 47
life force 171
limb regeneration 29, 30
 in salamanders 29
Logan, H.B. 106, 107
Lowen, A. 55, 72, 73

Macbeth 42
malpractice 2
manipulation 2, 6, 7, 39, 52, 53,
 65, 72-74, 95, 106, 190
massage 2, 11, 34-36, 38-40, 52,
 53, 55, 70, 116
mental imagery 2, 9, 23, 24
modern medicine 35-37, 45, 50,
 65, 79, 105, 130
Montagu, A. 61, 67, 69-71
moxibustion 35, 36
muscular armoring 55, 115

Naisbitt, J. 52
NASA 94
neck pain 51, 81, 156, 159, 160,
 169, 187
Newton, I. 45

nociceptive reflex 32, 34
nutrition 178

osteopathy 11, 52, 53

Palmer, D.D. 53, 56, 57
palpation 88, 89, 93, 95-98, 105,
 107, 126, 132, 133
 and sensory projection 92, 93
Pattison, J. 66
perception 2, 21, 22, 24, 73, 90,
 92, 93, 98, 101-105, 128
Pert, C. 22
physics 73, 99, 102, 104, 201
Pribram, K.H. 98, 102-104
psauoscopy, definition of word
 95
psyche 2, 3, 5, 8, 9, 14, 28, 32,
 54, 56, 57, 59, 79, 121, 122,
 123-126, 130, 131, 134, 135,
 137, 140, 143, 144, 149, 150,
 152, 153, 162, 166, 168, 170,
 179, 181, 186, 190, 192, 199,
 201
psychoanalysis 14, 54
psychology 2, 11, 54, 102, 104,
 202
psychoneuroimmunology 9
psychosomatic 3, 9, 13
psychosynthesis 14
psychotherapy 2, 5, 9, 12, 14,
 21, 25, 54, 55, 80, 122, 128,
 133, 134, 135, 161, 167, 169,
 173, 175, 178, 179, 181, 185,
 198, 199
pulse diagnosis 35, 36

reflex stimulation 2, 6, 39, 116
regeneration 29-32
 dedifferentiation 30, 31
 redifferentiation 30
Reich, W. 54-56, 115, 171, 201

relaxation 2, 4-8, 13, 15-17, 19,
    20, 24, 81-83, 85, 118, 124,
    126-128, 130, 132, 133, 141,
    144, 148, 150, 154, 157, 164,
    165, 167, 172, 174, 179, 184,
    187, 188, 189, 191, 197, 198
  and inner focussing 128, 132,
    141, 144, 150, 172
Roman emperors
  Adrian 42
  Vespasian 41, 50, 51
Rome 44, 47, 49
Rosenfeld, L. 62
royal touch 41-47, 50, 51
  Charles I 44
  Charles II 43, 44, 46, 51
  Charles X 45
  Edward IV 43, 44
  Edward the Confessor 42
  Elizabeth I 44
  Henry VI 43
  Mary Tudor 44
  Oliver Cromwell 44
  Queen Anne 50
  Robert the Pious 42
  William III 50

Sacro-Occipital Technique
    (S.O.T.) 114
Schroedinger, E. 100
Scrofula (the King's evil) 42-47
sexual abuse 2, 57, 158, 159,
    178, 179
Shakespeare, W. 42, 43
shaktipat diksha 48
shamanism 47, 96, 130, 131
Shealy, N. 128
sight 4, 12, 21, 29, 54, 72, 89,
    101, 102, 125, 126, 131, 133,
    153, 187, 191
Simonton, C.O. 9

smell 11, 18, 29, 67, 99, 101
soma 9, 14, 28, 59, 79, 121,
    123-126, 131, 143, 150, 152,
    166, 170, 179, 186, 190, 199,
    201
somatic imagery 24, 25, 89, 132,
    135, 143, 152, 179
  and automobile accident 19,
    21
  and colors 118, 138, 163
  imagery 144, 162
somatic memory 17-19, 22,
    25
somatic recall 22, 25
somatic therapy 2, 9, 11-13, 53,
    55-57, 88, 96, 105, 107, 115,
    116, 130, 135, 179
somatosensory system 21, 22
somatosynthesis 14, 17-19,
    21-27, 57, 80, 88, 98,
    105-107, 115, 117, 119-131,
    135-138, 140, 143, 146, 147,
    148-150, 152-155, 161-163,
    166, 169, 173-177, 184, 186,
    187, 191, 193, 195, 197, 201
  grounding the journey 54,
    174, 176
  open focus of guide 125, 126
  road map 122, 126
  the center 74, 83, 113, 124,
    127, 128, 152, 154, 160, 162,
    166, 167, 184, 186, 195, 196
  the guide 25, 26, 88-90, 93,
    95, 98, 105, 107, 115, 116,
    119, 120-129, 131, 132,
    135-138, 140, 141, 143, 144,
    146, 147, 150, 152, 154, 166,
    167, 169, 174, 175, 176, 177,
    183, 188, 193, 195, 198

the healing journey 7, 26, 32,
    43, 80, 82-84, 87, 88, 105,
    116, 120-132, 135-138, 140,
    143, 145-148, 150, 151,
    152-154, 160-163, 166-169,
    173-177, 179, 182, 183,
    186-190, 193, 195, 196, 198,
    199, 201
the journey from psyche to
    center 124-126, 152, 166,
    186, 190, 201
the journey from soma to
    psyche 123, 125, 126, 131,
    150, 152, 166, 170, 179, 186,
    190, 199, 201
the traveler 25, 26, 86, 88, 89,
    93, 95, 98, 105, 107, 108,
    110-112, 115-117, 119-129,
    132-138, 140-143, 146-154,
    156, 157, 160-162, 166-170,
    172, 173, 174-177, 184,
    186-190, 192-196, 198, 199
sound 11, 12, 19, 21, 22, 29, 54,
    56, 72, 90, 92, 94, 137
South Pacific 49
spinal misalignment 39
spine 6, 7, 17, 39, 48, 53, 57, 82,
    84, 85, 88, 93, 94, 105, 106,
    107, 108, 110-112, 114, 115,
    132, 134, 147, 187, 189, 197
still point 153, 162
subluxation 56
subpersonalities 148-152,
    156-158, 160, 166, 167, 176,
    179, 189, 190
surgery 35, 43, 117, 197
symbols 72, 134, 135, 187, 190,
    195
synesthesia 22

tactility 61

temple-sleep 38
therapeutic techniques
    image/counter-image
        146-148, 151, 187
    joint mobilization 115, 179
    modulation of human energy
        field 53, 106, 119
    occipital base release 85, 144,
        145
    soft tissue release 19-21, 25,
        83, 108, 110-113, 115, 135
    sustained pressure 116, 119
    therapeutic use of touch 96,
        105, 107, 117, 119, 153
    unfolding journey 143
    unwinding 25, 115, 116, 119,
        135, 147
    working with an inner
        healer 170, 172, 173, 176,
        190, 191, 192, 193
Therapeutic Touch 96, 105, 107,
    117, 119, 153
thigmotropism 27, 28
Tibet 49
Toftness, I.N. 93-96, 98
touch 1-3, 5-8, 11-18, 20-23,
    25-54, 56, 57, 59-77, 79-82,
    85, 86-90, 92, 93, 95-101,
    103-107, 112, 114, 117, 119,
    120-123, 126, 128-132,
    135-138, 141, 143, 150, 152,
    153, 154, 159, 160, 163, 165,
    170, 172, 175, 176, 183, 184,
    189, 192, 193, 196, 201, 202
    and animal development 67,
        68
    and biblical references 49
    and breast-feeding 68, 70
    and death/dying 32, 59, 68,
        71, 134, 144, 157, 179-184

and electromagnetic fields 31
and emotional development
71
and emotions 2, 16, 110, 120,
170, 174, 198
and fragmentation 79
and healing 48, 49
and human development 12,
32, 67-71
and human energy field 96,
98, 105-107, 117-119, 129,
132, 134, 135, 172, 179, 188
and human microwave field
94, 95, 108
and limb regeneration 31
and out-of-body experiences
2, 8, 48, 130, 131
and pain 1, 2, 5-8, 13, 15-17,
19-21, 24, 25, 28, 32, 34, 35,
39, 51, 54, 81, 82, 84, 87, 93,
97, 105, 106, 108, 110, 116,
119, 122, 124, 132, 134, 137,
138, 140, 144-147, 149-156,
158-161, 163-166, 169, 172,
173, 174, 178, 184-187, 189,
190, 192-196, 198, 199
and psychological issues 8,
21, 25, 55, 108, 110, 116,
117, 123, 138, 140, 141, 143,
148, 149, 152, 154, 161, 167,
169, 178, 184, 199
and sexuality 46, 59, 60, 62,
72, 73, 110
and spiritual issues 2, 90,
138, 140
and therapeutic rapport 12
as a reciprocal sense 12, 25,
68

language of 81, 136
touch boundaries 59, 60, 64,
71-76, 78-80, 90, 129, 194
absence of in mammy
lorries 77, 78
adolescent game of Trust
me? 59
boundary-making 73, 75, 76,
80
mind-body split 11, 74
riding a subway 4, 77, 78
self/not-self boundary
73-76, 78-80, 92
subjectivism 76, 77
touch taboo
doctor's white coat 51, 65
loss of objectivity 66
touch-piece 43
touchability 61, 62
traction 2, 6, 7, 144, 145, 161,
188, 190, 197, 199
transpersonal 52, 162-164,
166-170, 174, 196
higher self 125, 168, 186, 190,
196
spiritual self 164
trephination 35

unconscious 12, 13, 54, 56, 66,
87, 93, 135
universal intelligence 56, 171
Upledger, J.E. 114, 115

Wenen-nefer 40
Wilber, K. 74, 75
womb 11, 67-69
Worrall, O. 50, 51, 128, 129, 171

yoga 11

Photo: Wolfgang Jasper

About the Author

Dr. Clyde Ford was born in 1951 in New York City. He graduated from Wesleyan University (B.A.) in 1971 and worked as a systems engineer with the IBM Corporation until 1977 when he left to attend Western States Chiropractic College in Portland, Oregon. After being granted his doctorate of chiropractic in 1980, he moved to Richmond Virginia then Bellingham, Washington where he is currently in private practice. He is the former editor of *Leading Edge*, a bulliten for personal and social transformation, and past president of The Foundation for the Advancement of Chiropractic Research. He has professional training in psychotherapy from the Synthesis Education Foundation of Winchester, Massachusetts and the Psychosynthesis Institute of New York. He conducts workshops and seminars around the country. In 1987 he founded ISTAR, the Institute for Somatosynthesis Training and Research to continue the work presented in *Where Healing Waters Meet*.

For further information about workshops and seminars on somatosynthesis you can contact ISTAR:

ISTAR
P.O. Box 3056
Bellingham, Washington 98227
(206) 398-9355